DSLs in Boo

DSLs in Boo

DOMAIN-SPECIFIC LANGUAGES IN .NET

OREN EINI

WRITING AS AYENDE RAHIEN

MANNING

Greenwich
(74° w. long.)

For online information and ordering of this and other Manning books, please visit
www.manning.com. The publisher offers discounts on this book when ordered in quantity.
For more information, please contact

> Special Sales Department
> Manning Publications Co.
> Sound View Court 3B
> Greenwich, CT 06830
> Email: orders@manning.com

Manning Publications Co.
Sound View Court 3B
Greenwich, CT 06830

Development editor: Tom Cirtin
Copyeditor: Andy Carroll
Typesetter: Dottie Marsico
Cover designer: Leslie Haimes

ISBN 978-1-933988-60-3
Printed in the United States of America
1 2 3 4 5 6 7 8 9 10 – MAL – 15 14 13 12 11 10

For Mom
who told me it would take longer than I expected

brief contents

contents

preface

In 2007, I gave a talk about using Boo to build your own domain-specific languages (DSLs) at JAOO (http://jaoo.dk), a software conference in Denmark. I had been working with Boo and creating DSLs since 2005, but as I prepared for the talk, I was surprised to see just how easy it was to build DSLs with Boo. (I find that teaching something gives you a fresh perspective on it.)

That experience, and the audience's response, convinced me that you don't have to be a compiler expert or a parser wizard to build your own mini-languages. I realized that I needed to formalize the practices I had been using and make them publicly available.

One of the most challenging problems in the industry today is finding a way of clearly expressing intent in a particular domain. A lot of time and effort has been spent tackling that problem. A DSL is usually a good solution, but there is a strong perception in the community that writing your own language for a particular task is an extremely difficult task.

The truth is different from the perception. Creating a language from scratch would be a big task, but you don't need to start from scratch. Today, there are lots of tools and plenty of support for creating languages. When you decide to make an internal DSL—one that is hosted inside an existing programming language (such as Boo)—the cost of building that language drops significantly.

I routinely build new languages during presentations (onstage, within 5 or 10 minutes), because once you understand the basic principles, it is easy. Easy enough that it deserves to be a standard part of your toolset, ready to be used whenever you spot a problem that is suitable for a DSL solution.

That 2007 JAOO talk was the start of the journey that led to the creation of this book. Finishing up this project took longer than expected, but I am very happy to say that I have been successful in what I set out to do.

This book is meant to be an actionable guide, not a theory book. I go over the theory in the relevant places, but my goal is that, by the time you are halfway through the book, you'll be able to write your own DSLs.

acknowledgments

Like most books, this wasn't a solo effort. I would like to send my heartfelt gratitude to the people who made this book possible.

Thanks to Rodrigo B. de Oliveira, for creating the Boo language in the first place, and Cedric Vivier, Daniel Grunwald, Dmitry Malyshev, Greg Nagel, Joao Braganca, Martinho Fernandes, Paul Lang, and Avishay Lavie for helping to create such a wonderful language.

To the people who worked on and extended the Rhino DSL project, Simone Busoli, Nathan Stott, Jason Meckley, Craig Neuwirt, Tobias Hertkorn, Markus Zywitza, Adam Tybor, Paul Barriere, and Leonard Smith, thanks for making my job so much easier.

To everyone at Manning, especially publisher Marjan Bace and associate publisher Mike Stephens, thanks for your guidance, support, and patience. To development editor Tom Cirtin, copyeditor Andy Carroll, and proofreader Katie Tennant, thanks for being so patient with me, even when I took too long to get things done. Special thanks to technical proofreader Justin Chase for carefully reading the final manuscript once it was in production and for checking the code.

To the reviewers who read the manuscript numerous times during development, thanks for your comments and valuable feedback: Andrew Glover, Jon Skeet, Derik Whittaker, Freedom Dumlao, Justin Lee, Paul King, Matthew Pope, Craig Neuwirt, Mark Seemann, Steven Kelly, Robert Wenner, Garabed "Garo" Yeriazarian, and Avishay Lavie.

about this book

This book is meant for intermediate to advanced .NET developers who are interested in using domain-specific languages in their applications.

If you are new to language-oriented programming, this book will teach you how to create, build, and maintain your own languages.

If you are experienced with language-oriented programming, this book will give you all the practical knowledge necessary to easily build DSLs using the Boo programming language.

Note, however, that this book is focused on the practical side of building DSLs. While I talk about the theory underlying this field, I focus on practical aspects. If you are interested in learning more about DSLs, I also recommend reading Martin Fowler's forthcoming book on the topic: http://www.martinfowler.com/bliki/DomainSpecificLanguage.html. The book isn't finished yet, but much of the content can already be found on his site.

Roadmap

This book has five main sections.

Chapters 1–2 discuss DSLs in general, introduce the Boo language, and explain why I chose to use it as the basis for my DSL adventures.

Chapters 3–5 walk through the implementation of several different DSLs, their integration into applications, and all the various concerns you'll have to deal with when you add a DSL to your project.

Chapters 6–7 dive into advanced language manipulation and the infrastructure required to build an industry-strength DSL.

Chapters 8–11 go into the details surrounding a production-worthy DSL implementation: building testable languages and test languages, creating versionable DSLs, working with user interfaces for the languages, and documenting them.

Chapters 12–13 talk about implementation challenges for DSLs and walk through the steps of building a full real-world DSL example.

Two appendixes conclude the book. Appendix A is a basic Boo reference, familiarizing you with how to use Boo as a programming language, while appendix B covers the Boo language syntax.

Code conventions and downloads

All source code in listings or in text is in a `fixed-width font like this` to separate it from ordinary text. Source code for all working examples in this book is available for download from the publisher's website at www.manning.com/DSLsinBoo.

You can download the binary distribution of Boo from the Boo website at http://boo.codehaus.org. For more information on using Boo once you've downloaded it, please see page 23.

Author Online

The purchase of *DSLs in Boo* includes free access to a private web forum run by Manning Publications, where you can make comments about the book, ask technical questions, and receive help from the author and from other users. To access the forum and subscribe to it, point your web browser to www.manning.com/DSLsinBoo. This page provides information about how to get on the forum once you're registered, what kind of help is available, and the rules of conduct on the forum.

Manning's commitment to our readers is to provide a venue where a meaningful dialogue between individual readers and between readers and the author can take place. It's not a commitment to any specific amount of participation on the part of the author, whose contribution to the book's forum remains voluntary (and unpaid). We suggest you try asking him some challenging questions, lest his interest stray!

The Author Online forum and the archives of previous discussions will be accessible from the publisher's website as long as the book is in print.

about the author

Oren Eini is an independent consultant based in Israel. He is a frequent blogger at www.ayende.com/Blog/ under his pseudonym Ayende Rahien, and he's an internationally known presenter, having spoken at conferences such as DevTeach, JAOO, Oredev, NDC, and Progressive.NET.

Oren's main focus is on architecture and best practices that promote quality software and zero-friction development. He is the author of Rhino Mocks, one of the most popular mocking frameworks on the .NET platform, and he's also a leading figure in other well-known open source projects, including the Castle project and NHibernate.

Oren's hobbies include reading fantasy novels, reviewing code, and writing about himself in the third person. Oren is also a Microsoft MVP, a fact that he tends to forget when writing a bio.

about the cover illustration

The figure on the cover of *DSLs in Boo* is captioned "Le Dauber," which means *art student*. The illustration is taken from a 19th-century edition of Sylvain Maréchal's four-volume compendium of regional dress customs published in France. Each illustration is finely drawn and colored by hand. The rich variety of Maréchal's collection reminds us vividly of how culturally apart the world's towns and regions were just 200 years ago. Isolated from each other, people spoke different dialects and languages. In the streets or in the countryside, it was easy to identify where they lived and what their trade or station in life was just by their dress.

Dress codes have changed since then and the diversity by region, so rich at the time, has faded away. It is now hard to tell apart the inhabitants of different continents, let alone different towns or regions. Perhaps we have traded cultural diversity for a more varied personal life-certainly for a more varied and fast-paced technological life.

At a time when it is hard to tell one computer book from another, Manning celebrates the inventiveness and initiative of the computer business with book covers based on the rich diversity of regional life of two centuries ago, brought back to life by Maréchal's pictures.

What are domain-specific languages?

1

In the beginning, there was the bit. And the bit shifted left, and the bit shifted right, and there was the byte. The byte grew into a word, and then into a double word. And the developer saw the work, and it was good. And the evening and the morning were the first day. And on the next day, the developer came back to the work and spent the whole day trying to figure out what he had been thinking the day before.

If this story rings any bells, you're familiar with one of the most fundamental problems in computer science. The computer does what it is told, not what the programmer meant to tell it. Often enough, what the programmer tells it to do is in direct contradiction to what the programmer *meant* it to do. And that's a problem.

1

I've experienced this myself many times, and I'm not particularly incompetent. How, then, did I reach that point?

1.1   *Striving for simplicity*

Take a look at this piece of code:

```
for (p = freelist, oldp = 0;
     p && p != (struct chunk *)brkval;
     oldp = p, p = p->next) {
  if (p->len > nelems) {
      p->len -= nelems;
      q = p + p->len;
      q->next = 0;
      q->len = nelems;
      q++;
      return (void *)q;
  }
  if (p->len == nelems) {
      if (oldp == 0)
          freelist = p->next;
      else
          oldp->next = p->next;
      p->next = 0;
      p++;
      return (void *)p;
  }
}
```

You're among a decided minority if you can take a single glance at this code and deduce immediately what it's doing. Most developers would have to *decipher* this piece of code.

How does this connect to my difficulty in telling the computer what I want it to do? The problem is the level at which I instruct the computer what to do. If I am working down at the assembly level (or near assembly), I have to instruct the machine what to do in excruciating detail. The preceding piece of code was taken from the FreeBSD boot loader's malloc method, and there are good reasons it looks the way it does, but writing at this level has a big cost in productivity and flexibility.

Alternatively, I can instruct the computer to do things in higher-level terms, where it can better interpret what I want it to do.

As developers, we always want to achieve the simplest, clearest way to talk to the computer, regardless of the task at hand. Different tasks (low-level memory manipulation, for example) require us to work at different levels, but we always strive for readable, easily maintainable code. Within a given context, we may need to sacrifice those goals for other, more important goals (usually performance), but that should only done very cautiously.

And when we are not working on low-level code, we will, at some point, have to leave general-purpose programming languages behind to get the desired level of clarity. Building our own languages, each focused specifically on a single task, is a great way to achieve this simplicity and clarity.

What we'd like to find are clear, concise, and simple ways to instruct the machine what we want it to do, rather than to laboriously micromanage it.

1.1.1 Creating simple code

Producing code that's readable, maintainable, and simple is a great goal. But simple code is much harder to write than complex code. It's easy to throw code at a problem until it goes away. Simple code, on the other hand, is what you get when you remove all the complexity from the code. That isn't to say that it's complicated to write simple code; it's just that writing *complex* code is easy. The amount of effort it takes to decipher what a piece of code does is a good indication of how simple the code is.

Consider these two examples of getting the date in two weeks' time. Which is more readable?

- C# code: `DateTime.Now.AddDays(14);`
- C code: `time() + 1209600;`

I don't think there's any question about which is more readable. In fact, an even better solution would be this:

```
DateTime.Now.AddWeeks(2);
```

But this isn't part of .NET's Base Class Library (BCL) DateTime API.

Using higher-level concepts means you can concentrate more on what you want to be done, and less on how it should be done at the machine level. When using .NET or Java, for instance, I rarely need to concern myself with memory allocation.

That's helpful, but more often than not, you'll need to do more interesting things than merely calculate the date two weeks from now. You'll need to express concepts and algorithms in ways that make sense, and you'll need to be able to use them in projects of significant size and complexity. Having clearer ways to express those concepts translates directly into a more maintainable code base, which means reduced maintenance costs and an easier time changing and growing the system.

> **NOTE** It's considered polite to express intent in code in a manner that will make sense to the next developer who works with your code, particularly because that poor person may be you. A good suggestion that I take to heart is to assume that the next developer to touch your code will be an axe murderer who knows where you live and has a short fuse.

1.1.2 Creating clear code

Code may be clear about how it's doing things, but it might not be clear about what it's doing or why. Because we're assuming that the next developer will be a vicious killer with a nasty temper, we should make it easy to figure out what we've done and what we meant.

We can make our code easier to understand by using intention-revealing programming and concepts taken from domain-driven design, a design approach that says that your API, code structure, and the code itself should express intent, be expressed in the language of the domain, and generally have a high correlation with the problem domain that the application is trying to solve.

Even then, we quickly reach a point where our ability to express intent is hampered by the syntax of the language that we're using.

1.1.3 Creating intention-revealing code

Programming languages make it easy to tell the computer what it should do, but they can be less effective at expressing developer intent. For that matter, most general-purpose languages (such as C# or Java) are far less suited for a host of other tasks.

Let's consider text processing, for example. Suppose you want to validate an Israeli phone number like this: 03-9876543. You might do this with the code shown in listing 1.1.

Listing 1.1   Validating a phone number

```
public bool ValidatePhoneNumber(string input)
{
    if (input.Length != 10)
        return false;
    for (int i = 0; i < input.Length; i++)
    {
        if (i == 2 && input[i] != '-')
            return false;
        else if (char.IsDigit(input[i]) == false)
            return false;
    }
    return true;
}
```

Can you look at this code and understand what input it will accept without *deciphering* it? If you haven't noticed by now, I consider the need to decipher code bad.

Now let's look at a tool that's dedicated to text processing: regular expressions. Validating the phone number using a regular expression is as simple as the one-liner in listing 1.2.

Listing 1.2   Validating a phone number using regular expressions

```
public bool ValidatePhoneNumber(string input)
{
    return Regex.IsMatch(input, @"^\d{2}-\d{7}$");
}
```

In this case, the use of a specialized tool for text processing has made the intent much easier to understand, but you need to understand the tool. Anyone who knows regular expressions can glance at the code and figure out what input it will accept.

Another approach is to use masked input to define a mask for certain input, which would result in code like this:

```
Mask.Validate(input, "##-#######");
```

> **The challenges of specialized tools**
>
> Regular expressions are notorious for being write-only tools because the results can be difficult to read, particularly if you don't write them carefully.
>
> Using special tools to handle specialized tasks requires that you understand how to use the tools. If you don't understand regular expressions, and I hand you listing 1.2, how will you deal with it?
>
> We'll touch on this topic later in the book; most of chapter 11 is dedicated to techniques that can help people come to grips with custom languages.

Assuming you know that # is the character for matching a numeral, this is even easier to understand than the regular expression approach. (The .NET framework doesn't have any masked-input validation facilities beyond WinForms' `MaskedTestBox`.)

Querying and filtering are other situations where code is no longer sufficient. Let's say we want to retrieve data for all the customers in London. This isn't a query that you'll want to handle by yourself. Building an optimized query plan, instructing the data store which section of the data should be scanned, building manual filters for each individual query ... all of that can be quite tedious. It's quite a complex task, particularly if you want to handle it efficiently and in a transaction-safe manner.

It's far easier to send a SQL statement to the database and let it sort out how it wants to handle the request on its own. This allows us to speak at a much higher level of abstraction and ignore the details of how the data is retrieved.

So far, I have been consciously avoiding the use of the term *domain-specific languages*, but it's time we started discussing it.

1.2 *Understanding domain-specific languages*

Martin Fowler defines a domain-specific language (DSL) as "a computer language that's targeted to a particular kind of problem, rather than a general purpose language that's aimed at any kind of software problem" (http://martinfowler.com/bliki/DomainSpecificLanguage.html).

Domain-specific languages aren't a new idea by any means. DSLs have been around since long before the start of computing. People have always developed specialized vocabularies for specialized tasks. That's why sailors use terms like *port* and *starboard* and are not particularly afraid of *gallows*. Doctors similarly have a vocabulary that is baffling to the uninitiated, and weather forecasters have specific terms for various types of clouds, winds, and storms.

Regular expressions and SQL are similarly specialized languages:

- Both are languages designed for a narrow domain—text processing and database querying, respectively.
- Both are focused on letting you express what you mean, not how the implementation should work—that's left to some magic engine in the background.

The reason these languages are so successful is that the focus they offer is incredibly useful. They reduce the complexity that you need to handle, and they're flexible in terms of what you can make them do.

1.2.1 Expressing intent

From the beginning of computer programming, it was recognized that trying to express what you mean in natural language isn't a viable approach. A clearer, much more focused, way to express intent was needed—that's why we have code, which is unambiguous (most of the time) and easy for the computer to understand.

But while code may be unambiguous to a computer, it can certainly be incomprehensible to people. Understanding code can be a big problem. You tend to write the code once, and read it many more times. Clarity is much more important than brevity. By ensuring that our code is readable, clear, and concise, we make an investment that will benefit us both in the immediate future (producing software that is simpler and easier to change) and in the long term (providing easier maintainability and a clearer path for extensibility and growth).

But, as we've seen, code isn't always the clearest way to express intent. This is where intention-revealing programming comes into play, and one of the tools in that category is creating a DSL to clearly and efficiently express intent and meaning in code.

1.2.2 Creating your own languages

Most people assume that creating your own computer language is a fairly complex matter. This is because most of the literature out there assumes that you want to build a full-blown general language. This puts a lot of burden on you, as the language author.

It isn't simple to create a general language, but it's certainly possible. It just isn't something you'd want to do on a rainy afternoon or over a long weekend. The experience is out there, but the initial cost remains nontrivial.

But you don't always have to write your own language from scratch. You can utilize an existing language (called the *host language* or *base language*) to provide built-in language and runtime facilities, and then add more syntax and behavior on top

---

Building your own compiler

I stated that building your own compiler or interpreter isn't hard. This is true, to some extent. The main difficulties in going that route are the scope of the work and the fact that most of the work is arcane at worst and tedious at best. This is particularly true if you want to write a full-fledged language.

Writing a general-purpose language is a big task. You need to deal with the details of the syntax and worry about creating an execution engine (for interpreted languages) or generating IL (Intermediate Language) or machine code (for compiled languages). I don't consider it to be a complex task, but it is a big one.

> Building a single-purpose language is a far easier (and smaller) task, because the scope is much reduced. A good example of that can be seen in rSpec, a Ruby library for creating behavior-driven specifications. One of its capabilities is a story runner that accepts specifications written in English (http://blog.davidchelimsky.net/articles/2007/10/21/story-runner-in-plain-english). I suggest looking at how it works. It's quite ingenious in its simplicity.
>
> The problem with that approach for natural language processing is that you hit its limits quickly. It works only when the statements follow a rigid format, so although it may look like natural language, it is, in fact, nothing of the sort. If you want to make the language more intelligent, you have to accept the additional complexity of building a more full-featured language.
>
> I once consulted for a company that had built a DSL for defining business rules. They had over 100,000 lines of C++ code that they needed to maintain, and performance was a big concern. It became apparent that they could have switched the whole thing to an internal DSL (a DSL that's hosted in an existing language, which we'll talk about shortly) and saved quite a bit of time, effort, and pain.

of it. A popular example is Ruby on Rails, which is, in essence, a DSL for building web applications.

The tools for language-oriented programming had been improving for quite a while, but it was the introduction of Ruby on Rails—a wildly popular DSL that was recognized as such—that really started to get things rolling.

1.3 Distinguishing between DSL types

In the world of DSLs, we often distinguish between several types:

- External DSLs
- Graphical DSLs
- Fluent interfaces
- Internal or embedded DSLs

We'll discuss those types in turn, and look at their properties and uses.

1.3.1 External DSLs

When we talk about external DSLs, we're discussing DSLs that exist outside the confines of an existing language. SQL and regular expressions are two examples of external DSLs.

Building an external DSL means starting work from a blank slate. You need to define the syntax and required capabilities, and start working from there. This means that you have a lot of power in your hands, but you also need to handle everything yourself. And by "everything," I do mean *everything*, from defining operator precedence semantics to specifying how an `if` statement works.

Common tools for building external DSLs include Lex, Yacc, ANTLR, GOLD Parser, and Coco/R, among others. Those tools handle the first stage, translating text in a known syntax to a format that a computer program can consume to produce executable output. The part about "producing executable output" is usually left as an exercise for the reader. There are few tools to help you with that.

NOTE   One tool that comes to mind for producing executable output is the Dynamic Language Runtime (DLR), a Microsoft project that aims to give us dynamic languages in .NET. One basic underpinning of this project is a set of classes that specify the behavior of a program (the abstract syntax tree, or AST) that the DLR can turn into an executable. There are other such tools, for sure, but the DLR is the only one I know of in the .NET space.

Building rich external DSLs is similar to building a general purpose language. You need to understand compiler theory before starting on that path. If you're interested in that, I recommend reading *Compilers: Principles, Techniques, and Tools*, by Alfred V. Aho, Ravi Sethi, and Jeffrey D. Ullman, which is a classic book on the subject.

This book focuses on building languages on top of existing languages, not starting from scratch and going the whole way. Nevertheless, some background in compiler theory is certainly helpful, even when building a DSL that uses an existing language, so let's take a quick look at the process of building a language from scratch.

First, the grammar and syntax are often defined using a notation such as BNF (Backus-Naur Form) or a derivative, and then you use a tool to generate a parser. Once you've done that, you can run the parser over a code string, which will produce an abstract syntax tree (AST), which is the representation of the original string as an AST based on your definition of the language.

An example will make this clearer. Consider the code in listing 1.3, written in a fictional language.

Listing 1.3   An `if` statement in a fictional language

```
if 1 equals 2:
   print "1 = 2"
else:
   print "1 != 2"
```

The AST that was generated from the code in listing 1.3 is shown in figure 1.1.

You can then either build an interpreter that understands this AST and can execute it, or output an executable from the AST. Another common approach is to transform the AST into a semantic model that's easier to work with, but that has little correlation to the original text.

External DSLs are extremely powerful, but they also carry with them a significant cost. In general, I prefer to avoid going the external DSL route, mainly because of the cost, but also because internal DSLs serve well in most cases.

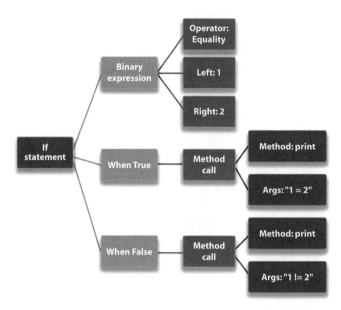

Figure 1.1 A hierarchical
representation of the AST
generated from a simple
`if` statement

I would use an external DSL for specifying languages that are too far afield from existing programming languages. SQL is a good example of a DSL you couldn't build as an internal DSL. You could build something similar, but you couldn't get it quite right, so an external DSL would be the right approach for writing your own SQL dialect.

1.3.2 Graphical DSLs

Another form of DSL is the graphical DSL. This is a DSL that uses shapes and lines to express intent rather than using text.

UML is a good example of a graphical DSL. UML is a DSL for describing software systems, and quite a lot of money and effort has been devoted to making UML the one true model from which you can generate the rest of the application. Figure 1.2 displays a small part of a typical UML diagram.

Customer
Id : long
Name : string
Orders : Set<Order>
AddOrder(order : Order) : void

Figure 1.2 UML class
diagram displaying the
`Customer` object

Graphical DSLs are great for expressing a lot of information in a concise way. Often, it's much easier to understand a problem when you see it than when it's explained in words. This visualization approach also allows for communication at a high level because of the physical limitations of the image. It's much easier to understand what's going on because there is less information, and you can see the big picture.

A lot of effort has been invested in making it possible to write your own graphical DSLs. Microsoft has the Visual Studio DSL Tools, which is a framework that allows you to build tools similar to the class designer and generate code with them.

There are quite a few examples of graphical DSLs that you've probably heard about:

- UML
- BizTalk orchestrations and maps

- SQL Server Integration Services
- Windows Workflow Foundation

I've had some experience with all of these graphical DSLs, and they all share common problems inherent to the graphical DSL model.

The whole point of a graphical DSL is to hide information that you don't want to see, so you can see the big picture. This means that you can't see the whole at the same time, which leads to a lot of time spent jumping between various elements on the DSL surface, trying to gather all the required data. Graphical DSLs are visually verbose; they often need a lot of screen real estate to express notions that take a few lines with a textual DSL.

And then there are important UI issues. Searching is difficult in a graphical DSL, as are search and replace operations. And mouse-driven development isn't a good idea, if only in consideration of your wrists.

Beyond that, there are serious difficulties working with graphical DSLs in a team environment. It's easy to pull out a code file and compare two versions (called a *diff*, or *diffing*), but this breaks down for graphical DSLs, even those that persist their data into XML files. Even assuming the XML persistence format is human-readable (and I haven't seen an example that was), comparing the XML defeats the whole purpose of using a graphical DSL in the first place. You need some way to express a diff graphically, and I haven't seen any good way to do that.

This makes graphical DSLs a problem in terms of source control. This is a huge issue as far as I am concerned, and I have run into this issue more than once, with no easy or good solutions in sight.

If you haven't guessed so far, I'm not a fan of graphical DSLs for programming. Graphical DSLs are great for *documentation*, but I find that they aren't very good for development when it comes to real-world scenarios.

1.3.3   *Fluent interfaces*

I had some doubts about including fluent interfaces in this list of DSL types because I think of them as degenerate internal DSLs for languages with little syntactic flexibility (such as C# or Java), which means their options for language extensibility are limited. Fluent interfaces are ways to structure your API so that operations flow naturally and provide more readable code. They tend to be valid only when used by developers during actual development, which limits their scope compared to other DSLs.

It's easier to demonstrate than explain, so take a look at listing 1.4, which runs a set of transformations on an image using a fluent interface API.

Listing 1.4 Fluent interface for specifying graphical transforms

```
new Pipeline("rhino.png")
    .Rotate(90)
    .Watermark("Mocks")
    .RoundCorners(100, Color.Bisque)
    .Save("fluent-rhino.png");
```

The implementation of a fluent interface is simple. The `Rotate()` method is shown in listing 1.5.

Listing 1.5 Implementation of a method in a fluent interface

```
public Pipeline Rotate(float degrees)
{
    RotateFilter filter = new RotateFilter();
    filter.RotateDegrees = degrees;
    image = filter.ExecuteFilter(image);
    return this;
}
```

On the surface, fluent interfaces are simply a type of method chaining, but they have implications for the readability of the operations, as well as for the instructive nature that can result from building good fluent interfaces. By carefully planning the return values, we can create a good language with high readability *and* we can gain the support of IntelliSense to aid in the writing of the language statements.

The fluent interface in listing 1.4 isn't particularly impressive, but listing 1.6 should be. This is valid C# 2.0 code, and even if you've never used it before, this code will probably be instantly readable.

Listing 1.6 Using a fluent interface for querying

```
User.FindAll(
    Where.User.City == "London" &&
    Where.User.RegisteredAt >= DateTime.Now.AddMonths(-3)
);
```

This code gives you all the users from London that registered in the last 3 months. Unfortunately, this fluent interface is based on code generation, operator overloading, and generics abuse; it was *very* hard to create and it isn't something I'd want to create again. (This code was written for C# 2.0; LINQ, in C# 3.0, makes this example look aged.)

Listing 1.7 is another example that shows the fluent interface to configure StructureMap.

Listing 1.7 Configuring the StructureMap container using a fluent interface

```
registry.AddInstanceOf<IWidget>()
  .WithName("DarkGreen")
  .UsingConcreteType<ColorWidget>()
  .WithProperty("Color").EqualTo("DarkGreen");
```

NOTE StructureMap (http://structuremap.sourceforge.net/) is an Inversion of Control (IoC) container, probably the oldest on .NET. An Inversion of Control container is a tool that helps you manage dependencies and lifetimes of objects in your application. You can think about them as very smart factories, although that doesn't do them justice. You can read more about IoC containers here: http://www.martinfowler.com/articles/injection.html.

And, finally, listing 1.8 shows an example for specifying regular expressions in a comparatively readable way.

> **Listing 1.8   Using a fluent interface to create a regular expression**

```
SmartRegex.Create("<div",
    SmartRegex.Space >= 0,
    "class='game'",
    SmartRegex.Space >= 0,
    ">");
```

Fluent interfaces are useful, and with C# 3.0 and VB.NET 9, we have some interesting options for expressing ourselves. The query syntax in listing 1.6 could easily be replaced by a LINQ query, but the other examples are still relevant. With the new capabilities like extension methods and lambdas, you can take fluent interfaces quite a long way.

Unfortunately, you usually can't take them far enough. Mainstream languages are too inflexible in their syntax to allow you the freedom to express yourself appropriately. I have tried this approach, and I have bumped into the limits of the language several times. This approach breaks down for the interesting scenarios.

This is particularly true when you want to express business requirements in a way that would make sense even to non-programmers. It would be good indeed if you could show businesspeople what you're doing, in a way that made sense to them.

This leads us directly toward the last item on our list, internal DSLs.

1.3.4   *Internal or embedded DSLs*

Internal DSLs are built on top of an existing language, but they don't try to remain true to the original programming language syntax. They try to express things in a way that makes sense to both the author and the reader, not to the compiler.

Obviously, the expressiveness of an internal DSL is limited by whatever constraints are imposed by the underlying language syntax. You can't build a good DSL on top of C# or Java; they have too much rigidity in their syntax to allow it. You probably could build a good DSL on C++, but it would probably include preprocessor macros galore, and I wouldn't place any bets on how maintainable it would be.

The popular choices for building internal DSLs are dynamic languages; Lisp and Smalltalk were probably the first common choices. Today, people mostly use Ruby, Python, and Boo. People turn to those languages for building DSLs because they have quite a bit of syntactic flexibility. For example, listing 1.9 is valid Ruby code.

> **Listing 1.9   A Rake build script, specifying tasks to run at build time**

```
task :default => [:test]
task :test do
   ruby "test/unittest.rb"
end
```

Listing 1.9 is part of a build script written using Rake, a build tool that uses a Ruby-based DSL to specify actions to take during the build process (http://rake.rubyforge.org/). Rake is a good example of using a DSL to express intent in an understandable manner. Consider the amount of XML you'd need to write using an XML-based build tool, such as NAnt or MSBuild, to do the same thing, and consider how readable that would be.

Other features that usually appear in dynamic languages are also useful when building DSLs: closures, macros, and duck typing.

The major advantage of an internal DSL is that it takes on all the power of the language it's written for. You don't have to write the semantics of an `if` statement, or redefine operator precedence, for instance. Sometimes that's useful, and in one of my DSL implementations I *did* redefine the `if` statement, but that's probably not a good thing to do in general, and it's rarely necessary.

A DSL built on top of an existing language can also be problematic, because you want to limit the options of the language to clarify what is going on. The DSL shouldn't be a full-fledged programming language; you already have that in the base language, after all.

The main purpose of an internal DSL is to reduce the amount of work required to make the compiler happy and increase the clarity of the code in question. That's the syntactic aspect of it, at least. The other purpose is to expose the domain. A DSL should be readable by someone who is familiar with the domain, not the programming language. That takes some work, and it's far more important than mere syntax; this is the core reason for building a DSL in the first place.

Or is it? Why do we need DSLs again?

1.4 Why write DSLs?

Why do you need a DSL? After all, you're reading this book, so you already know how to program. Can't you use "normal" programming languages to do the job, perhaps with a dash of fluent interfaces and domain-driven design to make the code easier to read?

So far, I've focused entirely on the *how*, which is somewhat hypocritical of me, because this entire book is going to focus on abstracting the *how*. Let's look at the *why* —the different needs that lead the drive toward a DSL.

There are several reasons you might want a DSL, and they're mostly based on the problems you want to solve. These are the most common ones:

- Making a technical issue or task simpler
- Expressing rules and actions in a way that's close to the domain and understandable to businesspeople
- Automating tasks and actions, usually as part of adding scriptability and extensibility features to your applications

We'll look at each of those scenarios in detail and examine the forces that drive us toward using DSLs and the implications they have on the languages we build.

1.4.1 Technical DSLs

A technical DSL is supposed to be used by someone who understands the development environment. It's meant to express matters more concisely, but it's still very much a programming language at heart. The main difference is that a programming language is more general, whereas a technical DSL is focused on solving the specific problem at hand. As such, it has all the benefits (and drawbacks) of single-purpose languages. Rake, Binsor, Rhino ETL, and Watir are examples of technical DSLs.

NOTE   As mentioned earlier, Rake is a build tool that uses a Ruby-based DSL to specify actions to be taken during the build process (http://rake.rubyforge.org/). Binsor is a DSL for defining dependencies for the Windsor IoC container (http://www.ayende.com/Blog/category/451.aspx). Rhino ETL is a DSL-based extract-transform-load (ETL) tool (http://www.ayende.com/Blog/category/545.aspx). And Watir is an automation DSL for driving Internet Explorer, mostly used for integration testing (http://en.wikipedia.org/wiki/Watir).

It makes sense to build a technical DSL if you need richer ways to specify what you want to happen. Technical DSLs are usually easier to write than other DSLs, because your target audience already understands programming—it takes less work to create a language that make sense to them.

In fact, the inclusion of programming features can make a sweet DSL indeed. We already saw a Rake sample (listing 1.9); listing 1.10 shows a Binsor example.

> **Listing 1.10   A Binsor script for registering all controllers in an assembly**

```
for type in AllTypesBased of IController("MyApplication.Web"):
    # Component is a keyword that would register the type in the container
    component type
```

It takes two lines to register all the controllers in the application. That's quite expressive. It's also a sweet merge between the use of standard language operations (`for` loops) and the DSL syntax (`component`).

This works well if your target audience is developers. If not, you'll need to provide a far richer environment in your DSLs. We usually call this type of DSL a business DSL.

1.4.2 Business DSLs

A business DSL needs to be (at the very least) readable to a businessperson with no background in programming. This type of DSL is mainly expressive in terms of the domain, and it has a lot less emphasis on the programming features that may still exist. It also tends to be more declarative than technical DSLs. The emphasis is placed on the declarative nature of the DSL and on matching it to the way the businesspeople think about the tasks at hand, so the programming features are not necessary in most cases.

For example, you wouldn't generally encourage the use of `for` loops in your business DSL, or explicit error handling, null checking, calling base class libraries, or any of the things that you would normally do in a technical environment. A business

DSL should be a closed system that provides all the expected usages directly in the language.

I can't think of a good example of a non-proprietary business DSL. There are business rule engines, but I wouldn't call them DSLs. They're one stage before that; they have no association to the real domain that we work with.

A good example of a business DSL that I have seen was created by a mobile phone company that needed to handle the variety of different contracts and benefits it offered. It also needed a short time to market, to respond rapidly to market conditions.

The end result was a DSL in which you could specify the different conditions and their results. For instance, to specify that you get 300 minutes free if you speak over 300 minutes a month, you would write something similar to listing 1.11.

Listing 1.11   A DSL for specifying benefits in a mobile phone company

```
when call_minutes_in_current_month > 300 and
              has_benefit "300 Minutes Free!!!":
       give_free_call_minutes 300, "300 Minutes Free!!!"
```

This DSL consists of a small language that can describe most of the benefits the company wants to express. The rest is a matter of naming conventions and dropping files in a specified folder, to be picked up and processed at regular intervals. We'll discuss the structure of the engine that surrounds the DSL itself in chapter 5.

Listing 1.11 still looks like a programming language, yes. But although a businessperson may not always be able to write actions using a business DSL, they should be able to read and understand them. After all, it's their business and their domain that you're describing. We'll see more complex examples later in the book, but for now let's keep this simple.

Using a business DSL requires business knowledge

This is something that people often overlook. When we evaluate the readability of a DSL, we often make the mistake of determining how readable it is to the layperson.

A business DSL uses business language, which can be completely opaque to a layperson. I have no idea what it means to adjust a claim, but presumably it makes sense to someone in the insurance business, and it's certainly something I would expect to see in a DSL targeted at solving a problem in the insurance world.

Why wouldn't a businessperson be able to write actions using a business DSL? One of the main reasons is that even a trivial syntax error would likely stop most nonprogrammers in their tracks. Understanding and overcoming errors requires programming knowledge that few businesspeople have. Although a DSL is supposed to be readable for nonprogrammers, it's still a programming language with little tolerance for such things as omitting the condition in an `if` statement, and many businesspeople would be unable to go over the first hurdle they faced.

It's important to know your audience—don't assume anything about your audience's ability or inability to write code. Although you might not expect them to understand programming, they may have experience in automating small tasks using VBA and Excel macros.

Matching the business DSL's capabilities to that of the expected audience will prove a powerful combination. You can provide the businesspeople with the tools, and they can provide the knowledge and the required perspective.

Conversely, creating a DSL that misses the target audience is likely to result in problems. In a business DSL, expressing the domain and the concepts in the language is only half the work; the other half is matching the language's capabilities and requirements to the people who will use it.

I suggest making the decision about whether you're creating a business-readable or a business-writable DSL as early in the game as you can possibly can. This decision will greatly affect the design and implementation of the DSL, and getting it wrong is likely to be expensive.

1.4.3   *Automatic or extensible DSLs*

Automatic or extensible DSLs may also be called IT DSLs. This type of DSL is often used to expose the internals of an application to the outside world.

Modern games are usually engines configured with some sort of scripting language. Another use for this style of DSL would be to get into the internals of an application and manage it. With such a DSL, you could write a script that would reroute all traffic from a server, wait for all current work to complete, and then take the server down, update it, and bring it up again.

Right now, it's possible to do this with shell scripts of various kinds, but most enterprise applications have a rich internal state that could be made at least partially visible. A DSL that would allow you to inspect and modify the internal state would be welcome. Many administrators would appreciate having more options for managing their applications.

Another way to look at this is to consider all the VBA-enabled applications out there, from Office to AutoCAD to accounting packages and ERP systems. VBA's extensibility enables users to create scripts that access the state of the system. The same thing can be done for enterprise applications using automation DSLs (at far less cost in licensing alone).

1.5   *Boo's DSL capabilities*

I've mentioned Lisp, Smalltalk, Ruby, Python, and Boo as languages that are well suited for writing internal DSLs, so why does this book focus on Boo? And have you even heard of this language? Boo has yet to become a household name (but just you wait), so we probably need to discuss what kind of language it is.

Boo is an object-oriented, statically typed programming language for the Common Language Infrastructure (CLI) with a Python-inspired syntax and a special focus on language and compiler extensibility. It's this focus on extensibility that makes it ideally

> ### Boo runs on Java as well—say hello to BooJay
>
> Boo is not just a CLR language; it's also a JVM language. You can learn more about Boo on Java in the BooJay discussion group: http://groups.google.com/ group/ boojay/.
>
> This screencast will introduce you to what BooJay is capable of: http://blogs. codehaus.org/people/bamboo/archives/001751_experience_boojay_ with_monolipse.html.

suited for building DSLs. That it runs natively on the Common Language Runtime (CLR; the technical name for the .NET platform) is a huge plus, because it means that your existing toolset is still relevant.

I dislike pigeonholing myself, but I'll readily admit that I mostly work on software based on the .NET Common Language Runtime. This is a common, stable platform[1] with a rich set of tools and practices. It makes sense to keep my DSL implementation within this platform because I already know most of its quirks and how to work around them. I can use my existing knowledge to troubleshoot most problems. Staying within the CLR also means that I'll have little problem when calling a DSL from my code, or vice versa—both the DSL and my code are CLR assemblies and interoperate cleanly.

Figure 1.3 shows an application that makes use of several DSLs. Those DSLs can access the application logic easily and natively, and the application can shell out to the DSL for decisions that require significant flexibility.

As much as I like the CLR, though, the common languages for it aren't well suited to language-oriented programming—they're too rigid. Rigid languages don't offer many options to express concepts. You have the default language syntax, and that's it.

Boo *is* a CLR language with a default syntax that's much like Python and with some interesting opinions about compiler architecture. Because it's a CLR language, it will compile down to IL (Intermediate Language—the CLR assembly language), and it will be able to access the entire base class library and any additional code you have lying around. It also will perform as fast as any other IL-based language. You don't sacrifice performance when you choose to use a DSL—at least not if you go with Boo.

In fact, you can debug your Boo DSL in Visual Studio, profile it with dotTrace (a really sweet .NET profiler from JetBrains: http://www.jetbrains.com/profiler/), and

Figure 1.3   DSLs used as integral parts of an application

---

[1]   Stable as long as you don't start playing with reflection emit and generics; there are dragons in that territory.

> **Using IronRuby or IronPython as host languages for DSLs**
>
> What about IronRuby and IronPython? They are CLR implementations of languages that have already proven to be suited for building DSLs.
>
> I have two major issues with using these host languages for my DSLs. The first is that, compared to Boo, they don't offer enough control over the resulting language. The second is that both languages run on the Dynamic Language Runtime, which is a layer on top of the CLR, which is what Boo runs on.
>
> This means that calling into IronRuby or IronPython code from C# code isn't as simple as adding a reference and making the call, which is all you need to do in Boo's case.

even reference it from any .NET language (such as C# or VB.NET). Similarly, your code (in any .NET language you care to name) will be able to make calls into the DSL code. This is the most common way to execute a DSL—by simply calling it.

What makes Boo special is that the compiler is open. And not open in the sense that you can look at the code, which isn't particularly useful unless you're writing compilers; what I mean is that you can easily change the compiler object model while it's compiling your code.

As you can imagine, this has some significant implications for your ability to use Boo for language-oriented programming. In effect, Boo will let you modify the language itself to fit your needs. I'll spend most of chapters 2 and 6 explaining this in detail, and you'll see what really made me choose Boo as the host language for my DSL efforts.

Boo also contains some interesting features for language-oriented programming, such as meta-methods, quasi-quotation, AST macros, and AST attributes.

As I mentioned, we'll explore Boo's language-oriented programming features in full in chapters 2 and 6. But for now, let's look at a few real-world DSLs written in Boo.

1.6   *Examining DSL examples*

Before we conclude this chapter, I want to give you a taste of the kind of DSLs you can create in Boo. This should give you some idea about the flexibility of the language.

1.6.1   *Brail*

Brail will probably remind you strongly of classic ASP or PHP. It's a text templating language, built by me, in which in you can mix code and text freely. Here's a sample:

```
<h1>My name is ${name}</h1>
<ul>
<%   for element in list: %>
    <li>${element}</li>
<%  end %>
</ul>
```

This example will output a header and a list in HTML format based on the input variables passed to it.

If you're interested, you can read up on Brail at the Castle Project: http://www.castleproject.org/monorail/documentation/trunk/viewengines/brail/index.html.

1.6.2   *Rhino ETL*

I built this DSL after I'd had enough of using an ETL tool that wasn't top-notch, to say the least. That ETL tool also used a graphical DSL as the building block, and the pain of using it on a day-to-day basis is one of the main reasons I dislike graphical DSLs.

NOTE   ETL stands for extract, transform, and load. It's a generic term for moving data around in a data warehouse. You *extract* the data from one location, *transform* it (probably with data from additional locations), and *load* it into its final destination. The classic example is moving data from a relational database to a decision-support system.

Rhino ETL employs the concept of steps, with data flowing from one step to the next. Usually the first step will extract the data from some source, and the last will load it to the final destination.

Here's an example of a full ETL process:

```
operation split_name:
    for row in rows:
        continue if row.Name is null
        row.FirstName, row.LastName = row.Name.Split()
        yield row

process UsersToPeople:
    input "source_db", Command = "SELECT id, name, email  FROM Users"
    split_names()
    output "destination_db", Command = """
        INSERT INTO People (UserId, FirstName, LastName, Email)
        VALUES (@UserId, @FirstName, @LastName, @Email)
        """:
        row.UserId = row.Id
```

This code gets the users list from the source database, splits the names, and then saves them to the destination database. This is a good example of a DSL that requires some knowledge of the domain before you can utilize it.

There's more information about Rhino ETL at http://www.ayende.com/Blog/category/545.aspx.

1.6.3   *Bake (Boo Build System)*

NAnt is an XML-based build system that works for simple scenarios, but it gets very complex very fast when you have a build script of any complexity. Bake, written by Georges Benatti, takes much the same conceptual approach (using tasks and actions), but it uses Boo to express the tasks and actions in the build script.

The resulting syntax tends to be easier to understand than the equivalent NAnt script at just about any level of complexity. XML has no natural way to express conditions and loops, and you often need those in a build script. It's much easier to read a build script when you're using a programming language to natively express concepts such as control flow. Interestingly enough, the ease of readability holds not only for complex build scripts, but also for simple ones, if only because XML-based languages have so much ceremony attached to them.

Here's a simple example that will create the build directory and copy all DLLs to it:

```
Task "init build dir":
    if not Directory.Exists("build"):
        MkDir "build"
    Cp FileSet("lib/*.dll").Files, "build", true
```

You can find out more about the Boo Build System at Google Code: http://code.google.com/p/boo-build-system/.

1.6.4   *Specter*

Specter is a behavior-driven development (BDD) testing framework, written by Andrew Davey and Cedric Vivier. It allows developers to build specifications for the object under test instead of asserting their behavior. You can read more about BDD here: http://behaviour-driven.org/.

Using Specter makes Boo behave in a way that's a better match for BDD. Here's an example for specifying how a stack (the data structure) should behave:

```
context "Empty stack":
 stack as Stack
 setup:
     stack = Stack()

 specify stack.Count.Must == 0

 specify "Stack must accept an item and count is then one":
    stack.Push(42)
    stack.Count.Must == 1
```

You can find out more about Specter here: http://specter.sourceforge.net/.

1.7   Summary

By now, you should understand what a DSL is. It used to be that the investment required to create a DSL was only justified for the big problems, but the tools have grown, and this book will help you understand how you can create a nontrivial language on a rainy afternoon.

Of all the DSL types presented in this chapter, I most strongly favor internal DSLs for their simplicity, extensibility, and low cost compared to the other approaches. Fluent interfaces are also good solutions, but they are frustrating when you bump into the limits of the (rigid) host language.

I have a strong bias against graphical DSLs for their visual verboseness, their complexity of use, and, most importantly, for the mess they often make out of source control. A graphical DSL doesn't lend itself to diffing and merging, which are critical in any scenario that involves more than a single developer.

Fortunately, this book isn't about graphical DSLs. It's about internal (or embedded) DSLs written in Boo. In chapter 2, we'll take a quick dive into Boo; just enough to get your feet wet and give you enough understanding of the subject to start building interesting languages with it.

Without further ado, let's get on with Boo.

An overview
of the Boo language

What is this Boo language anyway?

Boo is an object-oriented, statically typed language for the Common Language Runtime (CLR) with a Python-inspired syntax and a focus on language and compiler extensibility. (We'll discuss extensibility briefly in this chapter and in more detail in chapter 6.) Boo is an open source project released under the BSD license, which means you're free to take, modify, and use the language and its products in any way you want, without limitation, including for commercial use. (The license can be found at http://svn.codehaus.org/boo/boo/trunk/license.txt.)

Rodrigo B. de Oliveira started the project in early 2004, and since then it has grown significantly in popularity and features. The project is active and is continually evolving. As I write this, the released version of Boo is 0.9.1.

> **Getting Boo**
>
> You can download the binary distribution of Boo from the Boo website: http://boo.codehaus.org/.
>
> You can execute booish.exe from the bin directory (either by double-clicking it in Windows Explorer or issuing the command on the command line) to get a command interpreter that will allow you to experiment with Boo directly. It's convenient when you want to quickly try out some ideas, or verify an assumption.
>
> There is also booi.exe, which allows you execute Boo scripts without an explicit compilation step. And the compiler itself is invoked using boo.exe much as you can invoke the C# compiler by executing csc.exe.

NOTE Boo seems to be following the trend of many open source projects in that it isn't rushing toward a 1.0 release. Boo has been stable for a number of years, and I have been using it for production for the last 4 years. I have a high degree of trust in Boo, and it has not failed me yet.

Now that you know what Boo is, you're probably wondering why I chose to use it.

2.1   Why use Boo?

Boo is a CLR-based language, which means that when we use Boo, we benefit from the rich library that comes with .NET, JIT (just-in-time compilation) optimizations, and plenty of good tools. Even without extending the compiler, Boo has the following to offer:

- *Syntactic sugar for common programming patterns*—List, hash, and array literals, object initialization, string formatting, and regular expression matching are all first-class concepts in Boo. There is direct support for all of them in a natural manner.
- *Automatic variable declaration and type inference*[1]—The compiler takes care of things for you, so you don't have to type the same thing over and over again. Some would say that this is bad, due to the lack of explicit typing, but it's worth trying. In my experience, it works. Take a look at listing 2.1.

Listing 2.1   Exploring Boo's type inferencing

```
def random():
    return 4 # Selected by dice roll, guaranteed to be random

val = random()
```

---

[1] C# 3.0 has introduced the var keyword, which allows the C# compiler to do much the same for local variables. Boo supports this for just about everything (fields, properties, methods, local variables, and so on).

Why specify the type over and over again? The compiler can figure it out for itself and not bother you with it. If you want to get a compiler error, you can explicitly specify the type, as in listing 2.2.

Listing 2.2   Boo is statically typed—this code will cause a compiler error

```
val as string = random() # Will give error about type mismatch
```

- *Automatic typecasting*—The compiler will automatically cast variables to the appropriate type (if this is possible), without forcing you to explicitly cast variables. For example, when you try to pass a variable of type `Animal` to a method that requires a `dog` instance, the compiler will automatically cast it to a `dog`. The premise is that you would have to do this anyway. The following example shows what automatic typecasting does:

```
animal as Animal = Animal.CreateDog("Spot")
dog as Dog
dog = animal # Will automatically cast animal to Dog
```

- *Duck typing*—Boo is a strongly typed language, but you can ask the compiler to relax those constraints in certain situations and work like a dynamic language. This makes some things much more natural, because you can get into this dynamic invocation infrastructure and decide what to do at runtime. C# 4.0 will have some of the same capabilities when it comes out.

Let's see what we can do with the `XmlObject` in listing 2.3.

Listing 2.3   Using `IQuackFu` to get better syntax for working with XML

```
person = XmlObject(xmlDocument)
print person.FirstName
print person.LastName
```

This example resolves, at runtime, that we were asked to get the value of a property called `FirstName`, and then a property named `LastName`. This is easy to implement, as we'll see in section 2.4.9.

These features take care of some rough spots you might encounter when using string-based APIs, and they can be useful when building languages on top of Boo.

2.2   *Exploring compiler extensibility*

Boo is far more flexible than most other languages, and the option to reprogram the compiler is valuable not only for creating DSLs, but for taking care of tedious tasks that require repetitive code.

For example, suppose you want to implement the Singleton pattern. You'd need to do several things to make it happen:

- Ensure that the creation of the singleton is thread-safe
- Lazily initialize the singleton
- Make all the constructors private

- Ensure that serializing and deserializing the singleton will not create several instances of the singleton
- Create a static `Instance` property
- Have no static members on the singleton class

To do this in most languages, you'd have to follow an implementation pattern and write fairly repetitive code. In Boo, we can capture this implementation pattern in an AST attribute that will do all of that for us (more on AST attributes in chapter 6). Here's how you would define a singleton in Boo.

```
[singleton]
class MySingleton:
    pass
```

The `[singleton]` attribute isn't a built-in capability of Boo; it's a standard extension, and the capabilities to extend the language are also exposed to our code. This makes writing DSLs much easier.

By using a similar approach and the same language-extension capabilities, you can use `[disposable]`, `[observable]`, and other advanced techniques, such as aspect-oriented programming.

NOTE   There's lots to learn about Boo, but this book will focus on the things we need for building DSLs. You can find more information about useful things you can do with Boo here: http://docs.codehaus.org/display/BOO/Useful+things+about+Boo.

But before we discuss all the hoops we can make Boo jump through, we should look at the syntax.

2.3   Basic Boo syntax

Instead of explaining Boo's syntax by just printing its formal Backus-Naur Form (BNF), we'll look at a few sample programs. They should give you a feeling for the language.

Our first sample program will be, of course, Hello World. To make it a bit more interesting, we'll use WinForms for it. Listing 2.4 shows the code.

Listing 2.4   Hello World using WinForms

```
import System.Windows.Forms

f = Form(Text: "Hello, boo!")
btn = Button(Text: "Click Me!", Dock: DockStyle.Fill)
btn.Click += do(sender, e):  f.Close()
f.Controls.Add(btn)

Application.Run(f)
```

In this example, we start by importing the `System.Windows.Forms` namespace. This statement is similar to the `using` statement in C#, but in Boo this also instructs the compiler to load the `System.Windows.Forms` assembly if the namespace could not be found in the loaded assemblies.

Significant-whitespace versus whitespace-agnostic mode

If you've done any work with Python, you're probably aware that one of the major gripes against the language is the significant-whitespace issue. Python uses the indentation of the code to define control blocks. This means that you don't need curly braces or explicit block endings like end (in Ruby) or End If (in VB.NET).

The code looks like this:

```
if lives == 0:
    print "Game over!"
    game.Finish()
else:
    lives--
    print "${lives} more lives"
```

This is a major point of contention with Python, and because Boo uses the same convention, the same complaint has been raised against it as well. But having spent several years working with Boo, I can say that it rarely causes any problems.

"Rarely" isn't the same as "never," though. When I wrote Brail, a templating language using Boo, the whitespace issue *was* a major issue. I wanted to use the usual HTML formatting, but that messed up the formatting that Boo required.

Fortunately, Boo comes with a whitespace-agnostic mode, which you can utilize by flipping a compiler switch. When using whitespace-agnostic mode, the previous code would have to be written slightly differently:

```
if lives == 0:
    print "Game over!"
    game.Finish()
else:
    lives--
    print "${lives} more lives"
end
```

The only difference that you'll notice is the end at the end of the statement. This is because Boo will now use the structure of the code to figure out where control blocks begin and end. Usually, this means that a block starts when a statement ends with a colon (:) and ends with an end keyword.

When writing DSLs, I tend to use the significant-whitespace mode, and only go to the whitespace-agnostic mode when I find that the whitespace causes issues.

TIP   When you aren't sure how to do something in Boo, try doing what you would in C# (with the obvious syntax changes). In most cases, it will work, but note that it may not be the best way to do it in Boo.

Next, we create a Form and a Button. Boo supports property initialization at construction (C# 3.0 supports a similar notion, object initializers). Finally, we register the button Click event, add the button to the form, and start the application with the form as the main form.

Not bad for a quick Hello World application. If you wish, you can type the code in listing 2.4 directly into `booish` and experiment with the language.

Now, let's try something a tad more complicated, shall we? Listing 2.5 creates an HTTP server that allows you to download files from a directory.

Listing 2.5   An HTTP server in Boo

```
import System.Net
import System.IO

if argv.Length != 2:
    print "You must pass [prefix] [path] as parameters"
    return

prefix = argv[0]
path = argv[1]

if not Directory.Exists(path):
    print "Could not find ${path}"
    return

listener = HttpListener()
listener.Prefixes.Add(prefix)
listener.Start()

while true:
    context = listener.GetContext()
    file = Path.GetFileName(context.Request.RawUrl)
    fullPath = Path.Combine(path, file)
    if File.Exists(fullPath):
        context.Response.AddHeader("Content-Disposition", \
                                   "attachment; filename=${file}")
        bytes = File.ReadAllBytes(fullPath)
        context.Response.OutputStream.Write(bytes, 0, bytes.Length)
        context.Response.OutputStream.Flush()
        context.Response.Close()
    else:
        context.Response.StatusCode = 404
        context.Response.Close()
```

In this code we have a bit of argument validation, and then we set up an `HttpListener` and start replying to requests. This isn't the most interesting bit of code I have ever seen, but it does touch on a lot of different topics.

There are a few things that you should pay attention to in this example:

- The `argv` parameter is a string array (defined by Boo) that holds the command-line parameters passed by the user.
- The usage of `HttpListener` requires administrator privileges.
- You can execute the code using the following command from the command line (assuming that you save the code as http_server.boo):

    ```
    path\to\booi http_server.boo boo_server .\
    ```

    You can then go to http://localhost/boo_server/http_server.boo to download the http_server.boo file.

> ## That annoying semicolon
>
> One of the more annoying things when moving between languages is the semicolon. When I move between C# and VB.NET code, I keep putting semicolons at the end of VB.NET statements, and forgetting to end my C# code with semicolons.
>
> Boo has optional semicolons, so you can put them in or not, as you wish. This makes temporarily dropping into the language a far smoother experience, because you don't have to unlearn ingrained habits.

For anyone proficient in .NET, what we're doing should be familiar. The language may be a bit different, but the objects and methods we call are all from the Base Class Library (BCL). This familiarity is welcome. We don't need to learn everything from scratch.

Let's look at one last example before we get back to talking about DSLs. Listing 2.6 shows a simple implementation of GREP.

Listing 2.6   A simple GREP implementation

```
import System
import System.IO
import System.Text.RegularExpressions

# Get all files matching a specific pattern from a directory
# and all its subdirectories
# Note: string* is a shorthand to IEnumerable<string>
def GetFiles(dir as string, pattern as string) as string*:
    # Get all subdirectories
    folders = Directory.GetDirectories(dir)
    # For each subdirectory, recurse into that directory
    # and yield all the files that were returned
    for folder in folders:
        for file in GetFiles(folder, pattern):
            yield file
    # Yield all the files that match the given pattern
    for file in Directory.GetFiles(dir, pattern):
        yield file

# Argument validation
if argv.Length != 2:
    print "Usage: grep [pattern] [regex]"

filePattern = argv[0]
textPattern = Regex(argv[1])

# Get all the files matching the pattern in the current directory
for file in GetFiles(Environment.CurrentDirectory, filePattern):
    # For each file, read all the lines
    using sr = StreamReader(file):
        while not sr.EndOfStream:
            line = sr.ReadLine()
            # If the line match the given pattern, print it
```

```
if textPattern.IsMatch(line):
    print file, ":", line
```

In listing 2.6, `GetFiles` returns a type of `string*`, which is another Boo syntax short-cut. `string*` is the equivalent of `IEnumerable` of `string`. And more generally, `T*` is equivalent to `IEunumerable` of `T`, where `T` is any type. This code also uses `yield` to return results in a streaming fashion.

You can execute this code using the following command:

```
path\to\booi grep.boo *.cs TextBox
```

This will search the current directory for all the C# files that make use of TextBox.

More Boo information

This chapter offers a high-level overview of Boo. If you're new to the language, I recommend reading the appendixes to complete your knowledge of the language:

- Appendix A contains a Boo tutorial for beginners, which can guide you through the initial steps in learning the language.
- Appendix B contains a syntax reference comparing Boo with C#, which should help you to translate your C# knowledge to Boo.

In general, Boo should be fairly easy to grab and use if you're already familiar with a programming language of some kind.

I hope that this gave you a feel for the Boo language. Now let's continue exploring why Boo is a good language for writing DSLs.

2.4   *Boo's built-in language-oriented features*

Let's look at Boo's language-oriented features, starting with the simplest and moving on to the more complicated ones, always with an eye to how we can use them for building DSLs. The first few examples involve no changes to the compiler. Boo comes with a lot of features to support DSLs.

2.4.1   *String interpolation*

String interpolation is syntactic sugar on top of string builders, nothing more. This means that you can put an expression like `${}` inside a string, and anything inside the curly braces will be evaluated and appended to the string.

Consider this example:

```
name = "dear reader"
print "Hello ${name}"
```

This code will print "Hello dear reader". It's a direct translation of the following C# code (with no attempt to translate the semantics):

```
string name = "dear reader";
Console.WriteLine(
```

```
    new StringBuilder()
            .Append("Hello ")
            .Append(name)
    );
```

This is nice when you want to output text with variables, but without all the messy string concatenation.

Note that this works for static strings only, because it's a transformation that happens at compile time. You can't do something like the following and get the same experience:

```
str = "Hi ${" + PerferredNameFormat + "}"
print str.Evalute()
```

There is no way to take a string and evaluate it for string interpolation. If you need to dynamically change how you build strings at runtime, you'll need to use String-Builder directly.

2.4.2   *Is, and, not, and or*

Is, and, not, and or are keywords in Boo. The is keyword is the reference equality operator. And, not, and or have their usual meanings. By combining them, we can structure sentences that are valid Boo code while being very readable.

Here's an example:

```
customer.CurrentPlan is null and customer.RegisteredAt > SixMonthsAgo
```

This can be read almost like English and demonstrates that you can compose readable statements using those keywords.

2.4.3   *Optional parentheses*

The ability to skip specifying parentheses on method calls might look like a small feature, but it has a significant effect on readability.

Compare this,

```
SuggestRegisterToClub("Preferred")
```

and this:

```
SuggestRegisterToClub "Preferred"
```

Not much of a change, I'll admit, but the second version is easier to read. There is less syntactic noise for you to parse.

In fact, I would generally write it as follows, to make it even easier:

```
suggest_register_to_club "Preferred"
```

We'll revisit the idea of reducing the syntactic noise later in this chapter—the less noise, the more clarity. This gets even more interesting with anonymous blocks, which are another way Boo helps us reduce syntactic noise.

2.4.4 *Anonymous blocks*

Anonymous blocks are a feature of Boo that allows you to use a more natural syntax for passing delegates to a method. The way it works is quite simple: if the last parameter of a method is a delegate, you can start a new code block and the compiler will treat the new code block as the body of the delegate that you pass to the method.

What this means is that instead of using this C# code,

```
List<int> ints = GetListOfIntegers();
ints.ForEach(i => Console.WriteLine(i) );
```

we can use this Boo code:

```
ints = GetListOfIntegers()
ints.ForEach do(i): print i
```

If we want to execute an action and don't need parameters, we can do the same thing like this:

```
ints.ForEach:
    print "foo"
```

Those are fairly silly examples, but you'll use these techniques regularly when writing DSLs. Because the syntax flows more naturally, the DSL lets the user express intention more clearly and easily.

Suppose you wanted to perform some action when a new message arrives. You could write it like this:

```
msgBroker = MessageBroker()
msgBroker.WhenMessageArrives:
    print "message arrived"
```

In this instance, it's just another way to perform event registration, but I'm sure you can see the potential. It allows you to turn method calls into full-fledged keywords.

2.4.5 *Statement modifiers*

Statement modifiers are another tool for producing clearer code. By using them, you can turn several statements into a single sentence. You can use the following statement modifiers: `if`, `unless`, and `while`.

Consider this code:

```
if customer.IsPreferred:
    ApplyDiscount(0.5)
```

We can make it more readable by using a statement modifier, like this:

```
ApplyDiscount(0.5) if customer.IsPreferred
```

The first example has a very code-like structure, whereas the second flows more naturally. Statement modifiers allow you to change where you put the condition: instead of keeping it as an independent statement, you can make it part of the statement it applies to. This is a small change, moving the condition around, but like most of the topics we're discussing in this chapter, it can significantly enhance clarity when used properly.

In fact, we can make it even better by removing the parentheses and changing the method name:

```
apply_discount_of 0.5 if customer.IsPreferred
```

Some people feel that statement modifiers are harder to read, because they have to read to the end of the statement to figure out what is going on. For myself, I feel that this is a natural representation of the way we speak.

But this example points out another interesting usage pattern. Naming is different in code and natural language, and we can take advantage of that by using naming conventions.

2.4.6 *Naming conventions*

The CLR comes with clear guidelines about naming, and the BCL follows them closely. Names are in Pascal case for classes and members, and camelCase for parameters; abbreviations should be Pascal case unless they're two letters long, in which case both letters are capitalized, and so on. After a while, this style becomes an ingrained habit. But now I'm going to ask you to forget all of that. We aren't building an API to be consumed by other developers, who can ReadPascalCaseStatementsJustFine. We're building a language to be read, full stop.

When it's time to name your methods and classes, you should do so in the context of their usage, and their usage is in text, not in code. The previous example of changing `ApplyDiscount` to `apply_discount_of` is one example. It's easier to read `apply_discount_of` than the more visually condensed version.

Naming conventions and holy wars

The choice of naming conventions can be a heated topic. Some people swear by Pascal case, others think that underscores are the pinnacle of clarity, and others are well aware that camelCase is the way the universe was written. And so on.

I won't take sides in this argument. I'll just say that I have found underscores to be useful in reducing the density of some of my DSLs. As usual, you need to make your decision based on the wide variety of factors in your own scenario.

I urge you to consider your naming conventions carefully when you build a DSL. Regardless of your final choice, it's an important part of the way you structure your language.

This isn't just a matter of using underscores versus Pascal case. It's a matter of considering the method name in the context of the language. For instance, I might have several variants of a method name, depending on its usage, all forwarding to a single method. This can be done for clarity of intent in a particular usage, or as a way to specify additional intent.

Let's look at an example where we're publishing a message to various sources. We could have all of these methods call the same underlying method:

```
publish_message_to_group "administrators"

publish_message_to_owner

publish_message_to_user "joe"
```

If we were writing code, we'd probably use something like PublishMessage(destination), but the different method names provide additional clarity in different contexts. They allow us to be clearer about what we want to express.

Another way to provide multiple names for a single method is to extend the Boo compiler in such a way that it automatically translates from one naming convention to the other. The Boo compiler has rich support for that, and we'll discuss it extensively in chapter 6.

It might be easier to provide a DSL facade over your application code, to isolate the language-oriented naming from the CodeOriented naming. Extending classes using extension methods and properties is one way of gaining clarity in the DSL while still keeping the core code clear of different naming styles. We'll look at extension methods and properties in the next couple of sections.

2.4.7   *Extension methods*

Another way to employ naming conventions is to provide them externally, using extension methods. Classes in Boo are CLR classes, which means they follow the same laws that you're familiar with from C#. You can't add methods to a class or modify existing methods.[2] What you can do is to ask the compiler to pretend for you.

This Boo feature works like extension methods in C# 3.0, and it's interoperable with the C# 3.0 version. Boo is a bit more powerful, adding support for extension properties as well as extension methods. Here's a typical example of extending System.String:

```
class StringExtensions:
    [Extension]
    static def ToPascalCase(str as string):
        return char.ToUpper(str[0]) + str.Substring(1)
```

The definition of ToPascalCase here creates an extension method, which means that we can now call ToPascalCase as if it were an instance method on System.String, rather than a static method on a different class (and assembly). Unlike C#, where we only need to reference the class's namespace in the using block, in Boo we need to import the class itself. So in order to use the ToPascalCase extension method we need to write

```
import StringExtensions

"some string".ToPascalCase()
```

This is nice, but don't go overboard with it. I don't recommend writing extension methods to your own classes in regular code, but different rules apply to DSLs.

---

[2] Well, you probably *could* do this, if you really wanted to, but I don't recommend it. It would require modifying the compiler, and you'd still find that the CLR enforces some of those restrictions.

2.4.8 *Extension properties*

Extension properties are like extension methods, but they use properties.

For example, suppose we want to extend the IList interface to support the Length property. We could use the compiler support for extension properties to attach this property to everything that implements IList by using the following syntax:

```
class ListExtensions:
    [Extension]
    static Length[list as IList]:
        get:
            return list.Count
```

In general, extension properties can be used for the same reasons as extension methods: to get additional clarity without creating untidy code, and to create more expressive expressions. As with extension methods, you need to import the class that exposes the property before you can make use of the extension property. So, in order to use the Length extension property, we would write the following:

```
import System.Collections
import ListExtensions

a = ArrayList()
print a.Length
```

Extension properties are quite useful when we want to construct sentences. For example, we could extend the Int32 class so it knows about dates and times, making the following property chain valid:

```
2.minutes.from.now
```

This is done using extension properties and simple fluent interface, and it allows us to express complex values in a natural manner.

So what if, instead of extending a type by a single property or method, we could extend a type at runtime? Welcome to the world of duck typing …

2.4.9 *The IQuackFu interface*

If it walks like a duck and it quacks like a duck, then it must be an IQuackFu. Other languages call it duck typing or method missing (or message not understood) and many dynamic languages support it. Because Boo is a statically typed language (unless you explicitly tell the compiler that you want late-bound semantics), and because method missing is such a nice concept to have, Boo includes the IQuackFu interface to introduce this capability.

The IQuackFu interface, shown in figure 2.1, gives you the option to handle dynamic dispatch on your own, instead of having to rely on the language semantics.

Duck typing basically means that you don't care what the actual type of an object is. As long as it supports the operations you need (as long as it walks like a duck), you can treat it as a valid object (it is a duck).

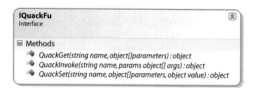

Figure 2.1 The `IQuackFu` interface is Boo's version of method missing.

So far, this sounds a lot like late-bound semantics (similar to VB.NET's behavior when you set `option strict off`), but there's more. By default, when you ask Boo to use duck typing, you'll get late-bound semantics, but `IQuackFu` also allows an object to take part in the decision about where to dispatch a call that cannot be made statically.

Don't worry if this doesn't quite make sense yet—it'll be clearer once we look at an example. Suppose we want to extract and display the first names from the XML in listing 2.7.

Listing 2.7   The input XML structure

```
<People>
    <Person>
        <FirstName>John</FirstName>
    </Person>
    <Person>
        <FirstName>Jane</FirstName>
    </Person>
</People>
```

We could do this using any number of XML processing options, but the amount of code required would make this awkward. We could also generate some sort of strongly typed wrapper around it if we had a schema for the XML. Or we could use a tool to generate the schema if we didn't have it already ... This is starting to look like a lot of work.

We could also do it as in listing 2.8. We're using a generic object here, so how can this work?

Listing 2.8   Using the XML object to output

```
doc = XmlObject(xmlDocument.DocumentElement)
for person as XmlObject in doc.Person:
    print person.FirstName
```

The code in listing 2.8 works because we intercept the calls to the object and decide how to answer them at runtime. This is what *method missing* means. We catch the call to a missing method and decide to do something smart about it (like returning the data from the XML document).

At least, this is how it works in dynamic languages. For a statically typed language, the situation is a bit different; all method calls must be known at compile time. That's why Boo introduced `IQuackFu`. Take a look at the implementation of `XmlObject` in listing 2.9, and then we'll look at how it works.

Listing 2.9   The XML object implementation—method missing over an XML document

```
class XmlObject(IQuackFu): # Implementing IQuackFu interface

    _element as XmlElement        # The element field

    # Get the XML element in the constructor and store it in a field
    def constructor(element as XmlElement):
        _element = element

    # Intercept any property call made to the object.
    # This allows us to translate a property call to navigate
    # the XML tree.
    def QuackGet(name as string, parameters as (object)) as object:

        # Get the node(s) by its name
        elements = _element.SelectNodes(name)

        if elements is not null: # Check that the node exists
            # Here we're being crafty. If there is only one node
            # selected, we'll wrap it in a new XmlObject and
            # return it. This allows us easy access throughout
            # the DOM.
            return XmlObject(elements[0]) if elements.Count == 1
            # If there is more than one, return a list of all
            # the matched nodes, each wrapped in an XmlObject.
            xmlObjects = List[of XmlObject]()
            for e as XmlElement in elements:
                xmlObjects.Add( XmlObject(e) )
            return xmlObjects

        else:

            return null

    # We don't support invoking methods, so we ignore this
    # method. We could also raise NotSupportedException here.
    def QuackInvoke(name as string, args as (object)) as object:
        pass # ignored

    # If we wanted two-way communication, we could have built
    # it into this method, but we don't, so we ignore this
    # method as well.
    def QuackSet(name as string, parameters as (object), value) as object:
        pass # ignored

    # This is to make it easier to work with the node.
    override def ToString():
        return _element.InnerText
```

This code doesn't implement the QuackInvoke and QuackSet methods, because they aren't relevant to the example. Implementing QuackGet is sufficient to make the point.

Listing 2.10 shows how we could use the XmlObject if we didn't have the compiler doing it for us.

Listing 2.10   Manually calling `IQuackFu` methods

```
doc = XmlObject(xmlDocument)
for person as XmlObject in doc.QuackGet("Person"):
        print person.QuackGet("FirstName")
```

When the compiler finds that it can't resolve a method (or a property) in the usual way, it then checks whether the type implements the `IQuackFu` interface. If it does, the compiler translates the original method call into a method call using `QuackGet`, `QuackSet`, or `QuackInvoke`. This means that we get to decide what will happen at run-time, which allows us to do some nice things. The `XmlObject` example is just one of the possibilities.

Convention-based methods are an interesting idea that's widely used in Ruby. Here's an example that should be immediately familiar to anyone who has dabbled in Rails' `ActiveRecord`:

```
user as User = Users.FindByNameAndPassword("foo", "bar")
```

That will be translated by the compiler to this:

```
user as User = Users.QuackInvoke("FindByNameAndPassword", "foo", "bar")
```

The `User`'s `QuackInvoke` method will parse the method name and issue a query by name and password.

This is a neat trick, with serious implications for writing DSLs. `IQuackFu` is usually the first tool that I reach for whenever I find that the standard mechanisms of the language aren't sufficient to express what I want.

There are also other tools that are useful, but we'll learn about them in chapter 6.

2.5   Summary

We've gone over the major benefits of Boo as a language for creating DSLs: its basic syntax and some of the things we can do with the built-in features.

In general, when building DSLs, I consider all of the aspects of Boo we've covered so far as the low-hanging fruit: easy to pick, good, and nearly all you need. You can build good DSLs by utilizing what the language gives you, without digging into Boo's more advanced options. Even when you do need to use some advanced options, you'll still need those regular language concepts in most of the DSLs you build. I recommend that you learn these options and think about how to use them effectively. But the basic Boo features aren't always enough, and they're certainly not the sum of what you can do using Boo.

I have chosen not to bore you with the usual language details, such as introducing `if` statements and explaining how loops work. Boo is simple enough that it shouldn't be too difficult to grasp the fundamentals based on the examples in this chapter. Because Boo runs on the CLR, it uses a familiar environment, so you're spared from learning that as well.

If you want a more structured approach to learning the language, take a look at appendix A, which contains a Boo language tutorial. Appendix B contains a syntax reference, which will allow you to translate between C# and Boo. I recommend at least skimming through appendix B.

As for reading Boo code, the overall structure of Boo means that it's similar to C#. In both you have classes, methods, operators, control statements, and so on. If you can read C# code, you can read Boo code. More information about Boo the language can be found on the Boo site (http://boo.codehaus.org/) and in the Boo language guide (http://boo.codehaus.org/Language+Guide).

We'll defer the dive into the deep end for a bit, and first discuss building an application with a DSL. Once we've covered the underlying concepts, we'll crack open the compiler and start telling it how it should behave.

For now, the next step is building a DSL-driven application.

The drive toward DSLs

In this chapter, we're going to look at the different types of DSLs that we can build and at how and when we should use them. We'll then take a problem—the need for a scheduling system—and begin solving it with a DSL—the Scheduling DSL. We'll start by looking at the problem, follow the reasoning that leads us to solving it using a DSL, and then decide on the syntax and implementation.

In this chapter, we'll build several implementations of the Scheduling DSL and go through the entire process of building a DSL for real use, although it will be a rather basic one.

3.1   *Choosing the DSL type to build*

The first step in building a DSL is deciding what type of a DSL to build. Our sample scenario will be scheduling tasks, so we'll take a look at several approaches to building a scheduling DSL, which will help us compare fluent interfaces and DSLs.

First, we need to consider the steps involved in scheduling tasks, from the usage perspective: defining named tasks, defining the repeatability of the task, and defining the set of actions that will occur when the task is executed. Here are some examples of each:

- Define named tasks
  + Crawl site
  + Back up database
  + Check that service is online
- Define when task should be executed
  + Once a day
  + Once a week
  + Every hour
- Define actions to occur when task is executed
  + Check URL response
  + Send email
  + Generate report

When we get around to writing the engine responsible for taking all three parts and making them into an executable, we'll focus on how to schedule tasks, how to handle errors, how to verify that tasks are completed, and so on. But from the point of view of the domain we're working on, those details aren't meaningful. When we define a new task, we should just deal with the scheduling semantics, not with implementation mechanics.

We could get much of this abstraction—separating the scheduling semantics from the scheduling implementation—by building facades and hiding the implementation details under the facades' abstraction, and we could get a fairly good syntax by using a fluent interface. Why build a DSL?

3.1.1   *The difference between fluent interfaces and DSLs*

If you have a fluent interface, you already have a DSL. It's a limited one, admittedly, but it's still a DSL for all intents and purposes. There are significant differences in readability between a fluent interface and a DSL, because you have a lot of freedom when you define the language for the DSL, but fluent interfaces have to work within the limits of a typically rigid language to work.[1]

---

[1] This, of course, assumes that we're talking about common static languages. Fluent interfaces in dynamic languages are a different matter, and are much closer to a DSL.

Because of those limitations, I tend to use DSLs and fluent interfaces for different tasks. I use a fluent interface when I need a touch of language-oriented programming, and I go with a DSL when I need something with a bit more flexibility.

We'll take a look at some code, and that should demonstrate the differences between fluent interfaces and DSLs. Please don't concern yourself with the implementation details for now; just look at the syntax.

First, listing 3.1 shows an example of a fluent interface.

Listing 3.1   Using a fluent interface to define a task to execute

```
new FluentTask("warn if website is down")
    .Every( TimeSpan.FromMinutes(3) )
    .StartingFrom( DateTime.Now )
    .When(() => new WebSite("http://example.org").IsNotResponding )
    .Execute(() => Notify("admin@example.org", "server down!"))
    .Schedule();
```

Listing 3.2 shows the DSL equivalent.

Listing 3.2   Using a DSL to define a task to execute

```
task "warn if website is down":
    every 3.Minutes()
    starting now
    when WebSite("http://example.org").IsNotResponding
    then:
        notify "admin@example.org", "server down!"
```

As you can see, the DSL code doesn't have to work to make the compiler happy, nor does it have the ugly lambda declaration in the middle of the code or all the syntactic baggage (parentheses). It would be difficult to take anything away from the DSL example without losing some meaning. There's little noise there, and noise reduction is important when we're talking about language-oriented programming. The less noise we have, the clearer the code is.

Now, remember that a fluent interface is also a DSL. This means that we can make the fluent interface example clearer. Tim Wilde was kind enough to do that for us on his blog (http://www.midnightcoder.net/Blog/viewpost.rails?postId=38), reaching the syntax outlined in listing 3.3.

Listing 3.3   A better fluent interface for scheduling tasks

```
Schedule.Task( "warn if website is down" ).
    Repeat.Every( 3 ).Minutes.
    Starting( DateTime.Now ).
    If( Web.Site( "http://example.org" ).IsNotResponding() ).
    Notify( "admin@example.org", "Site down!" );
```

But the catch, and there is always a catch, is that the complexity of the fluent interface implementation grows significantly as we try to express richer and richer concepts. In this case, the backend of the implementation got to eight classes and six interfaces, all for five lines of code, whereas the DSL implementation is considerably simpler. Toward the end of this chapter, we'll look at how to implement the Scheduling DSL, and the whole thing will be less than 150 lines, most of which are dedicated to enabling testing and running the backend engine.

Fluent interfaces tend to be harder to scale than DSLs. We haven't actually built a DSL yet, but we'll do that later in this chapter and you'll be able to judge for yourself. Does this mean that we should stop using fluent interfaces altogether? As usual, the answer is that it depends, but in general the answer is no.

3.1.2   *Choosing between a fluent interface and a DSL*

I'll admit that I tend to favor building DSLs over fluent interfaces, precisely because I leaned the other way in the past and got badly burned by trying to maintain something of that complexity in a rigid language. But there is a time and place for everything.

I tend to ask the following questions when I'm deciding which to choose:

- When will this DSL or fluent interface be used?
- Who will use the DSL or fluent interface?
- How flexible does the syntax need to be?

Fluent interfaces are usually useful only during the development process. A fluent interface is probably a good choice if you intend to use it while you write the code, because you won't have to switch between two languages and can take advantage of the IDE tooling. In contrast, if you want to allow modifications outside development (for example, in production), a DSL tends to be a much better choice.

This leads to the question of who will use the DSL or fluent interface. If domain experts are going to be the users, you'll probably want a full-blown DSL in place, because that will make it easier to work with the concepts of the domain. If the target audience is programmers, and the expected usage is during normal development, a fluent interface would be appropriate.

Last, but certainly not least, is the issue of the syntax that you want to use. DSLs are more expressive. Getting a fluent interface to be expressive can be prohibitive in terms of time and complexity.

One of most important differences between a DSL and a fluent interface shows up when you want to perform actions outside the direct development cycle. While a fluent interface is strongly tied to the development cycle, if only because we require an IDE, a build process, and to push binaries to production, with a DSL we are dealing with standalone scripts. It is very easy to treat them as such, edit them using a simple text editor (or using a dedicated tool, as discussed in chapter 10), and simply upload them to the production environment.

I am not a fan of treating DSL changes as mere configuration changes and thus skipping the test cycle, but in many organizations the ability to push such changes rapidly is a major selling point for a DSL over a fluent interface. Chapter 12 discusses pushing DSL changes to production in a disciplined, auditable, and controlled manner.

How to deal with language hopping

Some people have a theoretical issue with using more than one language at a time. I say "theoretical" because it's usually more theoretical than practical.

In the web world, people have little problem hopping between HTML, JavaScript, and server-side programming, so this disconnect isn't a big problem. In many enterprise applications, important parts of applications are written in SQL (stored procedures, triggers, complex queries, and the like), and here too we need to frequently move between code in C#, Java, or VB.NET and SQL queries. In my experience, language hopping has rarely caused any confusion (it has other issues, but this isn't the place to talk about them).

If you remain consistent in your domain terminology in both languages, and keep your language short and to the point, you shouldn't need to worry about problems as a result of language hopping.

Last, but not least, there is a hard limit to how much you can get from a fluent interface in terms of language-oriented programming. A DSL is much more flexible in this regard, and that is a major reason to favor a DSL over a fluent interface. On the plus side for fluent interfaces, you can take advantage of your existing tool chain (IDE, IntelliSense, and so on) instead of having to build your own.

Coming back to DSLs, let's explore the reasons and motives for building different types of DSLs, and how that affects the DSLs we're building.

3.2   *Building different types of DSLs*

As I mentioned in chapter 1, different types of DSLs are written for different purposes:

- *Technical DSLs*—Created to solve technical issues. You might use such DSLs to create build scripts, set up system configuration, or to provide a natural syntax for a technical domain (a DSL for behavior-driven design or for creating state machines).
- *Business DSLs*—Created to provide a common, executable language for a team (including domain experts) in a specific domain.
- *Extensibility DSLs*—Created to allow an application to be extended externally without modifying the application itself but by providing external scripts to add additional functionality. Usages include scripting, customer modifications, and so on.

These DSL types have different constraints and requirements that affect how you need to approach building them and where and how they are used in applications. We'll look at each type in depth, starting with technical DSLs.

3.2.1   *Building technical DSLs*

Technical DSLs are generally used to solve problems of clarity and complexity.

A build tool is an obvious example. Compiling all the code is a single step in the build process; copying all referenced assemblies to the output location is another step. We arrange those steps into groups that are called *targets*, which have dependency relationships between them. The job of the build script is to define the targets, the steps within the targets, and the dependencies between the different targets.

The process of building software is a complex one. Components' dependency management, complier options, platform choices, and many other issues need to be dealt with. In large projects needing a clear build process, the build scripts are a black art, feared by many and understood by few. This make them an excellent target for a technical DSL, because you can use the DSL to encapsulate the complexity and give even those who aren't familiar with the build the ability to understand and modify it.

Technical DSLs are built for technical people, usually developers. Having technical people as the audience greatly simplifies the task of building a good DSL, but creating a clear and expressive language is just as important for a technical DSL as for any other.

As a case in point, we can look at Apache Ant, a popular build tool in the Java world. When James Duncan Davidson created Apache Ant, it was perfectly logical to use an XML file to specify the syntax for the build script. After all, that's what XML is for, and using it avoided the need to create yet another parser. The problem is that this will work for awhile, and then you'll realize that you need conditionals and iterations and the like. The result can look like listing 3.4.

Listing 3.4   An Ant XML script with a `foreach` loop and not the best syntax

```
<foreach item="File" property="filename">
    <in>
        <items>
            <include name="${finished_spec.dir}\*.dll" />
        </items>
    </in>
    <do>
        <exec program="${build.dir}\document.exe"
            commandline="${filename} ${build.dir}\docs"/>
    </do>
</foreach>
```

James has reconsidered the decision to go with XML (http://weblogs.java.net/blog/duncan/archive/2003/06/ant_dotnext.html).

For comparison, listing 3.5 has the same functionality, but expressed using the Bake DSL.

Listing 3.5   A Bake script with a `for` loop

```
for file in Directory.GetFiles(finished_spec, "*.dll"):
    exec(Path: "${buildDir}\\document.exe",
                CmdLine: "${file} ${buildDir}\\docs")
```

Listing 3.4 and listing 3.5 perform the same action, executing a program for each DLL in a specific directory. The Ant script takes three times as many lines to express the same thing as the Boo Bake script, and the actual meaning of the script is lost in the XML noise.

This difference between the two styles can seem minor in such a small example, but consider how it affects your ability to read and understand what the script is doing in a real-world scenario.

TIP   Look at what we're iterating on in listing 3.5. We're using the standard CLR API in the DSL. This means that we have tremendous power in our hands; we don't need to supply everything to the DSL. We can make use of anything that already exists on the CLR, and, even more importantly, making use of the available API requires no additional effort.

As another example of a technical DSL where clarity is critical, consider listing 3.6, taken from a Binsor configuration file. (Binsor is a Boo DSL for configuring the Castle Windsor container.) This piece of code scans a set of assemblies and finds all the types that implement the `IController` interface.

Listing 3.6   Binsor script to scan a set of assemblies

```
for type in AllTypesIn("MyApp.Controllers", "MyApp.Helpers"):
        continue unless typeof(IController).IsAssignableFrom(type)
        component type
```

You can probably tell what the code in listing 3.6 is doing, even without a good understanding of how Binsor works. The combination between just enough DSL syntax and the ability to use standard programming constructs makes for a very powerful approach when building a technical DSL.

You aren't limited to just using loops—you have the full power of a programming language in your hands, which means that you can execute logic as part of configuration scripts. Even for simple configuration tasks, the ability to execute logic is invaluable. Consider the case of selecting a connection string for test or development. You could have several connection strings and select from them manually in the application code, or you could have an `if` statement in your configuration make the decision automatically.

The advantages of building a technical language are that you get the benefits of a DSL (clearer semantics and a higher focus on the task) and keep most of the power that you're used to having.

The disadvantage is that technical DSLs are still pretty close to programming languages, and as such tend to require programming skills to use. This is fine if you're targeting developers, but not if you want a DSL that a business expert can use. For those scenarios, you need a business DSL.

3.2.2 *Building business DSLs*

When you're building a DSL for a business scenario, rather than a technical one, you need to ask yourself a few questions. Who is going to write scripts using this DSL, and who is going to read those scripts?

> ### Talking with domain experts
>
> In one of my projects, I had an ex-developer as a business analyst. The domain was a complex one, and we often ran into subtleties. Being able to ping the analyst and go over code with him was invaluable. He could tell me if I was doing it right, because he could understand what the code was doing.
>
> This was an extremely rare situation, but it made my work much easier, because we could communicate on a level that both of us understood.
>
> Having a shared language and terminology with the domain experts is invaluable, but we can take it a few steps further by making that shared language be directly executable by the machine. With a business DSL, there is no translation gap between what the domain expert has told the developers and what the computer is executing.
>
> Not only that, but we can have the domain experts review the executable instructions (because they are written in a DSL that they can read) and tell us whether this is good or bad. Many domain experts already do some level of programming in the form of VBA or Microsoft Office programming. If they can work with that, they should be able to write using a DSL.

A business DSL doesn't necessarily have to be writable by the domain experts (business users, analysts, and the like). Building a DSL doesn't mean that you can offload all the work to the domain experts and leave it at that. The main purpose of a DSL is to facilitate better communication between the developers and the businesspeople.

Examples of business DSLs can be seen in rules engines of various dispositions. Usually those tools cost quite a bit of money and come with "easy to use and intuitive" designers and wizards.

Usually, business rules are simple condition and action statements. Imagine that we have a store and we want to calculate the final pricing on an order. The pricing business rules change frequently, and we'd like to have the businesspeople's direct input on those. Listing 3.7 shows how we can specify the rules for calculating the final pricing of an order using a DSL syntax.

Listing 3.7   A sample DSL for defining order-processing rules

```
when User.IsPreferred and Order.TotalCost > 1000:
    AddDiscountPercentage 5
    ApplyFreeShipping
when not User.IsPreferred and Order.TotalCost > 1000:
    SuggestUpgradeToPreferred
    ApplyFreeShipping
when User.IsNotPreferred and Order.TotalCost > 500:
    ApplyFreeShipping
```

Any businessperson could read and understand these rules. Getting this type of DSL to work takes about 10 minutes of work (the backend code for this DSL is only 68 lines long). The ability to easily define such a DSL means that you get a lot of flexibility for little cost.

NOTE Look at the difference between the second and third conditions in listing 3.7. The second uses `not User.IsPreferred` and the third uses `User.IsNotPreferred`. When building a DSL, you need to put aside some of your notions about good API design. What works for developers doesn't necessarily work well for language-oriented programming. Reading `not User.IsPreferred` is awkward for some people, so `User.IsNot-Preferred` is better from a readability standpoint.

3.2.3 Building Extensibility DSLs

You can use a DSL to extend an application. Consider the macro feature in Visual Studio or VBA in Excel. They're useful tools, and most big applications have something of that sort. Visual Studio has macros, Emacs has LISP, Office has VBA, many games use scripting for the "game logic," and so on.

Most of the approaches that we'll look at in this book could be called extensibility mechanisms, but true extensibility DSLs usually focus on enabling as much as possible, whereas in most DSLs we want a language that's expressive in a narrow domain. We'll talk about the implications of extensibility DSLs for an application in chapter 5.

Once you've decided to create a DSL, what's next? How do you go from the wish to be clear and expressive to having a DSL in hand?

3.3 Fleshing out the syntax

Let's imagine we haven't already seen the DSL syntax for the Scheduling DSL, and that we need to start building such a thing from scratch. Before we begin the actual implementation, we need to know what we want to do in our DSL:

- Define named tasks
- Specify what happens when a task is executed
- Define when a task should execute
- Describe the conditions for executing the task
- Define the recurrence pattern (how often we will repeat the task)

We also need to look at those goals from the appropriate perspective—the end user's. The *client* will pay for the DSL, but the *end users* are the people who will end up using the DSL. There is a distinct difference between the two. Identifying who the end user is can be a chore, but it's important to accurately identify who the users of the DSL will be.

One of the major reasons to build a DSL is to hide the complexities of the implementation with a language that makes sense to the domain experts. If you get the wrong idea about who is going to use the DSL, you will create something that is harder to use. The budgeting people generally have a much fuzzier notion about what their company is doing than the people actually doing the work. Once you have some idea about what the end users want, you can start the design and implementation.

I try to start using a declarative approach. It makes it easier to abstract all the details that aren't important for the users of the DSL when they are writing scripts. That means deciding what the DSL should do. After I have identified what I want to use the DSL for, I can start working on the syntax. It's usually easier to go from an example of how you want to specify things to the syntax than it is to go the other way.

One technique that I have found useful is to pretend that I have a program that can perfectly understand intent in plain English and execute it. For the Scheduling DSL, the input for that program might look like the following:

```
Define a task named: "warn if website is down", starting from now, running
    every 3 minutes. When website "http://example.org" is not alive, then
    notify "admin@example.org" that the server is down.
```

This syntax should cover a single scenario of using the Scheduling DSL, not all scenarios. The scenario should also be very specific. Notice that I've included the URL and email address in the scenario, to make it more detailed.

You should flesh out the DSL in small stages, to make it easier to implement and to discover the right language semantics. You should also make it clear that you're talking about a specific usage instance, and not the general syntax definition.

Once you have the scenario description, you can start breaking into lines, and indenting by action groups. This allows you to see the language syntax more clearly:

```
Define a task named: "warn if website is down",
     starting from now,
     running every 3 minutes.
     When web site "http://example.org" is not alive
     then notify "admin@example.org" that the server is down.
```

Now it looks a lot more structured, doesn't it? After this step, it's a matter of turning the natural language into something that you can build an internal DSL on. This requires some level of expertise, but mostly it requires knowing the syntax and what you can get away with.

We've already become somewhat familiar with the syntax of the Boo language and all the ways we can work with it in chapter 2. We'll look at more advanced options in chapter 6, and the syntax reference in appendix B can help you get familiar with what types of syntactic sugar you can build into your DSL.

3.4   *Choosing between imperative and declarative DSLs*

There are two main styles for building DSLs: imperative and declarative. These styles are independent of the DSL types we discussed in chapter 1 (external DSLs, graphical DSLs, and internal DSLs). Each of the three DSL types can be implemented using either style, although there is a tendency to use a more imperative approach for technical DSLs and a more declarative approach for business DSLs.

- An *imperative DSL* specifies a list of steps to execute (to output text using a templating DSL, for example). With this style, you specify what should happen.
- A *declarative DSL* is a specification of a goal. This specification is then executed by the supporting infrastructure. With this style, you specify the intended result.

The difference is really in the intention. Imperative DSLs usually specify *what to do*, and declarative DSLs specify *what you want done*.

SQL and regular expressions are examples of declarative DSLs. They both describe what you want done, but not how to do it. Build scripts are great example of imperative DSLs. It doesn't matter what build engine you use (NAnt, Rake, Make), the build script lists actions that need to be executed in a specified order. There are also hybrid DSLs, which are a mix of the two. They are DSLs that specify what you want done, but they also have some explicit actions to execute.

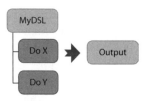

Figure 3.1 Standard operating procedure for imperative DSLs

Usually, with declarative DSLs, there are several steps along the way to the final execution. For example, SQL is a DSL that uses the declarative style. With SQL you can specify what properties you want to select and according to what criteria. You then let the database engine handle the loading of the data.

When you use an imperative DSL, the DSL directly dictates what will happen, as illustrated in figure 3.1.

When you use a declarative DSL, the DSL specifies the desired output, and there is an engine that takes any actions required to make it so. There isn't necessarily a one-to-one mapping between the output that the DSL requests and the actions that the engine takes, as illustrated in figure 3.2.

You have to decide which type of DSL you want to build. Imperative DSLs are good if you want a simple-to-understand but open-ended solution. Declarative DSLs work well when the problem itself is complex, but you can express the specification for the solution in a clear manner.

Regardless of which type of DSL you decide to build, you need to be careful not to leak implementation details into the DSL syntax. Doing so will generally make it harder to modify the DSL in the long run, and likely will confuse the users. DSLs should deal with the abstract concepts, such as applying free shipping, or suggesting registration as a preferred customer, and leave the *implementation* of those concepts to the application itself. This is an important concept that we'll come back to when we talk about unit testing in chapter 8.

Sometimes I build declarative DSLs, and more often hybrid DSLs (more on them in a minute). Usually the result of my DSLs is an object graph describing the intent of the user that I can feed into an engine that knows how to deal with it. The DSL portion is responsible for setting this up, and not much more.

I rarely find a use for imperative DSLs. When I use them, it's usually in some sort of helper functionality: text generation, file processing, and the like. A declarative DSL is more interesting, because it's usually used to express the complex scenarios.

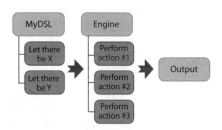

Figure 3.2 Standard operating procedure for declarative DSLs

I don't write a lot of purely declarative DSLs. While those are quite interesting in the abstract, getting them to work in real-world scenarios can be hard. But *mixing* the styles, creating a hybrid DSL, is a powerful combination.

A *hybrid DSL* is a declarative DSL that uses imperative programming approaches to reach the final state that's passed to the backend engine for processing. For example, consider this rule: "All preferred customers get 2 percent additional discount on large orders on Sunday." That rule is expressed in listing 3.8 using a hybrid of declarative and imperative styles (look at the third line):

Listing 3.8   A hybrid DSL, using both imperative and declarative concepts

```
when User.IsPreferred and Order.TotalCost > 1000:
    AddDiscountPercentage   5
    AddDiscountPercentage   2 if today is sunday
    ApplyFreeShipping
```

Note that this example uses the same syntax as before, but we're adding additional conditionals to the mix—we're mixing both styles. This is a silly example of the power of hybrid DSLs, but the ability to express control flow (loops and `if` constructs) and to have access to declarative concepts makes a hybrid DSL a natural for specifying behavior in more complex scenarios, and it can do so coherently.

Before we move on, listing 3.9 shows another approach, arguably a more declarative one, for the same problem.

Listing 3.9   A more declarative approach to specifying rules

```
applyDiscount 5.percent:
    when User.IsPreferred and Order.TotalCost > 1000
suggestPreferred:
    when not User.IsPreferred and Order.TotalCost > 1000
freeShipping:
    when Order.TotalCost > 500 and User.IsNotPreferred
    when Order.TotalCost > 1000 and User.IsPreferred
```

I find the example in listing 3.9 to be more expressive, because it explicitly breaks away from the developer mentality of `if`s and branches and forces you to think about actions and triggers, which is probably a better model for this particular problem.

The importance of clarity

In the initial draft of this book, one of the reviewers pointed out an inconsistency between listings 3.7 and 3.9. I've left the inconsistency in place to show how different syntaxes can change the way we understand the system.

If you look at the rules for free shipping, you can see that there's an interesting inconsistency. Preferred users get free shipping for orders above $1,000, whereas non-preferred users get free shipping for orders above $500.

In listing 3.7, you have to look at all the rules in order to understand what is going on. In listing 3.9, this inconsistency is explicit. In chapter 13, we'll talk extensively about how to make such concepts explicit.

I have been in situations where laying out the existing business rules close to one another (in a format like listing 3.9) has highlighted logical problems in what the business was doing, though sometimes they went ahead with the inconsistency. I try to avoid using the term *business logic*, because I rarely find any sort of logic in it.

Nevertheless, both examples perform the exact same operations, and are equivalent in terms of complexity and usage. In fact, there is a one-to-one mapping between the two.

That's enough theory; let's pull the concepts of a DSL apart, and see how it works.

3.5   Taking a DSL apart—what makes it tick?

We've looked at building DSLs from the point of view of the outward syntax—how we use them. What we haven't done is cover how they're structured internally—how we build and integrate them into our applications.

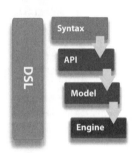

In general, a DSL is composed of the building blocks shown in figure 3.3.

A typical DSL is usually split into several distinct parts:

Figure 3.3   A typical DSL structure

- *Syntax*—This is the core language or the syntax extensions that you create.
- *API*—This is the API used in the DSL; it is usually built specifically to support the DSL and its needs.
- *Model*—This is the existing code base we reuse in our DSL (usually using a facade). The difference between the API and the model is that the model usually represents the notions in our application (such as `Customer`, `Discount`, and so on), whereas the API focuses on providing the DSL with convenient ways to access and manipulate the model.
- *Engine*—This is the runtime engine that executes the DSL and processes its results.

The language and the API can be intrinsically tied together, but there is a fine line separating the two. The API exposes the operations that DSL users will use in the application. Usually you'll expose the domain operations to the DSL. You express those operations through the language, but the API is focused on enabling a good syntax for the operations, not on providing the operations themselves.

We'll deal with language construction in the next two chapters, and we'll see an example of it in the next section. Broadly, we need to understand what features of the language we can use and what modifications we're able to make to the language to better express our intent. Often, this is directly related to the API that we expose to the DSL. As I mentioned earlier, if you're working in a domain-driven design manner, you're in a good position to reuse the same domain objects in your DSL (although that causes problems, such as versioning, which we'll look at in chapter 9). Often,

> **Keeping the layers separated**
>
> Several times in the past I have tried to combine different parts of the DSL—typically the syntax and the API—usually to my regret. It's important to keep each layer to itself, because that brings several advantages.
>
> It means you can work on each layer independently. Enhancing your API doesn't break the syntax, and adding a method call doesn't require dealing with the internals of the compiler.
>
> You can use the DSL infrastructure from other languages, as well. Why would you want to do that? Because this will avoid tying your investment in the DSL into a single implementation of the syntax, and that's important. You may want to have several dialects of a single DSL working against a single infrastructure, or you may decide that you have hit the limits of the host language and you need to build an external DSL (or one using a different host language). You'll still want to use the same infrastructure across all of them. Having an infrastructure that is not tied to a specific language implementation also means that you can use this infrastructure without any DSL, directly from your application.
>
> A typical example of using the DSL infrastructure without a DSL language would be an infrastructure that can also be used via a fluent interface to the application and via a DSL for external extensibility.

though, the API will be composed of facades over the application, to provide the DSL with coarse-grained access into the application (fine-grained control is often *too* fine grained and is rarely useful in a DSL).

The execution engine is responsible for the entire process of selecting a DSL script and executing it, from setting up the compiler to executing the compiled code, from setting up the execution environment to executing the secondary stages in the engine after the DSL has finished running (assuming you have a declarative DSL).

Extending the Boo language itself is probably the most powerful way to add additional functionality to a DSL, but it's also the most difficult. You need to understand how the compiler works, to some extent. Boo was built to allow that, but it's usually easier to extend a DSL by adding to the API than by extending the Boo language. When you need to extend Boo to enrich your DSL, those extensions will also reside in the engine and will be managed by it.

The API is part of the DSL. Repeat that a few times in your head. The API is part of the DSL because it composes a significant part of the language that you use to communicate intent.

Having a clear API, one that reflects the domain you're working in, will make building a DSL much easier. In fact, the process of writing a DSL is similar to the process of fleshing out a domain model or ubiquitous language in domain-driven design. Like the domain itself, the DSL should evolve with your understanding of the domain and the requirements of the application.

DSLs and domain-driven design are often seen together, for that matter.

> ### Use iterative design for your DSLs
>
> When sitting down to design a DSL, I take one of two approaches. Either I let it grow organically, as new needs arise, or I try to think about the core scenarios that I need to handle, and decide what I want the language to look like.
>
> There are advantages to both approaches. The first approach is the one I generally use when I am building a language for myself, because I already have a fairly good idea what kind of a language I want.
>
> I use the second approach if I'm building a DSL for general consumption, particularly to be used by non-developers. This isn't to say you need to spend weeks and months designing a DSL. I still very much favor the iterative approach, but you should seek additional input before you start committing to a language's syntax. Hopefully, this input will come from the expected audience of the DSL, which can help guide you toward a language that's well suited for their needs. Then, once you start, assume that you'll not be able to deliver the best result in the first few tries.
>
> We'll tackle the problem of DSL maintenance and versioning in chapter 9, and the techniques described there will help you build DSLs that can be modified in response to your increasing understanding of the domain and the requirements that you place on the DSL.
>
> If you build a DSL when you're just starting to understand the domain, and you neglect to maintain it as your understanding of the domain and its needs grows, it will sulk and refuse to cooperate. It will no longer allow you to easily express your intent, but rather will force you to awkwardly specify your intentions.

3.6 *Combining domain-driven design and DSLs*

Domain-driven design (DDD) is an approach to software design that's based on the premise that the primary focus should be on the domain and the domain logic (as opposed to focusing on technological concerns) and that complex domain designs should be based on a model.

If you aren't familiar with DDD, you may want to skip this section, because it focuses specifically on the use of DSLs in DDD applications.

TIP If you're interested in DDD, I highly recommend that you read *Domain-Driven Design* by Eric Evans and *Applying Domain-Driven Design and Patterns* by Jimmy Nilsson. Those books do an excellent job of describing how to flesh out and maintain a domain model.

3.6.1 *Language-oriented programming in DDD*

The reason for using language-oriented programming is that humans are good at expressing ideas using a spoken language. While spoken language is generally very imprecise, people usually settle on a set of terms and phrases that have specific meanings in a particular context.

Ubiquitous language and DSLs

Ubiquitous language is a term used in DDD to describe the way we talk about the software. The ubiquitous language is a spoken language that's structured around the domain model and is used by all members of the team when talking about the domain.

A ubiquitous language isn't a DSL, and a DSL isn't a ubiquitous language. A ubiquitous language is used to make communication clearer. Terms from the ubiquitous language are then used in the code of the system.

A DSL, on the other hand, can be seen as taking the ubiquitous language and turning it into an executable language. A DSL isn't always about a business domain, but when it is, and when you're practicing DDD, it's almost certain that your DSL will reflect the ubiquitous language closely.

In short, the ubiquitous language is the language of communication inside a team, whereas a DSL is a way to express intent. The two can (and hopefully will) be merged in many scenarios.

In some fields, the domain terms are very explicit. In a Sarbanes-Oxley tracking system, the domain terms are defined in the law itself. In many fields, some of the terms are well defined (such as in accounting) but other terms are often more loosely defined and can vary in different businesses or even different departments. The term *customer* is probably the quintessential example of a loosely defined term. I once sat in a meeting with two department heads, watching them fight for 3 hours over how the system would define a customer, without any satisfactory result.

When you're building software, you usually need to talk to the domain experts. They can help clarify what the domain terms are, and from there you can build the ubiquitous language that you'll use in the project.

Once you have the ubiquitous language, you can start looking at what you want to express in the DSL, and how you can use the ubiquitous language to express that. From there, you follow the same path we outlined in section 3.3: break it up according to the semantics, and then see what the language will allow you to get away with.

We'll spend chapters 4 and 5 mostly dealing with how much we can get away with. But before we get into that, let's look at the result of combining DSLs and DDD. You may have heard that the whole is greater than the sum of its parts.

3.6.2   *Applying a DSL in a DDD application*

It seems natural, when thinking about DSLs, to add DDD to the mix, doesn't it?

Figure 3.4 shows a set of DSLs in a domain-driven application. In most applications, you'll have a set of DSLs, each of them targeted at one specific goal. You'll also usually have a DSL facade of some kind that will translate the code-driven API to a more language-oriented API.

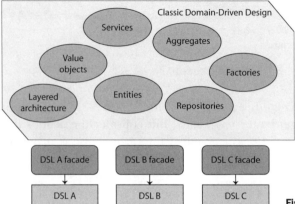

Figure 3.4 DSLs used in a DDD context

There are quite a few domains where DDD doesn't make sense. In fact, most of the DSLs that I use daily aren't tied to a DDD implementation. They're technical DSLs, used for such things as templating, configuration, ETL (extract, transform, and load), and so on.

Technical DSLs rarely require a full-fledged domain model or a ubiquitous language because the model used is usually implicit in the assumptions that we have as software developers. A templating DSL doesn't need anything beyond text-processing instructions, for example. A configuration DSL needs little beyond knowing what it configures.

But when it comes to business DSLs, we're in a much more interesting position. Let's look at an example and start by assuming that we've defined a domain using the techniques that Eric Evans suggests in his book, *Domain-Driven Design.*
Assuming that we have a CLR application (written in C#, VB.NET, or Boo) and assuming we're writing the DSL in Boo, we have immediate and unlimited access to the domain. This means that, by default, our DSL can immediately take advantage of all the work that went into building the ubiquitous language and the domain model.

All the ideas about the domain model and ubiquitous language are directly applicable and exposed to the DSL. Think back to the business DSL example in listing 3.7, repeated here in listing 3.10.

What if I don't know DDD already?

If you haven't read Evans' book or are not familiar with the terminology used, DDD calls for creating a ubiquitous language shared by all the stakeholders in the project (which explicitly includes the developers and the businesspeople).

The ubiquitous language is not used solely for communication with the businesspeople; it is part and parcel of the actual structure of the code. The more closely the language matches the way the businesspeople think about the processes to be performed, the more closely the software will meet the needs of the business.

> **Listing 3.10   A DSL that uses an existing DDD-based domain model**

```
when User.IsPreferred and Order.TotalCost > 1000:
    AddDiscountPercentage  5
    ApplyFreeShipping
when User.IsNotPreferred and Order.TotalCost > 500:
    ApplyFreeShipping
```

Notice that we're using both `IsPreferred` and `IsNotPreferred`—having both of them means that you get better readability. But consider the actions that are being performed when the condition specified in the when clause is matched. We aren't modifying state, like this:

```
Order.TotalCost = Order.TotalCost - (Order.TotalCost * 0.05) #apply discount
```

That would probably work, but it's a bad way to do it. It's completely opaque, for one thing. The code is clear about what it does, but there is no hint about the business logic and reasoning behind it. There is a distinct difference between applying a discount for a particular sale offer and applying a discount because of a coupon, for example, and this code doesn't explain that. It's also probably wrong from the domain perspective, because you will almost certainly want to keep track of your discounts.

In the domain, we probably would have something like this:

```
Order.ApplyDiscountPercentage(5)
```

That would be valid code that we could put into action as well. But in the DSL, because we already know what the applicable operations are, we can make it even more explicit by specifying the discount as an operation with a known context. This makes those operations into part of the language that we use when writing functionality with the DSL.

Now, let's get back to the Scheduling DSL that we started to build at the beginning of this chapter. Let's dive into the implementation details.

3.7   *Implementing the Scheduling DSL*

Listing 3.11 will refresh your memory about what the Scheduling DSL looks like.

> **Listing 3.11   Sample code from the Scheduling DSL**

```
task "warn if website is down":
    every 3.Minutes()
    starting now
    when WebSite("http://example.org").IsNotResponding
    then:
        notify "admin@example.org", "server down!"
```

It doesn't look much like code, right? But take a look at the class diagram in figure 3.5.

This is the implicit base class for the Scheduling DSL. An *implicit base class* is one of the more common ways to define and work with a DSL. We'll spend some time talking about this in chapter 4.

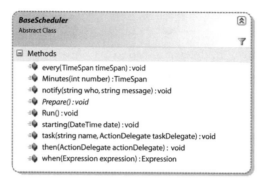

**Figure 3.5   Class diagram of
BaseScheduler, the implicit
base class for the Scheduling DSL**

For now, please assume that the DSL code you see is being magically placed in the Pre-pare() method of a derived class. This means that you have full access to all the methods that the BaseScheduler exposes, because those are exposed by the base class.

What this means, in turn, is that you can now look at the DSL and the class diagram and suddenly understand that most of what goes on here involves plain old method calls. Nothing fancy or hard to understand—we're merely using a slightly different syntax to call them than you usually do.

We're adding a minor extension to the language here. Two methods in the Base-Scheduler aren't part of the API, but rather are part of the language extension:

- Minutes()—This is a simple extension method that allows us to specify 3.Min-utes(), which reads better than TimeSpan.FromMinutes(3), which is how we would usually perform the same task.
- when(Expression)—This is a meta-method, which is a method that can modify the language. It specifies that the expression that's passed to it will be wrapped in a delegate and stored in an instance variable. We'll see exactly how this works in chapter 4.

That doesn't make much sense right now, I know, so let's start taking this DSL apart. We'll use the exact opposite approach from what we do when we're building the DSL. We'll add the programming concepts to the existing DSL until we fully understand how this works.

Let's start by adding parentheses and removing some compiler syntactic sugar. Listing 3.12 shows the results of that.

Listing 3.12   The Scheduling DSL after removing most of the syntactic sugar

```
task("warn if website is down", do() :
    self.every( self.Minutes(3) )
    self.starting ( self.now )
    self.when( WebSite("http://example.org").IsNotResponding)
    self.then( do():
        notify( "admin@example.org", "server down!")
    )
)
```

A couple of notes about this before we continue:

- `self` in Boo is the equivalent of `this` in C# or Java or of `Me` in VB.NET.
- `do():` is the syntax for anonymous delegates in Boo.

That looks a lot more like code now (and a lot less like a normal language). But we're not done yet. We still need to resolve the `when` meta-method. When we run that, we'll get the result shown in listing 3.13.

Listing 3.13   The Scheduling DSL after resolving the when meta-method

```
task("warn if website is down", do() :
    self.every( self.Minutes(3) )
    starting ( self.now )
    condition = do():
        return WebSite("http://example.org").IsNotResponding
    then( do():
        notify( "admin@example.org", "server down!")
    )
)
```

As you can see, we completely removed the `when` method, replacing it with an assignment of an anonymous delegate for the instance variable. This is the only piece of compiler magic we've performed. Everything else is already in the Boo language.

Meta-methods and anonymous blocks

Take a look at the `when` and `then` methods. Both of them end up with a similar syntax, but they're implemented in drastically different ways. The `when` method is a meta-method. It changes the code at compilation time. The `then` method uses an anonymous block as a way to pass the delegate to execute.

The reason we have two different approaches that end up with nearly the same end result (passing a delegate to a method) has to do with the syntax we want to achieve.

With the `when` method, we want to achieve a keyword-like behavior, so the `when` method accepts an expression and transforms that to a delegate. The `then` keyword has a different syntax that accepts a block of code, so we use Boo's anonymous blocks to help us out there.

We'll talk about those things extensively in chapters 4 and 6.

Now we can take the code in listing 3.13 and make a direct translation to C#, which will give us the code in listing 3.14.

Listing 3.14   The Scheduling DSL code, translated to C#

```
task("warn if website is down", delegate
{
    this.every( this.Minutes(3) );
    this.starting ( this.now );
    this.condition = delegate
    {
```

```
        return new WebSite("http://example.org"). IsNotResponding;
    };
    this.then( delegate
    {
        this.notify( "admin@example.org", "server down!");
    });
});
```

Take a look back at the original DSL text in listing 3.11, and compare it to listing 3.14. In terms of functionality, they're the same, but the syntactic differences between them are huge, and we want a good syntax for our DSL.

We've skipped one important part; we haven't talked yet about what the implicit base class will do. The result of the implicit base class resolving its base class is shown in listing 3.15, and the details of what the implicit base class is doing are discussed in section 3.8.

Listing 3.15 The full class that was generated using the implicit base class

```
public class MyDemoTask ( BaseScheduler ):
        def override Prepare():
            task("warn if website is down"), def():
                # the rest of the code
```

Now that we have a firm grasp of what code we're getting out of the DSL, we need to get to grips with how we can run this code.

3.8   *Running the Scheduling DSL*

So far we've focused on the transformations we're putting the code through, but we haven't talked yet about how to compile and execute a DSL. Remember, we aren't dealing with scripts in the strict sense of the word; we have no interpreter to run. We're going to compile our DSL to IL, and then execute this IL. The code that it takes to do this isn't difficult, just annoying to write time after time, so I wrapped it up in a common project called Rhino DSL.[2]

> **The Rhino DSL project**
>
> The Rhino DSL project is a set of components that turned out to be useful across many DSL implementations. It contains classes to aid in building a DSL engine, implicit base classes, multifile DSLs, and so on.
>
> We're going to use Rhino DSL throughout this book; it's an open source project, licensed under the BSD license, which means that you can use it freely in any type of application or scenario. We're also going to spend chapter 7 dissecting Rhino DSL, to ensure that you understand how it works, so you could implement it on your own, if you ever need to.

---

[2] Rhino [Project Name] is a naming convention that I use for most of my projects. You may be familiar with Rhino Mocks, for example, which is part of the same group of projects as Rhino DSL. There is no connection to Mozilla's Rhino project, which is a JavaScript implementation in Java.

Compilation is expensive, and once we load an assembly in the CLR, we have no way of freeing the occupied memory short of unloading the entire AppDomain. To deal with these two problems, we need to do at least some caching up front. Doing this on a DSL-by-DSL basis is annoying, and it would be nice to get the cost of creating a DSL down as much as possible.

For all of those reasons, Rhino DSL provides the `DslFactory` class, which takes care of all of that. It works closely with the `DslEngine`, which is the class we derive from to specify how we want the compilation of the DSL to behave.

Again, none of this is strictly necessary. You can do it yourself easily, if you choose to, but using Rhino DSL makes it easier and allows us to focus on the DSL implementation instead of the compiler mechanics.

We've already looked at the `BaseScheduler` class. Now let's take a peek at the `SchedulingDslEngine` class. Listing 3.16 shows the full source code of the class.

Listing 3.16   The implementation of `SchedulingDslEngine`

```
public class SchedulingDslEngine : DslEngine
{
    protected override void CustomizeCompiler(
        BooCompiler compiler,
        CompilerPipeline pipeline,
        string[] urls)
    {
        pipeline.Insert(1,
            new ImplicitBaseClassCompilerStep(
                typeof (BaseScheduler),
                "Prepare",
                // default namespace imports
                "Rhino.DSL.Tests.SchedulingDSL"));
    }
}
```

As you can see, it doesn't do much, but what it does do is interesting. The method is called `CustomizeCompiler`, and you're going to learn a whole lot more about customizing the compiler in chapter 4. For now, keep in mind that Boo allows you to move code around during compilation, and the `ImplicitBaseClassCompilerStep` does that.

The `ImplicitBaseClassCompilerStep` will create an implicit class that will derive from `BaseScheduler`. All the code in the file will be placed in the `Prepare` derived method. We can also specify default namespace imports. In listing 3.16, you can see that we add the `Rhino.DSL.Tests.ShedulingDSL` namespace. This namespace will be imported to all the DSL scripts, so we don't have to explicitly import it. VB.NET users are familiar with this feature, using the project imports.

We're nearly at the point when we can execute our DSL. The one thing that's still missing is the `DslFactory` intervention. Listing 3.17 shows how we can work with that.

Listing 3.17 Executing a Scheduling DSL script

```
//initialization
DslFactory factory = new DslFactory();
factory.Register<BaseScheduler>(new SchedulingDslEngine());

//get the DSL instance
BaseScheduler scheduler = factory.Create<BaseScheduler>(
                          @"path/to/ValidateWebSiteUp.boo");

//This is where we run the code from the DSL file
scheduler.Prepare();

//Run the prepared scheduler
scheduler.Run();
```

First, we initialize the `DslFactory`, and then create and register a `DslEngine` for the specific base type we want. Note that you should only do this once, probably during the startup of the application. This usually means in the `Main` method in console and Windows applications, and in `Application_Startup` in web applications.

We then get the DSL instance from the factory. We pass both the base type we want (which is associated with the `DslEngine` that we registered and the return value of this method), and the path to the DSL script. Usually this will be a path in the filesystem, but I have seen embedded resources, URLs, and even source control links used.

Once we have the DSL instance, we can do whatever we want with it. Usually, this depends on the type of DSL it is. When using an imperative DSL, I would tend to call the `Run()` or `Execute()` methods. With a declarative DSL, I would usually call a `Prepare()` or `Build()` method, which would execute the code that we wrote using the DSL, and then I would call the `Run()` or `Execute()` method, which would take the result of the previous method call and act upon it. In more complex scenarios, you might ask a separate class to process the results, instead of having the base class share both responsibilities.

In the case of the Scheduling DSL, we use a declarative approach, so we call the `Prepare()` method to get whatever declarations were made in the DSL, and then we run the code. The `Run()` method in such a DSL will usually perform some sort of registration into a scheduling engine.

And that's it—all the building blocks that you need to write a good DSL. We're going to spend a lot more time discussing all the things we can do with DSLs, how we can integrate them into real applications, and version, test, and deploy them, but you should now have an overall understanding of what's involved.

3.9   Summary

We've gone over quite a bit of information in this chapter. We contrasted the implementation of a simple problem (scheduling tasks) using both fluent interfaces in C# and a full-blown Boo-based DSL, and we saw that it's very easy to take a DSL further than a fluent interface. And that's aside from the syntactic differences between the two solutions.

We also explored why we might want to build DSLs and what types of DSLs we can build: technical, business, and extensibility DSLs.

Then we rolled up our sleeves and went to work building the Scheduling DSL, from the initial syntax, to implementing the DSL base class, to creating the DSL engine and running the code.

Along the way we took a quick peek at combining DSLs and DDD, explored the differences between imperative and declarative DSLs, and generally had fun. We covered (at a high level) just about everything you'll need to create a useful DSL.

But not quite everything. We're still focused at too high a level. It's time to get down into the details and start practicing what we've discussed so far. That's up next.

Building DSLs

In this chapter, we'll look at how to design an application that uses DSLs to do much of its work. We'll cover several of those DSLs in detail (and leave others for later), and we'll explore how to build, instantiate, and execute those DSLs in the context of our application. We're going to focus on two types of DSLs, the ones most commonly used in business applications: technical DSLs and business DSLs.

Technical DSLs are generally used as bootstrapping and configuration mechanisms to make it easier to modify a part of a system. In general, those DSLs enable recurring tasks, usually of a one-off nature. Scripting is a common use for technical DSLs—configuration or build scripts, for example. Combining the power of a flexible language with a DSL designed for the task at hand makes for a powerful tool. Everything you do with a technical DSL can be done using code, but the DSL should make it easier and simpler. A DSL makes it easy to produce a one-off solution to a problem.

Note that a one-off solution isn't necessarily throwaway code. It's a solution that you usually need once in an application. Configuring the Inversion of Control container is done once per application, for example, but it's a *critically* important part of the application, and it's something that you'll modify often as the application grows. Similarly, you tend to have one build script per project, but you want it to be of very high quality.

Business DSLs tend to be more declarative than technical DSLs and often focus on business rules and the actions to be taken when the conditions of those rules are met. A business DSL defines policy, whereas the application code defines the operations. Policy is usually where most changes are made; the operations of a system are mostly fixed.

For example, a business DSL could define the rules for processing orders—rules that would affect the following domain objects:

- Discounts
- Payment plans
- Shipping options
- Authorization rules

The application code would execute the business DSL scripts in order to get the policy decisions that apply for a particular scenario. It would then take the policy decisions and apply them to the system. We'll see an example of that when we build the Quote-Generation DSL.

You're not limited to a single DSL per application. In fact, you'll probably have several, both technical and business DSLs. Each will handle a specific set of scenarios (processing orders, authorizing payments, suggesting new products, and so on).

Before you can start writing a DSL, though, you need to understand the domain and what kind of DSL you want. That's what the next section is about.

4.1   Designing a system with DSLs

In the rest of this book, we'll concentrate on building a system with DSLs in mind. To ensure that the domain is familiar to all, we'll use an online shop as our example. This will give us a rich domain to play with and allow us to define several different DSLs to show a variety of uses. We'll probably go a tad overboard with DSL usage in order to demonstrate all sorts of DSLs, so you can take that into consideration. You'll likely not make use of so many DSLs in a single application in real life.

There are cases where you'll want to design a system as nothing but a set of DSLs, each handling a specific task, and have the users manage the set of scripts that define the actual behavior of the application. In that type of scenario, you would reverse the usual roles of application code and DSLs—the application code would be focused on infrastructure concerns and the requirements of the DSL. This approach would probably work best in backend processing systems. Creating a UI on top of a DSL is certainly possible, but you're likely to hit the point of diminishing returns. Good UIs are complex, and a DSL that's complex enough to create a good UI is a programming language. You would probably want to work with an existing programming language rather than a DSL.

I find that the best approach is to use a DSL to define policy, and application code to define the framework and operations that are executed by the system.

Building such a system turns out to be almost trivial, because all you need to do is write the basic operations that the system is supposed to perform (which are usually fairly well understood), and then you can play around with the policy at will. Those operations, in our sample application, are things such as applying discounts, notifying users, and processing payments.

If you have done your job well, you'll likely be able to sit down with the customer and define the policy, and let them review it at the same time. How you notify users about an action in the application will rarely change, but when and why you do it may be changed more regularly. The same holds true for discount calculations; *how* you apply a discount is well known, but the business rules governing *when* you give a discount change regularly.

We don't want to deal with UIs or persistence in our example system, so we'll deal strictly with the backend processing only and fake services for the other parts of the system. We can use DSLs for several purposes in this scenario:

- Message translation and routing
- Authorization
- Quote generation

We'll start with the easiest, routing and translating messages.

4.2 Creating the Message-Routing DSL

Suppose we have a backend order-processing system that uses messages as the primary means of communication. Several external systems will communicate with the order-processing system, including a web application, business partners, administration tools, and the company's warehouse system, and all of those will be built by different teams, with different schedules, priorities, and constraints. The backend system is the black hole in the middle, around which all the other systems orbit.

The Message-Routing DSL needs to take an incoming message and dispatch it to the correct handler in the application. Message translation and routing is a simple domain, but it usually looks fairly nasty in code. This is especially true if you want to take versioning into consideration, or if you want to deal with heterogeneous environments.

4.2.1 Designing the Message-Routing DSL

Let's start with the simplest alternative: an endpoint that can accept JSON-formatted messages and process them. We'll take a peek at the big picture first, in figure 4.1.

We'll start from an external application that sends a JSON message to a given endpoint. This endpoint will take the JSON string, translate it to a JSON object, and pass it to the routing module. The routing module will use a set of DSL scripts to decide how

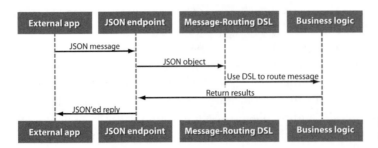

Figure 4.1   Routing messages using DSL

to route each message to the business component responsible for handling the message. The business component will perform its job, and can return a reply that will be sent to the client. So far, this is a fairly typical messaging scenario. We only need to add asynchronous messages and we can call ourselves enterprise developers.

Now let's consider the Message-Routing DSL part of figure 4.1. These are the responsibilities of the routing modules:

- Accept messages in a variety of formats (XML, JSON, CLR objects, and so on)
- Translate messages from external representation to internal representation
- Dispatch internal messages to the appropriate handler

We now know what we need to build; we're left with deciding on the syntax.

The main reason that we want to use a DSL here is to keep the system flexible and make it easy to add new messages and transformations. This DSL will be used by technical people, most probably the developers on the project. This, in turn, means that we can use a technical DSL here. Each script using this DSL will probably have the following responsibilities:

- Deciding whether the script can handle the message
- Transforming the message to the internal message representation
- Deciding where to dispatch the message

IMPLEMENTING THE MESSAGE-ROUTING DSL

With that in mind, we can start writing a draft of the Message-Routing DSL syntax, as shown in listing 4.1.

Listing 4.1   Initial draft of the Message-Routing DSL

```
# decide if this script can handle this message
return unless msg.type == "NewOrder" and msg.version == "1.0"

# decide which handle is going to handle it
HandleWith NewOrderHandler:
    # define a new list
    lines = []
    # add order lines to the list
    for line in msg.order_lines:
        lines.Add( OrderLine( line.product, line.qty ) )
    # create internal message representation
    return NewOrderMessage(
```

```
      msg.customer_id,
      msg.type,
      lines.ToArray(OrderLine) )
```

This is a good place to start. It's straightforward to read and to write, and it satisfies all the requirements we have. It's a highly technical DSL, but that's fine, because it will be used by technical people.

NOTE   It's easy to create technical DSLs, because you don't have to provide a lot of abstraction over what the language offers. You mostly need to provide a good API and good semantics.

Let's get to the implementation, starting with the routing part. How do we get the messages in the first place? We need to handle several message types without placing undue burden on the developers. After all, avoiding the need to write adapters or translators for them is exactly why we went with the DSL route. But we also want to keep our DSL implementation as simple as possible. If I need to

Figure 4.2   The `Router` class

do things like `xmlDocument.SelectNodes("/xpath/query")` in the DSL on a routine basis, I probably have an abstraction issue somewhere.

Let's take a look at figure 4.2, which shows how we can resolve this issue. As you can see, we have a single method here, `Route()`, that accepts an `IQuackFu`. We covered `IQuackFu` in chapter 2—it allows us to handle unknown method calls at runtime in a smart fashion. We used it to build the `XMLObject` before, and here we can use it to separate the implementation of the message from its structure. This means that we don't care if the message is XML, JSON, or a plain CLR object. We can treat it as a standard object, and let the `IQuackFu` implementation deal with the details. This gives us maximum flexibility with a minimum of fuss.

NOTE   `Route()` has a string as its return type. In real-world scenarios, we'd probably want to return a message as well, but for our purposes, a string works just fine.

Now we can get down to building the DSL. We'll use Rhino DSL to take care of all the heavy lifting of building the DSL. Don't worry about understanding all of it; the whole of chapter 7 discusses Rhino DSL and how to use it.

We'll start with a typical first step; defining the implicit base class that will be the basis of our DSL. Listing 4.2 shows the entire code of the base class.

Listing 4.2   The base class for the Message-Routing DSL

```
/// <summary>
/// This delegate is used by the DSL to return the
/// internal representation of the message
/// </summary>
```

```
public delegate object MessageTransformer();

public abstract class RoutingBase
{
    protected IQuackFu msg;
    public string Result;

    public void Initialize(IQuackFu message)
    {
        msg = message;
    }

    /// <summary>
    /// Routes the current message. This method is overridden by the
    /// DSL. This is also where the logic of the DSL executes.
    /// </summary>
    public abstract void Route();

    public void HandleWith(Type handlerType, MessageTransformer transformer)
    {
        IMessageHandler handler =
            (IMessageHandler) Activator.CreateInstance(handlerType);
        Result = handler.Handle(transformer());
    }
}
```

How does it work? The Message-Routing DSL script will be compiled into a class that inherits from `RoutingBase`, and all the code in the script will go into the `Route()` method, while the `msg` field will contain the current message during execution.

Implicit Base Class

The Implicit Base Class is one approach to building a DSL. With this approach, we define a base class in the application code, and then a compiler step in Boo will turn the DSL script into a class that's derived from the defined base class. Hence the *base class* moniker. The *implicit* part of the name comes from the fact that there is no reference to the class in the DSL script itself—it's implicit.

There are three major advantages to this approach.

The first is that we can refer to DSL script instances using the base class, by utilizing standard OOP principals.

The second is that the base class can expose methods and properties that are useful in the DSL. This means that the base class itself composes part of the language that we're creating. We'll discuss the mechanics of building this in more detail in chapter 6, but the concept itself is important.

The last advantage is that if the class is implicit, we can replace it. This is extremely helpful when we want to test a DSL or version it.

Using an implicit base class allows us to define the language keywords and constructs (as we did with the Scheduling DSL in chapter 2) easily.

When we execute the `Route()` method, the DSL code is executed. The second line in listing 4.1 (return if the message is not the expected type or version) checks to see if the message is a match, and if it isn't, the message is ignored without performing any action.

Then we have the `HandleWith NewOrderHandler` and the code beneath that. Here we're using Boo's ability to infer things for us. In this case, we pass the type name as the first parameter, and Boo will turn that into a `typeof(NewOrderHandler)` for us. The code underneath the `HandleWith` line uses implicit blocks to pass the delegate that will transform the message to its internal representation.

We now need a way to compile this DSL. We do it using a DSL engine, as shown in listing 4.3.

Listing 4.3   The Message-Routing DSL engine

```
public class RoutingDslEngine : DslEngine
{
    protected override void CustomizeCompiler(
        BooCompiler compiler,
        CompilerPipeline pipeline,
        string[] urls)
    {
        // The compiler should allow late bound semantics
        compiler.Parameters.Ducky = true;
        pipeline.Insert(1,
            new ImplicitBaseClassCompilerStep(
                // the base type
                typeof (RoutingBase),
                // the method to override
                "Route",
                // import the following namespaces
                "Chapter4.MessageRouting.Handlers",
                "Chapter4.MessageRouting.Messages"));
    }
}
```

NOTE The DSL engine is part of the Rhino DSL set of tools, and it's discussed extensively in chapter 7. A DSL engine contains the configuration required to change the behavior of the Boo compiler to support our DSL.

That's it. Our DSL is ready to roll, almost. We just need to hook it up to the `Router` class, as shown in listing 4.4.

Listing 4.4   The `Router` class handles message dispatch for the application

```
public static class Router
{
private static readonly DslFactory dslFactory;

static Router()
{
    dslFactory = new DslFactory();
```

```
        dslFactory.Register<RoutingBase>(
                    new RoutingDslEngine());
    }

    public static string Route(IQuackFu msg)
    {
        StringBuilder messages = new StringBuilder();
        RoutingBase[] routings =
                dslFactory.CreateAll<RoutingBase>(
                Settings.Default.RoutingScriptsDirectory
            );
        foreach (RoutingBase routing in routings)
        {
            routing.Initialize(msg);
            routing.Route();
            if (routing.Result != null)
                messages.AppendLine(routing.Result);
        }
        if(messages.Length==0)
        {
            return "nothing can handle this message";
        }
        return messages.ToString();
    }
}
```

Listing 4.4 gives us a few concepts to discuss. In the constructor, we create a new DSL factory and register our Message-Routing DSL engine, but the important parts are in the `Route(msg)` method.

We ask the DSL factory to give us all the DSL instances in a specific folder (`Create-All` will return instances of all the scripts in the given path). This is a nice way of handling a set of scripts (though it tends to break down when you have more than a few dozen scripts—at that point, you'll want better management of them, and we'll discuss this in chapter 5). We get back an array of `RoutingBase` instances from `CreateAll`, which we iterate over and run. This gives all the scripts a shot at handling the message.

The last pieces we're missing are the JSON endpoint and the `JsonMessageAdapter`. We'll start from the endpoint, because this is simple ASP.NET stuff. We create an HTTP handler class that accepts the messages and then sends them to be routed. Listing 4.5 shows how it's done.

Listing 4.5   The JSON endpoint

```
public void ProcessRequest(HttpContext context)
{
    //verify that we only allow POST http calls
    if (context.Request.RequestType != "POST")
    {
        context.Response.StatusCode = 400;
        context.Response.Write("You can only access this URL using POST");
        return;
    }
    // translate from the post body to a JSON object
```

```
byte[] bytes = context.Request.BinaryRead(context.Request.TotalBytes);
string json = Encoding.UTF8.GetString(bytes);
JsonSerializer jsonSerializer = new JsonSerializer();
JsonReader reader = new JsonReader(new StringReader(json));
JavaScriptObject javaScriptObject =
        (JavaScriptObject)jsonSerializer.Deserialize(reader);

// send the JSON object to be routed
string returnMessage =
        Router.Route(new JsonMessageAdapter(javaScriptObject));
context.Response.Write(returnMessage);
}
```

This code deals mostly with unpacking the data from the request and deserializing the string into an object. The important part happens on the second-last line: we call `Router.Route()` and pass a `JsonMessageAdapter`. This class is responsible for translating the `JavaScriptObject` into an `IQuackFu`, which is what we expect in the Message-Routing DSL.

The code for `JsonMessageAdapter` is in listing 4.6.

Listing 4.6 The `JsonMessageAdapter` implementation

```
public class JsonMessageAdapter : IQuackFu
{
    private readonly JavaScriptObject js;

    public JsonMessageAdapter(JavaScriptObject js)
    {
        this.js = js;
    }

    public object QuackGet(string name, object[] parameters)
    {
        object value = js[name];
        JavaScriptArray array = value as JavaScriptArray;
        if(array!=null)
        {
            return array.ConvertAll<JsonMessageAdapter>(
            delegate(object obj)
            {
                return new JsonMessageAdapter(
                            (JavaScriptObject) obj);
            });
        }
        return value;
    }
}
```

This listing only shows the `QuackGet()` method and ignores `QuackSet()` and `Quack-Invoke()`, because they aren't implemented. About the only interesting thing here is how we deal with arrays, because we need to convert them to `JsonMessageAdapter` arrays.

That's all, folks. Honest. We need around 200 lines of code to build this, and it takes about an hour or so.

Go back to listing 4.1 and look at the DSL that we wrote. We can now use it to process JSON messages like the one in listing 4.7.

Listing 4.7   A JSON message that can be handled by our DSL

```
{
    type: "NewOrder",
    version: "1.0",
    customer_id: 15,
    order_lines:
        [
            { product: 3, qty: 5 },
            { product: 8, qty: 6 },
            { product: 2, qty: 3 },
        ]
}
```

Extending this infrastructure—to deal with XML objects, for example—is a simple matter of creating an `XmlMessageAdapter` (or using the `XmlObject` that we created in chapter 2) and adding a new endpoint that can accept it.

You have probably figured out that the Message-Routing DSL is a very imperative DSL, but it's more than just its syntax; it also does a lot. Calling `Router.Route()` takes care of everything from invoking the DSL logic to selecting the appropriate handlers, executing them, and returning the results. After calling the Message-Routing DSL, there isn't much left to be done.

In the space of a few pages, we created a DSL, implemented the structure around it, and are ready to put it to use. It wasn't complex, and we didn't even have to use any of the advanced options that are at our disposal.

The reason it was so simple is mostly that we can get away with having a very technical language. This means we could utilize the built-in syntactic sugar in Boo to get a nice DSL, but not much more. Nearly everything we did was to create infrastructure code and run the DSL.

The next DSL we'll build—the Authorization DSL—will have a much higher focus on the language than the infrastructure. The infrastructure is mostly the same from one DSL implementation to the next, so we don't need to focus on that any longer.

4.3   *Creating the Authorization DSL*

Most complex applications have equally complex authorization rules, often complex enough to be their own domain. Authorization is a critical chore in an application. You can't avoid it, but it's almost always annoying to deal with, and it can be *very* complex. Worse, any bugs in the security system are critical by definition. Trying to understand why a certain operation was allowed (or denied) can be a complex endeavor.

We're going to build a DSL for making policy decisions about permissions in an application. Getting security right is important, and security systems also have to be flexible. All in all, it seems like a good fit for a DSL.

This is the specification for our Authorization DSL:

- Limit the problem domain to reduce complexity.
- Flexibility is important.
- Clarity is critical.

The specification could use some more work, but let's try to define the requirements we have for the Authorization DSL:

- It must be able to ask the security system if an operation is allowed.
- It must be able to ask the security system if an operation on a specific entity is allowed.
- It must output reasonable information from the security system to allow easy debugging.

In this list, an *operation* is something that the application does that needs to be secured. Viewing customer information or authorizing a client to go above a credit limit are both examples of operations in our online shop example.

I tend to use simple structured strings to represent operations. Here are two examples:

- `"/customer/orders/view"`
- `"/customer/beyond_credit_limit/authorize"`

If this reminds you of paths in a filesystem, that's no coincidence. This is a natural way to think about operations in our domain. It's also a simple approach that supports tooling well.

Enough with the chitchat—let's see some code.

4.3.1 *Exploring the Authorization DSL design*

This time, we'll start from the application and move to the DSL, rather than the other way around. We'll start with the `Authorization` class, which is the gateway to our security infrastructure. It's shown in figure 4.3.

The `Authorization` class contains two methods: one for checking an operation, and the second for checking an operation on an entity. The `WhyAllowed()` method lets you retrieve the reason for a certain operation being allowed or denied.

One thing to note is that the `IsAllowed()` methods return a nullable `boolean`. This allows the method to return `null` when the security system has no opinion on the subject. If that happens, the application needs to decide whether the operation is allowed by default or is forbidden by default. This is a matter for the business logic specific to each operation and cannot be dictated by the DSL implementation.

Now let's think about what kind of authorization rules we're going to need. We're going to use the Command pattern in the DSL—this is a fairly common approach in DSL building, and implicit base classes will usually implement the command patterns. The Command pattern is a design pattern in which an object represents a single

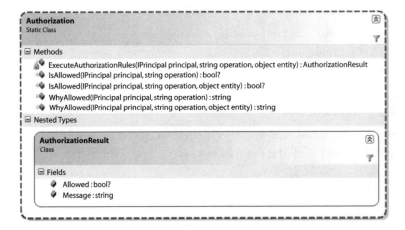

Figure 4.3   The `Authorization` class, the gateway to the Authorization DSL

action (a command) in the application. For more details about the Command pattern, see the explanation at the Data & Object Factory (http://www.dofactory.com/Patterns/PatternCommand.aspx). Figure 4.4 shows the `AuthorizationRule` class.

There are a couple of interesting things to note about the implementation of this class:

- The `CheckAuthorization()` method and the `Operation` property are both abstract, so derived classes (and our DSL) have to implement them.
- The `Allow()` and `Deny()` methods are the only ways for the derived class to affect the state of the rule. Both methods accept a `reason` string, which means that we're automatically documenting the reason for the decision.

For the moment, we'll skip over the DSL implementation (which we'll get to in the next section). We'll assume that it exists and look at how we're going to use it.

Listing 4.8 shows the `ExecuteAuthorizationRules()` method. It's a private method in the `Authorization` class that performs the bulk of the work for the class.

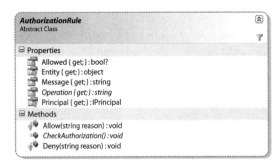

Figure 4.4   The base class for the Authorization DSL—`AuthorizationRule`

```
private static AuthorizationResult ExecuteAuthorizationRules(
    IPrincipal principal,
    string operation,
    object entity)
{
    // get all the authorization rules
    AuthorizationRule[] authorizationRules =
            dslFactory.CreateAll<AuthorizationRule>(
              Settings.Default.AuthorizationScriptsDirectory,
              principal,
              entity);
    foreach (AuthorizationRule rule in authorizationRules)
    {
      // check if the current rule operation equals
      // the requested operation, we don't care about casing
        bool operationMatched = string.Equals(
            rule.Operation, operation,
            StringComparison.InvariantCultureIgnoreCase);
      // move on if this is not so.
        if (operationMatched == false)
            continue;

      // execute the rule
        rule.CheckAuthorization();
      // return the result if the rule had any.
        if (rule.Allowed != null)
        {
            return new AuthorizationResult(
                rule.Allowed,
                rule.Message
                );
        }
    }
    // return a default (negative) result if
    // no rule matched this operation
    return new AuthorizationResult(
        null,
        "No rule allowed this operation"
        );
}
```

By now, you can probably guess what the DSL looks like, right?
Listing 4.9 shows the DSL engine for the Authorization DSL.

Listing 4.9 The Authorization DSL engine implementation

```
public class AuthorizationDslEngine : DslEngine
{
    protected override void CustomizeCompiler(
      BooCompiler compiler,
      CompilerPipeline pipeline,
      Uri[] urls)
    {
```

```
        // The compiler should allow late-bound semantics
        compiler.Parameters.Ducky = true;
        pipeline.Insert(1,
            new ImplicitBaseClassCompilerStep(
            // the base type
                typeof(AuthorizationRule),
            // the method to override
                "CheckAuthorization",
            // import the following namespaces
                "Chapter4.Security"));
    }
}
```

You may have noticed that the AuthorizationDslEngine displays a stunning similarity to the RoutingDslEngine. This is almost always the case, because most of the hard work is done in the Rhino DSL code. This leaves us with what is basically configuration code.

4.3.2　*Building the Authorization DSL*

Now let's take a look at our DSL, shall we? We want to implement the following rules:

- Users can log in between 9 a.m. and 5 p.m.
- Administrators can always log in.

The script in listing 4.10 satisfies those requirements.

Listing 4.10　A simple authorization script for account login

```
operation "/account/login"

if Principal.IsInRole("Administrators"):
    Allow("Administrators can always log in")
    return

if date.Now.Hour < 9 or date.Now.Hour > 17:
    Deny("Cannot log in outside of business hours, 09:00 - 17:00")
    return
```

This looks almost boringly standard, right?[1] We make use of the Boo date keyword to reference System.DateTime, which we haven't seen before, but that isn't very interesting.

There is one interesting thing here: the first line isn't something that we've seen so far. We know that we need to provide an implementation of the Operation property, but how can we do it?

It's done using a macro, which takes the first argument of the macro, generates a property, and returns that argument from the property. The code for this is shown in listing 4.11.

---

[1]　The job of an architect is to make everyone in the team expire out of sheer boredom. The more complexity we can shift into the infrastructure, the less complexity we need to deal with during our day-to-day coding.

Listing 4.11 `OperationMacro` creates a property returning its first argument

```
public class OperationMacro : GeneratePropertyMacro
{
    public OperationMacro()
        : base("Operation")
    {
    }
}
```

The `GeneratePropertyMacro` that we inherit from is the class that does all the work. We only need to extend it and pass the desired property name. The end result of this line,

```
operation "/account/login"
```

is this code:

```
Operation:
    get:
        return "/account/login"
```

And that's it, more or less. We can now ask the authorization system questions, which will be answered by the DSL. We can execute the code in listing 4.12 to do just that.

Listing 4.12 Using the authorization system

```
WindowsPrincipal principal = new WindowsPrincipal(
                                    WindowsIdentity.GetCurrent());
bool? allowed = Authorization.IsAllowed(principal, "/account/login");
Console.WriteLine("Allowed login: {0}", allowed);
Console.WriteLine(Authorization.WhyAllowed(principal, "/account/login"));
```

Note that in listing 4.8, we assumed a denied-unless-allowed policy. This means that our scripts don't have to explicitly deny anything—they can simply not allow it. This is a nice option to have in certain circumstances.

Let's try another example to see how useful our DSL is. Suppose we want to specify that only managers can approve orders with a total cost of over $10,000. Listing 4.13 shows the DSL script that validates this rule.

Listing 4.13 Authorization script that ensures only managers can approve costly orders

```
operation "/order/approve"

if Principal.IsInRole("Managers"):
    Allow("Managers can always approve orders")
    return

if Entity.TotalCost >= 10_000:
    Deny("Only managers can approve orders of more than 10,000")
    return

Allow("All users can approve orders less than 10,000")
```

TIP   Boo supports the use of the underscore character as a thousands separator in integers. This makes it easier to read big numbers.

Listing 4.14 shows how we can use this script.

Listing 4.14   Using the authorization script for approving orders

```
bool? allowed = Authorization.IsAllowed(principal,
            "/order/approve", order);
Console.WriteLine("Allowed login: {0}", allowed);
Console.WriteLine(Authorization.WhyAllowed(principal,
                "/order/approve", order));
```

In only a few pages, we've built ourselves a flexible authorization system. It isn't production-ready yet—we need to add all the usual error handling, edge cases, tuning, and priming—but it's a great example of using a DSL to easily extend your application.

The Authorization DSL is a more declarative example than the Message-Routing DSL. While the syntax is very imperative, the end result of the Authorization DSL is a value that is then processed by the application.

4.4   The "dark side" of using a DSL

We also need to explore the dark side of using DSLs such as the Authorization DSL. Our system allows us to easily express authorization rules related to business logic, but it suffers from a couple of weaknesses. It doesn't have a friendly UI; we can't do much with it except by editing the code.[2] And it doesn't really permit programmatic modification—if you find yourself generating DSL scripts on the fly, you probably need to rethink your DSL editing strategy.

Most security systems are based on the concepts of users and roles for a reason. Those are easy to handle UI–wise, and it's easy to programmatically add a user to a role or remove a user from a role. The same approach won't work using a DSL. You could certainly use roles in the DSL, and you could do other smart things (the DSL has access to the application, so you could store the state in a database and let the DSL query that). But a good DSL is intentionally limited, to reduce the complexity that you have to deal with.

If a task is awkward to deal with, you build a DSL to handle the complexity. If the DSL is awkward to deal with, you may want to rethink your approach.

Let's see how we can integrate a DSL with a user interface, shall we? The secret is to separate the responsibilities so the DSL is based on rules, and the rules feed on the data from the UI. The Quote-Generation DSL is a good candidate for a DSL that can accept data from the user. We'll discuss it next. In chapter 10, we'll do the reverse, taking the DSL output and working with it in the UI.

4.5   The Quote-Generation DSL

Let's say that our online shop sells enterprise software, and our customers want to buy our system. The price will vary depending on the options they want, the number of

---

[2]   This is not strictly true. You can build a designer for this, but that's not really what this sort of DSL is meant to do.

expected users, the underlying platform, the application dependencies, and a host of other things. Generating the quote can get pretty complex. Quote generation is also an extremely fluid field; quotes and the rules governing them change frequently, making this task a good candidate for a DSL.

NOTE I used the software sales example here because it's easy to understand, but you could use the same approach to generate quotes for custom cars, house purchasing, and so on.

Figure 4.5 shows an example of a quote-generation UI for a single application. It doesn't represent all the options that exist in the application. This is much more than a UI—there is a full-fledged logic system here. Calculating the total cost is the easy part; first you have to understand what you need.

Let's define a set of rules for the application. It will be clearer when we have the list in front of us:

- The Salaries module requires one machine for every 150 users.
- The Taxes module requires one machine for every 50 users.
- The Vacations module requires the Scheduling Work module.
- The Vacations module requires the External Connections module.
- The Pension Plans module requires the External Connections module.
- The Pension Plans module must be on the same machine as the Health Insurance module.
- The Health Insurance module requires the External Connections module.
- The Recruiting module requires a connection to the internet, and therefore requires a firewall from the recommended list.
- The Employee Monitoring module requires the CompMonitor component.

This example is still too simple. We could probably come up with 50 or more rules that we would need to handle. Handling the second-level dependencies alone (External Connections, CompMonitor, and so on) would be a big task.

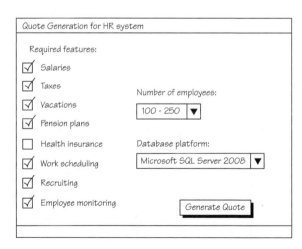

Figure 4.5 The quote-generation UI allows us to pass information from the application to the DSL.

Now that we've established that this is a complex field, let's think about how we could utilize a DSL here. We have a set of independent rules that affect the global state, which makes this a great candidate for a DSL. We can define each of the rules in its own script, and execute them as we'd normally do. This gives us the flexibility that we want.

But unlike the previous two examples (the Message-Routing and Authorization DSLs), we aren't dealing with a primarily technical DSL here. The Quote-Generation DSL is a business-facing DSL. Some of the information may be technical, but a lot of it is related to business requirements, and the DSL will reflect that.

Business-facing DSLs tend to take a bit more work to create than technical DSLs. So far, we haven't paid much attention to the language itself—it was fairly obvious what it was supposed to be, because the target audience was developers. Now we need to *think* about it, and we need to explore a few possibilities.

The code in listing 4.15 solves the Quote-Generation DSL problem using the same approach that we have taken so far.

Listing 4.15   A technical DSL for quote generation

```
if has( "Vacations" ):
    add "Scheduling"

number_of_machines["Salary"] = (user_count % 150) +1
number_of_machines["Taxes"] = (user_count % 50) +1
```

This could work, but trying to express something like "must reside on the same machine as another module" would be complex. The whole thing ends up looking like code, and we won't gain much in the process.

4.5.1   *Building business-facing DSLs*

The rules listed previously for our application include a few basic conditionals, numbers of users, and dependencies. We can make them (and any other common requirements) part of our DSL.

Listing 4.16 shows one way to specify the rules from the previous list.

Managing DSL snippets

I've mixed a few rules together in listing 4.15 to make it easier to see what's going on. When the scripts are this small, we're likely to want to handle them in a way that's a bit different than the one file per script that we have had so far.

In this case, most rules will end up being a line or two long. Those are what I call snippets—they're simple to write, and we're going to have a lot of them. The combination of all those snippets gives us a rich behavior, as all the small pieces come together to perform a single task.

We'll discuss the management of a system composed of many small snippets in chapter 5.

Listing 4.16 Business-facing, declarative DSL for solving the quote-generation problem

```
specification @vacations:
    requires @scheduling_work
    requires @external_connections

specification @salary:
    users_per_machine 150

specification @taxes:
    users_per_machine 50

specification @pension:
    same_machine_as @health_insurance
```

This looks much better. This is a purely declarative DSL that allows us to specify easily the information that we want, and to defer any decisions or calculations to the engine that runs the application.

TIP When I originally created this example, I hadn't intended to create a declarative DSL. But sometimes the model insists on a given approach, and it's usually worth going along with it to see what the result is.

Let's explore the implementation of this DSL.[3] The implicit base class for this DSL is the `QuoteGeneratorRule`, shown in figure 4.6.

We need to note a few things about `QuoteGeneratorRule`. The first is that we use a strange naming convention for some of the methods (`requires`, `same_machine_as`, `specification`, and `users_per_machine` do not follow the standard .NET naming convention). This is the easiest way to get *keywords* in the DSL. We can take more advanced routes, like convention-based mapping, but doing so requires us to perform our own method lookup, and that isn't trivial. Changing the naming convention on the implicit base class is the easiest, simplest solution for the problem. Note that the `specification()` method accepts a delegate as the last parameter, so we're using anonymous blocks again, like we did in the Message-Routing DSL `Handle` method.

The second thing to note is all the @ signs scattered through the DSL (listing 4.16). Those are called *symbols*, and they translate to string literals without the annoying

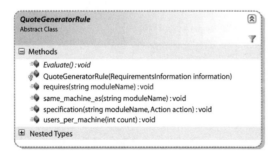

Figure 4.6 Implicit base class for the Quote-Generation DSL

---

[3] I am not going to implement the quote-generation engine, because this is both complex and beyond the scope of the book.

quotes. This may seem like a small thing, but it significantly enhances the readability of the language.

Boo doesn't support symbols natively, but they're trivial to add. In fact, the functionality is already there in Rhino DSL, which makes our DSL engine boring once again. Listing 4.17 shows what we need to add to the engine to support symbols.

Listing 4.17   Adding support for symbols

```
public class QuoteGenerationDslEngine : DslEngine
{
    protected override void CustomizeCompiler(
      BooCompiler compiler,
      CompilerPipeline pipeline,
      Uri[] urls)
    {
        pipeline.Insert(1,
            new ImplicitBaseClassCompilerStep(
                typeof(QuoteGeneratorRule),
                "Evaluate",
                "Chapter4.QuoteGeneration"));
    // add symbols support
        pipeline.Insert(2, new UseSymbolsStep());
    }
}
```

The last thing that's worth noting about the QuoteGeneratorRule class is that it accepts a RequirementsInformation class. This allows it to understand what context it runs in, which will be important later on.

The QuoteGeneratorRule class is responsible for building the object model that will later be processed by the quote-generation engine. We aren't going to write a quote-generation engine, because it is not fairly simple to do, and building it requires absolutely no DSL knowledge. Listing 4.18 shows the implementation of a few of the methods in the QuoteGeneratorRule class.

Listing 4.18   A few interesting methods from the `QuoteGeneratorRule` class

```
public void specification(string moduleName, Action action)
{
    this.currentModule = new SystemModule(moduleName);
    this.Modules.Add(currentModule);
    action();
}
public void requires(string moduleName)
{
    this.currentModule.Requirements.Add(moduleName);
}
```

The end result of evaluating a rule is an object model describing the requirements for a particular quote. For each module, we have a specification that lists what the required modules are, what other modules must run on the same machine, and how many users it can support. A different part of the application can take this description and generate the final quote from it. This DSL was pretty easy to build, and we have a nice syntax, but why do we need a DSL for this? Isn't this a good candidate for using XML?

4.5.2 *Selecting the appropriate medium*

We could have expressed the same ideas with XML (or a database) just as easily as with the DSL. Listing 4.19 shows the same concept, expressed in XML.

Listing 4.19 The Quote-Generation DSL expressed in XML

```
<specification name="vacation">
    <requires name="scheduling_work"/>
    <requires name="external_connections"/>
</specification>

<specification name="salary">
    <users_per_machine value="150"/>
</specification>

<specification name="taxes">
    <users_per_machine value="50"/>
</specification>

<specification name="pension">
    <same_machine_as name="health_insurance"/>
</specification>
```

We have a one-to-one mapping between the DSL and XML. The Quote-Generation DSL is a pure declarative DSL, which means that it only declares data. XML is good for declaring data, so it isn't surprising that we'd have a good match between the two.

Personally, I think the DSL syntax is nicer, and the amount of work it takes to get from a DSL to the object model is small compared to the work required to translate from XML to the same object model. But that's a personal opinion. A pure declarative DSL is comparable to XML in almost all respects.

It gets interesting when we decide that we don't want a pure declarative DSL. Let's add a couple of new rules to the mix, shall we?

- The Pension Plans module must be on the same machine as the Health Insurance module if the user count is less than 500.
- The Pension Plans module requires a distributed messaging backend if the user count is greater than 500.

Trying to express *that* in XML can be a real pain. Doing so would involve shoving programming concepts into the XML, which is always a bad idea. We could try to put this logic into the quote-generation engine, but that's complicating it for-no good reason.

Using our DSL (with no modification), we can write it as shown in listing 4.20.

Listing 4.20   Dealing with business logic in the DSL

```
specification @pension:
    if information.UserCount < 500:
        same_machine_as @health_insurance
    else:
        requires @distributed_messaging_backend
```

This is one of the major benefits of using DSLs—they scale well as the application complexity grows.

Now all we're left with is writing the backend for this, which would take the data we've built and generate the pricing. That's a simple problem, with all the parameters well specified. In fact, throughout the whole process, there isn't a single place where there's overwhelming complexity. I like that.

Code or data?

Some people attempt to use DSLs in the same way they would use XML. They use them as data storage systems. Basically, the DSL is relegated to being a prettier version of XML.

From my point of view, this is a waste of time and effort. It's the ability to make decisions that makes DSLs so valuable. Making all the decisions in the engine code will complicate the engine with all the decisions that we may ever need to make. Putting the decisions in the DSL and feeding the final result to the engine means that the engine is much simpler, the DSL scripts are *not* more complex, and we still get the flexibility that we want.

4.6   Summary

We started this chapter by defining a domain model, and then we built a DSL or three, representing three different approaches to building DSLs.

- The Message-Routing DSL is an example of an imperative DSL. It's executed to perform some goals.
- The Authorization DSL is a more declarative example (but still mostly imperative). It's executed to produce a value, which is later used.
- The Quote-Generation DSL is a mostly declarative example. It produces an object graph that's later taken up by the processing engine.

We've also seen why such DSLs are useful: they can contain logic, which affects the outputted object graph.

We also have another observation to make. Consider the following methods:

- `QuoteGeneratorRule.Evaluate()`
- `RoutingBase.Route()`
- `AuthorizationRule.CheckAuthorization()`

As you would discover if you could refer to *The Illustrated Design Patterns Spotter Guide*,[4] we have a match: the Command pattern. As a direct result of using the Implicit Base Class approach, we get an implementation of the Command pattern. This means we get a lot of the usual strengths and weaknesses of using the Command pattern, and it also means that the usual approaches to solving those issues are applicable.

NOTE I tend to use the Command pattern often, even outside of writing DSLs. It's a good way to package functionality and handle complexity in many areas.

In section 4.1, we talked about building a system using DSLs, and we did so by creating three DSLs. In many applications, you won't have a single DSL, but several, each for a particular domain and task. You can use the same techniques (and sometimes similar syntax) to tailor a language to its particular domain. All of those languages work together to create a single application.

We've now built our share of DSLs, and even written a DSL script or two. But we haven't talked about how to manage them in any meaningful way. We've focused on the details, so now it's time to take a broader look and see how to make use of a DSL in an application. In the next chapter, we'll look at how to integrate a DSL with an application, develop with it, and go to production with it. We'll look at the overall development lifecycle.

---

[4] Such a book doesn't, unfortunately, exist.

Integrating DSLs into your applications 5

We've covered a lot of ground, but only at the micro level so far. We've talked about how to build a DSL, how to ensure you have a good language, what the design parameters are, and so on. But we haven't yet touched on the macro level: how to take a DSL and integrate it into an application. Chapter 4 covered this at the micro level (building the languages themselves), but in this chapter we're going to discuss all that surrounds a DSL in an application. We'll talk about when and where to integrate a DSL, how to handle errors, how to handle dependencies between scripts, and how to set up a DSL structure that will be easy to work with.

5.1 Exploring DSL integration

The first thing we'll do is explore a DSL-integrated application to see what it looks like. That will give you an idea of the things you need to handle.

Figure 5.1 shows the DSLs integrated into our online shop example. We explored some of those DSLs in chapter 4 from the language-building perspective. Now we'll explore them from the application-integration perspective. This will be somewhat easier, because you've already seen how to make the calls to the DSL scripts. But in chapter 4 we were focusing on the language, and the integration approaches we used were trivial.

Figure 5.1   The integrated DSLs in our online shop example

Let's take the Message-Routing DSL as our first example. Listing 5.1 shows the integration of the Message-Routing DSL into the application. To refresh your memory, this method is part of the `Router` class, which dispatches incoming messages to the application services using the DSL scripts.

Listing 5.1   `Router.Route()` integrates the Message-Routing DSL into the application

```
public static string Route(IQuackFu msg)
{
    RoutingBase[] routings =
        dslFactory.CreateAll<RoutingBase>(
            Settings.Default.RoutingScriptsDirectory
        );
    foreach (RoutingBase routing in routings)
    {
        routing.Initialize(msg);
        routing.Route();
    }
    //removed for brevity's sake
    return null;
}
```

The `Route()` method seems almost ridiculously simple, right? It just grabs all the items from the specified directory and executes them all. For simple scenarios, dumping everything into a single directory works; take a look at figure 5.2 to see what such a directory might look like.

This looks good, right? But what happens if I don't need to handle just five messages? What happens if I need to handle a hundred, or twelve thousand? I assume that, like me, you won't want to hunt down one file in a huge directory. Also, if we have a large number of DSL scripts, and we scan all of them for every message that we route, we're going to have a performance issue on our hands.

Figure 5.2   A sample directory of Message-Routing DSL scripts

NOTE   Having a large number of scripts in a single directory will also have other effects. Rhino DSL batch compiles all scripts in a directory, and compiling takes time. This is a one-time cost, but it's a real cost.

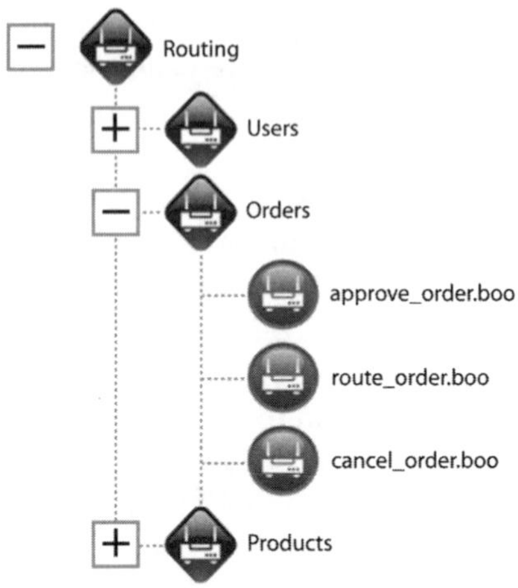

Figure 5.3   A directory structure mirroring our messaging structure

It's clear that we need some sort of structure in place to select which DSL scripts we're going to run. We already store the scripts in the filesystem, and filesystems long ago solved the problem of organizing large number of files using directories. So we could create a directory for all related scripts, and that would immediately give us a natural structure. But we'll still need to scan all the scripts for a match, right?

Well, not if we're smart about it. We can use the filesystem structure as a mirror of our messaging structure. Figure 5.3 shows a directory structure based on this idea. Now, when we get a message, we can check to see which broad category it's relevant for, and then execute only the scripts that are in that directory.

In fact, we can take that one step further by saying that the filename should match the message name. This way, once we have the message, we know which script we should run to handle it. Using a naming convention like this is an important friction-free way to integrate a DSL into your applications. A naming convention like that is a special case of using the convention over configuration principle.

Convention over configuration is a design paradigm that states that we should only have to explicitly specify the unusual aspects of our application. Everything that is conventional should be implicitly understood by the application. You can read more about it here: http://en.wikipedia.org/wiki/Convention_over_configuration.

5.2   *Naming conventions*

One of the key reasons for using a DSL is to reduce the effort required to make changes to the application. The main focus when building a DSL is usually on the language and the resulting API, but it's as critical to think about the environment in which the DSL will be used.

The Message-Routing DSL, for example, has a problem. It can't handle large numbers of messages with the approach that we've taken. Just scanning through all the scripts would take too much time.

To solve this problem, we can use a naming convention. Let's assume that we receive the message shown in table 5.1.

Table 5.1   A sample message

Key	Value
Type	orders/new_order
Version	1.0
CustomerId	15
TotalCost	$10

> **What about encapsulation?**
>
> It seems like the directory structure for our DSL scripts is directly responsible for the type of messaging that we send, so isn't this a violation of encapsulation?
>
> Well, not really. What we have here is a hierarchical structure for our messages, which is mirrored in both the DSL scripts and the message types. This doesn't break encapsulation; it simply lets us see the exact same thing from different perspectives.

Not a realistic message, I admit, but bear with me. Table 5.1 shows a structured message format with a field called `Type`, whose value is the name of the message-routing script to be run. This allows the Message-Routing DSL engine to go directly to the relevant script, without having to execute all the routing scripts.

Once we have read the message type, we can try to find a matching script by name, first for `<type>_<version>.boo` and then for `<type>.boo`. This means that we can match script versions to message versions for free as well, if we have different versions of particular message types that need different script versions.

When we need to handle a new type of message, we know immediately where to put the script that handles this message and how to name the script file. The reverse is also true. When we need the script that handles a given message type, we know where to look for it. This is the power of conventions, and I urge you to find a good convention when it comes to integrating your DSLs into applications.

TIP   When you come up with a convention, be sure to document it and how you got to it! A convention is only as good as it is *conventional*. If you have an *uncommon* convention, it is not only useless, it is actively harmful.

The naming convention and structure outlined here is important if you expect to have a large number of scripts, but it's of much less importance if you only have a few. Examples of DSLs where you might have few scripts are application-configuration DSLs, build-script DSLs, code-generation DSLs, and so on. In those cases, the DSL is usually composed of a single script (maybe split into several files, but conceptually a single script) that is used in narrow parts of the application or application lifecycle.

In those cases, the structure of the script files isn't relevant; you're only ever going to have a single one of those scripts, so it doesn't matter. The only interesting aspect of those DSLs from the application-integration perspective is how you execute them, and we more or less covered that already in chapter 4.

Let's look at another example of conventions in the context of the Authorization DSL (which was discussed in chapter 4). Listing 5.2 shows an example script for that DSL to refresh your memory.

Listing 5.2   A simple Authorization DSL script

```
operation "/account/login"

if Principal.IsInRole("Administrators"):
    Allow("Administrators can always log in")
    return

if date.Now.Hour < 9 or date.Now.Hour > 17:
    Deny("Cannot log in outside of business hours, 09:00 - 17:00")
    return
```

In the first line of listing 5.2, the operation name has an interesting property. It's already using a hierarchical structure, which is ideally suited for the type of convention-based structure we have been looking at.

Listing 5.3 shows how we can take advantage of the hierarchical nature of authorizable operations to handle the simple scenario where you have one script per operation and need to match them up.

Listing 5.3   Using operation names as conventions for the script names

```
private static AuthorizationResult ExecuteAuthorizationRules(
    IPrincipal principal,
    string operation,
    object entity)
{
    //assume that operations starts with '/'
    string operationUnrooted = operation.Substring(1);
    //create script path
    string script = Path.Combine(
                Settings.Default.AuthorizationScriptsDirectory,
                operationUnrooted+".boo");
    // try get the executable script
    AuthorizationRule authorizationRule =
        dslFactory.TryCreate<AuthorizationRule>(script, principal, entity);
    if(authorizationRule == null)
    {
        return new AuthorizationResult(false,
                "No rule allow this operation");
    }
    // perform authorization check
    authorizationRule.CheckAuthorization();
    return new AuthorizationResult(
        authorizationRule.Allowed,
        authorizationRule.Message
        );
}
```

The code is even simpler than the version in chapter 4 (see listing 4.8 for comparison), and it's obvious what is going on. But I did say that this was for the simplest scenario.

Consider a more complicated case where we have multiple rules for authorizing an operation. The /account/login operation, for instance, might be ruled by work hours, rank, remote worker privilege, and other factors. Right now, if we want to express all of this in the account/login.boo script, it's fairly simple, but what happens when it grows? What happens if we want to split it up based on the different rules?

Again, we run into problems in scaling out the complexity. Never fear, though—there is a solution. Instead of putting all the logic for the operation inside account/login.boo, we'll split it further, so the login operation will be handled by three different scripts:

- account/login/work-hours.boo
- account/login/remote-workers.boo
- account/login/administrators.boo

This allows us to separate the rules out into various well-named files, which reduces the number of balls we have to juggle whenever we need to edit an operation's logic.

In this case, `ExecuteAuthorizationRules()` will look almost identical to listing 4.8, except that it will append the operation to the base directory name when it searches for all the relevant scripts.

Our problems aren't all solved yet: what happens if we have dependencies and ordering requirements for the different scripts? Let's say that administrators should always have access, even outside of work hours. If the work-hours rule is executed first, access will be denied.

We need some way to specify ordering, or at least dependencies.

5.3 *Ordering the execution of scripts*

Fairly often, we'll need to execute scripts in some order. Security rules, where the first rule to allow or deny is the deciding one, are good examples. Many business rules follow the same pattern. This means we need to handle ordering in our DSL whenever we have to execute more than a single script for a certain action. (If we're executing only a single script, we obviously don't need to handle ordering.)

In general, there are several ways to enforce ordering in script execution:

- Providing no guaranteed ordering
- Ordering by naming
- Ordering with script priorities
- Ordering by external configuration

We'll look at each of these in order.

5.3.1 *Handling ordering without order*

Handling ordering by forgoing order is a strategy that surprises many people. The main idea here is to set things up in such a way that explicit ordering of the scripts isn't mandatory.

Let's take the example of authorization rules; we can decide that it's enough to have at least a single rule that says that we're allowed to perform an operation. (This may not be a good idea from the point of view of an authorization system, but it will suffice to make my point.) With this system, we don't care what the execution order is;

we want to aggregate all the results and then check whether any authorization rule has allowed us in. This is probably the least-expensive approach (you don't have to do anything), but it has serious implications.

For example, it requires that the scripts have no side effects. You can't perform any state changes in the script because we execute all of them. If the script will change the state of the application, we must know that it is valid to execute, and not just rely on discarding results that we don't care about. For something like the Authorization DSL, this is not only acceptable but also highly desirable. On the other hand, doing this with the Message-Routing DSL is impossible.

For that matter, you could argue that this approach isn't appropriate for authorization either, because authorization rules are generally naturally ordered. In most cases, we can't avoid some sort of ordering, so let's explore some of the other options.

5.3.2   *Ordering by name*

This is somewhat related to the naming-convention approach we used earlier. When you order scripts by name, you need to name your scripts in order. For example, in the Authorization DSL example, we'd have the following script names:

- account/login/01-administrators.boo
- account/login/02-work-hours.boo
- account/login/03-remote-workers.boo

This is a simple approach, and it works well in practice. In our code, we execute each script until we get a decisive answer. In fact, listing 4.8, unmodified, supports this exact model (Rhino DSL ensures that you get the script instances in ascending alphabetical order).

Although this works, it isn't a favorite approach of mine. I don't like this naming scheme because it's a bit painful to change the order of scripts, particularly if you want to add a new first script, which necessitates renaming all the other scripts (unless you plan ahead and leave enough gaps in your numbering system).

This isn't too onerous a task, but it is worth exploring other options, such as script priorities.

5.3.3   *Prioritizing scripts*

Script prioritization is a fancy name for a simple concept: giving each script a priority number and then executing each script according to its priority order. Figure 5.4 shows the main concept.

In the DSL, we make use of a generated property (like the Authorization DSL's Operation property) to set the priority in the script. Listing 5.4 shows an example of how it works.

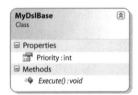

Figure 5.4   A base class for a DSL that supports script prioritization

Listing 5.4   A DSL script using prioritization

```
# specifying the priority of this script
priority 10

# the actual work done by this script
when order.TotalCost > 10_000:
    add_discount_precentage 5
```

Now all you have to do is sort the scripts by their priority and execute the top-ranking script. Listing 5.5 shows the gist of it.

Using priorities encoded in the scripts does mean that we have to compile and execute a full directory to figure out the order in which we will execute the scripts. This isn't as big a problem as it might sound at first, because we aren't dealing with all the scripts, just the much smaller number of scripts for a particular operation.

Listing 5.5   Executing the highest priority script

```
MyDslBase [] dslInstances = Factory.CreateAll<MyDslBase>( pathToScripts );
Array.Sort(dslInstances, delegate (MyDslBase x, MyDslBase y)
{
      // reverse order, topmost first
      return y.Priority.Compare(x.Priority);
});
dslInstances[0].Execute();
```

This is trivial to implement, both from the DSL perspective and in terms of selecting the highest priority script to execute. Usually, you won't simply execute the highest priority script; you'll want to execute them all in order until you have a valid match.

In the case of the Authorization DSL, you'd execute all the scripts until you get an allow or deny answer from one of the scripts. A "doesn't care" response will cause the application to try the next script in the queue.

Script prioritization does have some disadvantages:

- You have to go into the scripts to retrieve the priority order. This can be cumbersome if there are many scripts.
- You have no easy way of avoiding duplicate priorities, which happens when you assign the same priority to more than one script.
- Changing script priorities requires editing the scripts, which might cause problems if you want to reprioritize them at runtime. We had a similar issue when ordering using a naming convention.
- Responsibilities are mixed. The script is now responsible for both its own ordering and whatever action it's supposed to perform.

For these reasons, you might consider using a completely different approach, such as handling the ordering externally.

5.3.4   *Ordering using external configuration*

External ordering of scripts is useful mainly when you want to control ordering (and execution) at runtime, probably programmatically, using some sort of user interface that allows an administrator to configure it.

We'll talk more about this approach when we get to section 5.8, where we'll consider how to manage and administer a DSL. For now, let's focus on the implementation itself.

The simplest way to set up external configuration is to have a `files.lst` file in the scripts directory, which lists all the relevant scripts in the order they're required. We can get this by overriding the `GetMatchingUrlsIn(directory)` method in our DSL engine. Listing 5.6 shows the code for doing just that.

Listing 5.6   Getting an ordered list of scripts from a file

```
public override Uri[] GetMatchingUrlsIn(string directory)
{
    string fileListing = Path.Combine(directory, "files.lst");
    string[] scriptsToRun = File.ReadAllLines(fileListing);
    return Array.ConvertAll<string, Uri>(scriptsToRun,
        delegate(string input)
        {
                return new Uri(Path.Combine(directory, input));
        });
}
```

Other options include putting the information in an XML file or a database, but the overall approach is the same.

This is the most flexible solution, but it does come with its own problems. Adding a new script is now a two-step process: creating the script file and then adding it to whatever external configuration system you have chosen. My main concern in that situation is that handling the external configuration system will take a significant amount of time, not because it takes a long time to update, but because it's another step in the process that can be forgotten or missed. You can avoid that by making the external configuration smart (by adding more conventions to it), but it's still something to consider.

Now that we have ordering down pat, it's time to consider reuse and dependencies between scripts.

5.4   *Managing reuse and dependencies*

Quite often, you'll write a piece of code that you want to use in several places. This is true of DSLs too. There are several ways of reusing code when you're using a DSL.

The first, and most obvious, method is to remember that you're using Boo as the DSL language, and that Boo is a full-fledged CLR language. As such, it's capable of calling your code without any hassle. That works if you want to express the reusable piece in your application code.

Often, though, you'll want to take a piece of the DSL code and reuse *that*. Doing so allows you to take advantage of the benefits of using a DSL, after all. In this situation, reuse is more complex.

The first thing you need to recall is that although we have been calling the DSL files "scripts," they don't match the usual script terminology. They're compiled to IL in an assembly that we can then load into an `AppDomain` and execute. The DSL itself does fancy footwork with the compiler, after all.

Because the DSL is compiled to assemblies, we can reference the compiled assembly and use that. Boo makes it easy, because it allows you to create an assembly reference from code, not using the compiler parameters.

Listing 5.7 shows a piece of reusable code that we want to share among several scripts.

Listing 5.7 A reusable piece of DSL code

```
import System.Security.Principal

class AuthorizationExtension:
    # here we use an extension property to extend the IPrincipal interface
    [Extension]
    static IsManager[principal as IPrincipal] as bool:
        get:
            return principal.IsInRole("Managers")
```

We need to compile it to an assembly (by adding the `SaveAssembly` step to the pipeline, or by executing `booc.exe`) and save it to disk. This gives us the CommonAuthorizationMethods.dll assembly. Listing 5.8 shows how we can use that.

Listing 5.8 Using an `import` statement to create an assembly reference

```
# import the class and create assembly reference
import AuthorizationExtension from CommonAuthorizationMethods.dll
# use the extension property
if Principal.IsManager:
    Allow("Managers can always log in")
    return

if date.Now.Hour < 9 or date.Now.Hour > 17:
    Deny("Cannot log in outside of business hours, 09:00 - 17:00")
```

This works well, but it forces you to deal with the compiled assembly of the DSL scripts. This is possible, but it's awkward. It would be better to preserve the feeling that we're working in an infrastructure-free environment. Having to deal with assembly references hurts this experience.

Luckily, there's another way of dealing with this. Script references use the exact same mechanism that we have looked at so far (compiling the referenced script, adding a reference to the compiled assembly, and so on), but it's transparent from our point of view. Listing 5.9 does exactly the same thing as listing 5.8, but it uses script references instead of assembly references.

Listing 5.9   Using an `import` statement to create a script reference

```
# create the script reference
import file from CommonAuthorizationMethods.boo
# import the class
import AuthorizationExtension
# use the extension property
if Principal.IsManager:
    Allow("Managers can always log in")
    return

if date.Now.Hour < 9 or date.Now.Hour > 17:
    Deny("Cannot log in outside of business hours, 09:00 - 17:00")
```

As you can see, they're practically identical. The only difference is that we use the `import file from <filename>` form to add a script reference, and we need a second `import` statement to import the class after we create the script reference. (We need to import the class so it will be recognized for looking up extension properties.)

Script references aren't part of Boo

Script references are another extension to Boo; they aren't part of the core language. You can enable support for script references by adding the following statement in the `CustomizeCompiler()` method in your `DslEngine` implementation:

```
pipeline.Insert(2, new AutoReferenceFilesCompilerStep());
```

It's important to understand that script references aren't `#include` statements. What happens is that the code is compiled on the fly, and the resulting assembly is referenced by the current script. (It's actually a bit more involved than that, mostly to ensure that you only compile a script reference once, instead of multiple times.) This allows you to reuse DSL code between scripts, without causing issues with the usual include-based approach (such as increased code size and compilation time).

Speaking of which, it's time to take another look at an issue that most developers see as even more important than reuse: performance.

5.5   *Performance considerations when using a DSL*

A lot of programmers will tell you that their number-one concern is performance. I personally give positions 0 through 7 to maintainability, but that doesn't excuse bad performance, so let's talk about it a bit.

TIP   There is also much to learn from the wisdom of the ages: "We should forget about small efficiencies, say about 97% of the time: premature optimization is the root of all evil" (Donald Knuth).

Let's consider what effect using a DSL will have on the performance of an application. Here are some costs of integrating a DSL into an application:

- Script compilation
- Script execution

- Script management
- Memory pressure

5.5.1 *Script compilation*

Script compilation is the most easily noticeable issue. This is particularly true when you're compiling large amounts of code or continuously reinterpreting the same code.

If you're rolling your own DSL, you should be aware of this; make sure that you cache the results of compiling the DSL. Otherwise you'll pay a high price every time you execute a script. Rhino DSL takes care of that for you already, so this isn't something that you'll generally need to worry about.

> **TIP** One of the major problems with caching is that you need to invalidate the cache when the underlying data changes. If you decide to roll your own caching infrastructure, make sure you take this into account. You don't want to have to restart the application because you changed a script.

We'll look at Rhino DSL's caching and batching support in chapter 7.

5.5.2 *Script execution*

Script execution tends to be the least time-consuming operation when using a DSL. The DSL code is compiled to IL, and, as such, it enjoys all the benefits that the CLR has. This means that the DSL code is optimized by the JIT (just-in-time) compiler, runs at native speed, and in general has little runtime overhead.

This doesn't mean that it isn't possible to build slow DSL scripts. It means that the platform you choose to run on won't be an issue, even if you want to use a DSL in a common code path, where performance is an important concern.

Another important advantage of building your DSL in Boo is that if performance problems result from script execution, you can pull out your favorite profiler and pinpoint the exact cause of the issue. It looks like basing the DSL on a language that's compiled to IL has significant advantages.

DSL startup costs

One thing that might crop up is the startup cost of the DSL. Compilation does take time, even if the results of the compilation are cached after the first round.

For many applications, this isn't an important consideration, but for others, the startup time can be a make-or-break decision regarding DSL usage.

For scenarios where startup time is critical, you can retain all the advantages that the DSL offers but also get the best startup speed by precompiling the DSL. (We'll look at precompilation in chapter 12.) By using precompilation, you lose the flexibility of changing scripts on the fly, but you still have the richness of the language and you get a startup cost that's near zero.

5.5.3   Script management

Script management is probably the main cause for performance issues when using a DSL. By *script management* I mean the code that decides which scripts to execute. For example, having to execute 500 scripts when we could execute 2 will cost us.

We spent some time exploring naming conventions and how to structure our DSL previously in this chapter. Then we talked about the advantages from the point of view of organization and manageability of the DSL.

Those aren't the only benefits of good organization; there is also the issue of performance. Good organization often means that we can pinpoint exactly which script we need to run, instead of having to speculatively run many scripts.

5.5.4   Memory pressure

The last performance issue we need to consider is memory pressure. But these aren't memory issues in the traditional C++ sense; our DSLs aren't going to suffer from memory leaks, and garbage collection will still work the way you're used to. By *memory pressure*, I mean *assembly leakage*. This is probably going to be a rare event, but as long as we're talking about performance...

The DSL code that we use is compiled to IL, which resides in an assembly, which is loaded into an `AppDomain`. But an `AppDomain` can't release assemblies, so once you load an assembly into an `AppDomain`, you can't unload it without unloading the entire `AppDomain`. Because you probably want to have automatic refresh for scripts (so that when you change the script, it's automatically compiled on the fly), you need to pay attention to that. Each compilation causes a new assembly to be loaded,[1] which can't be unloaded.

If you have many script changes, and you have a long-running application, all those assemblies being loaded can eventually cause memory issues. The usual solution is to segregate the DSL into a separate `AppDomain` and reload it after a certain number of recompilations have occurred.

This solves the problem, and it has other advantages besides reducing the number of in-memory assemblies. For example, it segregates the DSL from the rest of the application, which allows you to add security measures and protect yourself from rogue scripts. This segregation is our next topic.

5.6   Segregating the DSL from the application

Although having a DSL (or a set of DSLs) in place can make many things much easier, DSLs bring their own set of issues. You're letting external entities add code to your application, and if you, or your team, are the ones adding those scripts, it's all well and good. If it's a separate team or business analysts who are doing so, you need to take precautions against unfortunate accidents and malicious attacks.

---

[1] Well, that's not technically correct, but it's close enough for now. We'll get to the technicalities in chapter 7.

There are several vectors of attack that can be used when you have DSL code running in your application. These are the most common ones (but by no means the only ones):

- Malicious actions, such as deleting or corrupting data, installing malware, and the like
- Denial of service, hogging the CPU, leaking memory, or trying to kill the host application by triggering faults in the runtime or the OS

There are several options for limiting what a script can do, such as building your own security infrastructure to separate the DSL from the rest of the application, limiting the time that a script can run, or executing it under a lower security context.

5.6.1 Building your own security infrastructure

The first option is to dig into the compiler and try to build your own security infrastructure by disallowing all calls except a certain permitted set.

For myself, I am extremely nervous about doing such things. Rolling your own security is almost always a bad thing. You *are* going to miss something, and few solutions will be able to protect you from the code in listing 5.10.

> **Listing 5.10 A trivial malicious script**

```
# Denial of service attack using a DSL
# this script never returns and takes 100% CPU
while true:
    pass
```

You can try to detect that, but you'll quickly get into the halting problem (proving that for all input, the program terminates in a finite amount of time), and Alan Turing[2] already proved in 1935 that it can't be solved.

That said, we don't have to roll our own security (nor should we). We can use the security infrastructure of the platform.

5.6.2 Segregating the DSL

The problem of segregating the DSL from the application is a subset of protecting a host application from add-ins. There is a lot of information available on that topic, and because we're using IL all the way, everything that's relevant to an add-in is also relevant to a DSL. It isn't possible to cover all the options that the CLR offers to control add-ins. That's a topic for whole book on its own, but we can touch on the high points.

The first thing to realize is that the unit of isolation on the CLR is the `AppDomain`, both in terms of loading and unloading the assembly, as we mentioned earlier, and in terms of permissions, safety, boundaries, and so on. In general, when the time comes to erect a security boundary, you'll usually create a new `AppDomain` with the desired

---

[2] Alan Turing (1912–1954) was a British mathematician and computer scientist and is considered to be the father of modern computer science.

permission set and execute the suspected code there. Listing 5.11 shows how we can do that.

Listing 5.11 Creating a sandboxed `AppDomain`

```
// Create local intranet permissions
// This is what I would generally use for DSL
Evidence intranetEvidence = new Evidence(
    new object[] { new Zone(SecurityZone.Intranet) },
    new object[] { });
// Create the relevant permission set
PermissionSet intranetPermissions =
    SecurityManager.ResolvePolicy(intranetEvidence);

AppDomainSetup setup = new AppDomainSetup();
setup.ApplicationBase = AppDomain.CurrentDomain.BaseDirectory;

// create a sandboxed domain
AppDomain sandboxedDomain = AppDomain.CreateDomain(
    "DSL Domain", intranetEvidence, setup,
    intranetPermissions);
// Create an instance of a class that we can use to execute
// our DSL in the remote domain
DslExecuter unwrap = (DslExecuter)
    sandboxedDomain.CreateInstanceAndUnwrap(
        typeof(DslExecuter).Assembly.FullName,
        typeof(DslExecuter).FullName);
```

The `DslExecuter` is something that you'll have to write yourself; its code will depend on what you want done in the sandboxed domain. Using a separated `AppDomain` with lower security settings, you're mostly protected from whatever malicious acts the scripts can perform. You can enhance that by applying code access security policies, but those tend to be fairly complex, and I have rarely found them useful. Since you're running the scripts in a separate `AppDomain`, they can't corrupt application state. This is almost the perfect solution.

It's *almost perfect* because there are two additional vectors of attack against which the CLR doesn't give us the tools to protect ourselves. Unhandled thread exceptions and stack overflows are both exceptions that the runtime considers critical, and they'll cause the termination of the process they occurred on. And there are also denial of service attacks like the example in listing 5.10.

It's important to note that those critical exceptions will kill the *process*, not just the responsible `AppDomain`. There are no easy solutions for this problem, and the two options I have found aren't ideal. The first involves writing unmanaged code to host the CLR, so you can control how it will behave under those scenarios. The second is spinning off another process and handling the possibility of it crashing by spinning it up again.

Neither option makes me happy, but that's the way it is. Most of the time, I believe that running DSL code in a separate `AppDomain` is an acceptable risk and carry on without the additional complexity each option involves.

5.6.3   Considerations for securing a DSL in your application

As a result, when it comes time to protect my applications from rogue scripts, I focus on two main subjects:

- Protecting the application by limiting what the script can do (using a separate `AppDomain` with limited permissions)
- Protecting the application by limiting how long a script can run (executing scripts with a timeout, and when the time limit is reached, killing the thread executing the DSL code and reporting a failure)

Most of the time, I don't bother with all of that. It all depends on the type of application that you write, the people who are developing the scripts, what level they're at, and how trustworthy they are.

Table 5.2 outlines the options you have for segregating the DSL, and the implications of each option.

In general, I would recommend that you go with the first approach (no segregation) unless you have solid reasons to do otherwise. In nearly all scenarios, this is the easiest and simplest way to go, and it will handle most requirements well.

Table 5.2   Summary of segregation options

Segregation approach	Implications	Suitable for
No segregation— run DSL code in the same `AppDomain`	Fastest performance DSL code runs under the same privileges as application code Frequent changes in DSL scripts may necessitate application restart	This is ideal when the DSL code has the same level of trust as the application code itself. But if you expect to have frequent changes to the DSL scripts, you may want to consider the next level to prevent assembly leakage.
High segregation— run DSL code in a different `AppDomain`	High level of separation from the application Permissions can be tuned down, so the DSL can do little Can reload the `AppDomain` after a certain number of recompilations Slower performance (cross-`AppDomain` communication is slower than just calling a method on an object in the current `AppDomain`)	This is appropriate when the DSL code isn't as trusted as the application code and you want to ensure separation between the two. It's also important when you suspect that you'll have many changes in the scripts and you want to be able to perform an `AppDomain` restart when needed. Malicious scripts can take down the application if they *really* try.
Complete segregation— run DSL code in a separate process	High cost for communication between processes High level of separation from the application Permissions can be tuned down as needed Supports `AppDomain` reloading DSLs can't take application down	This is suitable when you do not trust the DSL or when you want to ensure even greater separation of application and DSL. It requires you to take care of recovering the process if it dies.

> **Handling isolation with System.AddIns**
>
> `System.AddIns` is a namespace in .NET that offers support for those scenarios when you want to run untrusted plug-in code in your application. I haven't had time to investigate it in detail, but it supports isolation on the `AppDomain` and process levels, and it takes care of much of the grunt work.
>
> If isolation is important for your application, I suggest taking a look at `System.AddIns` before rolling an isolation layer independently.

Even the main reason for moving to the other approaches (`AppDomain` reload, and the subsequent assembly unload that frees the loaded assemblies) isn't a real issue in most systems. Most script changes happen during development, when the application is rarely operating continuously for significant enough amounts of time to cause problems.

In practice, I have found the problem of DSL segregation to be a minor concern. The handling of script errors is a far bigger concern.

5.7   Handling DSL errors

In general, errors in DSLs are divided into two broad categories: compilation errors (which might include problems with the syntax or with transformation code), and runtime errors when executing scripts. We'll look at the second one first, since it's the more familiar.

5.7.1   Handling runtime errors

As you can imagine, because a DSL compiles to IL, any runtime error will be an exception. This means that you already know how to handle it. You just use a `try ... catch` block when you execute the DSL code, and handle the error according to your exception policies. That's it, almost.

There is one issue to deal with. Because the whole purpose of the DSL is to give you a better way to express yourself, the DSL code and what is executing aren't necessarily the same. In fact, they're often radically different.

Take a look at listing 5.12, which shows a Message-Routing DSL script that will cause a runtime exception.

> **Listing 5.12   A Message-Routing DSL script that will cause a runtime exception**

```
HandleWith NewOrderHandler:
    zero = 0
    print 1/zero # will cause error
```

When you execute this script, you'll get the exception in listing 5.13.

Listing 5.13 The exception message from executing listing 5.12

```
System.DivideByZeroException: Attempted to divide by zero.
    at RouteNewOrder.Route$closure$1()
            in Source\Scripts\Routing\RouteNewOrder.boo:line 7
    at CompilerGenerated.$adaptor$___callable0$MessageTransformer$0.Invoke()
    at RoutingBase.HandleWith(Type handlerType,
            MessageTransformer transformer)
            in Source\BDSLiB\MessageRouting\DSL\RoutingBase.cs:line 55
    at RouteNewOrder.Route()
            in Source\Scripts\Routing\RouteNewOrder.boo:line 5
    at Router.Route(IQuackFu msg)
            in Source\BDSLiB\MessageRouting\Router.cs:line 32
    at JSONEndPoint.ProcessRequest(HttpContext context)
            in Source\BDSLiB.EndPoints\JSON.EndPoint.ashx.cs:line 29
```

In this case, it's pretty clear what's going on. We have a divide by zero error. But where did it happen? In `RouteNewOrder.Route$closure$1()`, of all places. How did we get that?

This is a good example of the type of changes between DSL and IL that can confuse you when you try to figure out exactly where the error is. In this case, because of the structure of the Message-Routing DSL, the code inside the handle statement is a closure (or block or anonymous delegate), which explains why it has this strange name.

When you want to analyze exactly where this error happened, the method name isn't much help—you won't be able to make the connection between the method name and the code in the DSL unless you're well versed in the internals of the Boo compiler. I know that I certainly can't.

But while we don't know which statement in the DSL caused the error, we do have the line-number location in the file that caused the error (and this is why we'll look at lexical info in detail in chapter 6). This location information allows us to go to the file and see exactly where the error occurred. This is incredibly useful when you need to deal with errors.

Now that I have the error, what do I do with it?

This section discusses how to get the error and how to catch the exception. But what should you do with the error once you get it?

You can start from the assumption that you'll have errors in your scripts and runtime errors when you execute them. As such, error handling should be a key consideration when designing your DSLs.

One approach is to let the error bubble up, and let the application code handle this. Another is to consider a DSL script that failed compilation to be invalid and ignore the error, whereas an error in executing the script would be passed to higher levels.

There is no one-size-fits-all solution here. You need to tailor the error-handling strategy to the purpose of the DSL.

That's about all you need to do to deal with runtime errors. And with the one caveat of finding the exact error location, we handle DSL errors in the same way we handle application code errors.

Now we can talk about compilation errors and how to handle them.

5.7.2 *Handling compilation errors*

Compilation errors are divided into three broad categories: syntax errors, invalid code, and errors thrown by extensions to the compiler.

Syntax errors are caused by mistakes like forgetting to put a colon at the end of an `if` statement. They will usually cause an error of the "unexpected token" variety.

Invalid code is when you use correct syntax but the code is wrong. Calling `int.LaunchRocket()` is valid syntax, but `int` doesn't have a `LaunchRocket()` method (at least not the last time I checked), so it will generate an error similar to this one: "ERROR: 'LaunchRocket' is not a member of 'int'."

There isn't much that can be done for those first two categories of errors, although Boo is smart enough in many cases to suggest alternatives for misspelled identifiers. For example, trying to call `int.Prase()` will generate the following error: "ERROR: 'Prase' is not a member of 'int'. Did you mean 'Parse'?"

The third category of compilation error is errors that are thrown from your extensions to the compiler. This code is run as part of the compilation process, and errors in this code will be reported as compilation errors. These errors (unless they're intentional) are plain old bugs, and should be treated as such. The compiler will show the exception information from your extensions, which will allow you to pinpoint the issue and create a fix for it. You could also execute the compiler while in the debugger and debug your compiler extensions.

5.7.3 *Error-handling strategies*

Now that we've covered error management in DSLs specifically, I want to recommend a few best practices for handling those errors.

First, you should log all errors (compilation and runtime errors) to someplace where you can analyze them later. This is particularly true after you go to production. This log should be accessible to the developers.

> **TIP** I was once denied read privileges to the production application logs, which meant that I had to *guess* what the problem was. Make sure that you log the errors to an operation database that is explicitly defined as accessible to developers, rather than the production database, where regulatory concerns may prevent developer access.

Second, refer to management of faulty DSL scripts (ones that cannot be compiled). If a script fails to compile, you should make a note of that and ignore it until the next time it has been changed (in which case you can try compiling it again).

Attempting to execute a script that compiles successfully but fails every time it is executed is a waste of CPU cycles, so allowing a script a certain number of consecutive

---

Circuit breakers

When you suspend a script that keeps failing, you're using the Circuit Breaker pattern.[3] It's used to minimize the effects of failure in one part of a system on the rest of the system.

You'll probably want to set a time limit for the script's suspension, after which it's valid for execution again (or after it has been changed, presumably fixing the error). Also, make sure you take into account that the input might have caused the error; if a script fails on invalid input, it isn't the script's fault.

Note that this technique is not always appropriate. For example, if the authentication module is throwing errors, it's probably a bad idea to disable authentication and allow full access for everyone. But it's often a good way to stop propagating failures.

---

failures and then suspending its execution would also be a good idea. Keep in mind, though, that suspending a script that contains critical business logic is probably not a good idea. At that point, you would want the entire application to come to a screeching halt until someone can fix it.

I can't stress how important it is that administrators should be notified when scripts are turned off. For example, they should see when account/login.boo has been disabled because it keeps throwing errors (perhaps because the LDAP directory was taken down). Something like this certainly requires administrator intervention.

This brings us to the last topic for this chapter—administrating our DSL integration.

5.8   *Administrating DSL integration*

When I talk about administrating an application's DSL integration, I'm really talking about several related tasks.

Usually, you'll administer DSLs using the administration section of your application, although sometimes you will use a custom application for administering the DSLs in an application. We'll discuss building such tools in chapter 10.

Administrating the DSL and the DSL scripts consists of several tasks:

- *Reviewing logging and auditing information*—Logging is particularly important when it's related to errors, but other information is also important. You can use this information to track the usage of certain scripts, check the timing of scripts, review the success of particular operations, and so on.
- *Reviewing information about suspended and ignored scripts*—This information will let you know which scripts have failed to run, so you can fix them. *Ignored scripts* are those with compiler errors, whereas *suspended scripts* are those that tripped the circuit breaker and have been disabled for a time.

---

[3] Circuit Breaker is the name of a pattern in *Release It! Design and Deploy Production-Ready Software* by Michael T. Nygard. I highly recommend this book. It's available from http://www.pragprog.com/titles/mnee.

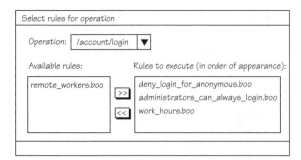

Figure 5.5   An administration screen for specifying which rules to execute on an operation

- *Configuring the order of scripts*—We looked at the ordering of scripts in section 5.3. In your application administration UI you can configure the mechanism that you use to set the script execution order, which gives you more flexibility at deployment time.

- *Configuring which scripts should run for certain actions*—You can treat scripts as part of the rules in the system, and work with them dynamically. This approach, of dynamic rule composition, is useful when you have rapidly changing environments. With DSLs, making changes is easy, and providing a user interface to decide which scripts to run in response to what actions makes change management easy (we'll talk about DSL change management in chapter 12). Figure 5.5 shows a sample user interface that could be used to administer such rules.

- *Updating scripts*—You can also use the administration section of the application to update scripts, but this should be considered carefully, because production code changes are not something you want to make *too* easy. Change management and source control are two things that you definitely want in place for DSLs, and we'll discuss them in chapter 12.

The list just enumerates common tasks that come up in most DSL implementations. I generally implement each of those on an as-needed basis, and there are others (audit information, for example) that you might want to implement as well. The DSL administration should be considered as part of the DSL design, and chapter 12 talks extensively about that topic.

5.9   *Summary*

We've covered quite a bit of ground in this chapter. We talked about the macro concerns of using a DSL in your application and how the DSL solution can scale easily as the complexity of the application grows.

We looked at using naming and ordering conventions to allow our DSLs to find the appropriate scripts to run and the order in which to run them with as little work as possible. Reducing the work required to find the right set of scripts to handle a certain action is important, both in terms of the amount of work that the DSL has to do and our own mental processes when we try to add a new script or find out how particular scripts work.

We also explored the reuse, performance, and segregation aspects of using a DSL. In all three cases, we saw that compiling the scripts to IL gives us the advantages of native CLR code, which means that we can take advantage of all the CLR services, from easily reusing scripts, to profiling a DSL, to using the built-in sandboxing features of the runtime.

We also looked at error handling. Again, because our DSLs are based on Boo, which compiles to IL, we can use all our familiar tools and concepts.

Looking at the big picture, you should now be starting to see how you can plug a DSL implementation into an application to make the implementation of policies more convenient, readable, and dynamic.

Throughout this chapter, we continued building the DSL, looking at how to deal with the compiler and use Rhino DSL. We touched briefly on cache invalidation, script references, and some other goodies, but we haven't looked at those topics in detail. It's now time to discover exactly what the compiler can do for us. That's the topic of the next chapter.

Advanced compiler
extensibility approaches

6

Boo offers a rich set of extensibility mechanisms that you can use. We'll look at them for a couple of reasons: to make sure you understand what is possible, and to expose you to the way they can be used to create easily readable, intuitive, and natural DSLs.

But before we can start talking about compiler extensibility, we need to look at the compiler itself and define some common terms. A lot of Boo's capabilities are exposed in ways that only make sense if you understand these concepts. I'll assume compilers aren't your area of expertise and make sure that you can understand and use the capabilities we'll look at.

You won't need this knowledge on a day-to-day basis. You can build most DSLs without going deep into the compiler, but it's important to understand how things work under the hood. There are some situations when it's easier to go into the compiler and make a change than work around the problem with the tools that are exposed on the surface.

The basic structure of the Boo compiler is the *pipeline*—it's how the compiler transforms bits of text in a file into executable code.

6.1 *The compiler pipeline*

When the compiler starts to compile a set of files, it runs a set of steps to produce the final assembly. This series of steps is called the compiler *pipeline*.

Figure 6.1 shows a partial list of the steps in a standard compilation. Right now, a typical Boo compiler pipeline has over 40 steps, each of which performs a distinct task. When you write a step, you only have to focus on that particular task, nothing else.

TIP There are several Boo compiler pipelines that you can choose from, but switching pipelines is fairly advanced stuff, and not something you usually need to do for DSLs.

Let's focus on the first step, parsing the code. In this step, the parser reads the code and outputs a set of objects that represent that code. We've seen that done in chapter 1, when we talked about abstract syntax trees (ASTs). ASTs are the object models that the compiler uses to represent the code.

The parser takes code like this,

```
if 1 == 2:
    print "1 = 2"
else:
    print "1 != 2"
```

and turns it into an object model that looks like figure 6.2.

You can think of AST as the compiler's DOM, such as the XML and HTML DOM that you're probably already familiar with. Like them, the AST can be manipulated to get different results. In fact, this is what most of the compiler steps do. The first step, parsing, takes the code and translates it to AST; all the other steps scan and transform the AST. There are several extension points into the compiler pipeline, from custom compiler steps to meta-methods, and from AST attributes to AST macros. We will discuss all of them in this chapter.

Manipulating the AST takes some getting used to. I have shocked people when I suggested changing if statement semantics as one of the options for extending the

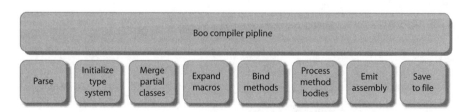

Figure 6.1 A selection of Boo's compiler steps

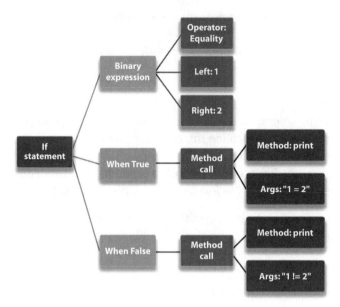

Figure 6.2   Abstract syntax tree of an `if` statement

language. Hopefully, when we go over all the extensibility options in the compiler, it will become clearer. Mind you, you'll want to exercise some self-control when doing this. Although an `if` loop is an interesting idea, it seems to bother some people.

Now let's use what we've learned about the compiler and look at how it works and how we can modify it.

6.2   Meta-methods

The first level of extending the compiler is easy—we covered it in chapter 2 when we talked about duck typing and `IQuackFu`. The next level is when we start working with the compiler's AST that represents your source code and from which the compiler generates the IL to build assemblies. And the first step in that direction is building meta-methods.

A *meta-method* is a shortcut into the compiler. It's a method that accepts an AST node and returns an AST node. *AST node* is a generic term for all the types of nodes that compose the AST.

Let's implement an assert method. But, because Boo already has an `assert` statement, we'll use "`verify`" as the method name. Listing 6.1 shows the method implementation in its entirety.

> **Listing 6.1   Implementing the `verify` method**

```
[Meta]
static def verify(expr as Expression):
    return [|
        unless $expr:
            raise $(expr.ToCodeString())
    |]
```

Exploring the AST

We'll do a lot of work in this chapter and the rest of the book that touches the AST directly, and I highly recommend that you explore it yourself. Although I can explain the concepts behind the methods we're going to use, there is no substitute for experience, particularly when it comes to understanding how to use the AST.

The best way to explore it is to ask the Boo compiler to print the resulting AST from a given piece of code. You can do that by including the `PrintAst` step in the compiler pipeline.

Another option is to use quasi-quotation (discussed later in this chapter) and .NET Reflector (http://www.red-gate.com/products/reflector/) to get an understanding of how the AST is composed and used. I suggest spending some time familiarizing yourself with the AST. It's important to get a good understanding of how the compiler works so you can fully utilize the compiler's capabilities.

The code in listing 6.1 creates a new keyword in the language. We can use it to ensure that a given condition is true; if it isn't true, an exception will be thrown. We can use `verify` in the following manner:

```
verify arg is not null
```

The `verify` implementation instructs the compiler to output a check and to raise an exception if the check fails. For now, please ignore any syntax you don't understand. I've used quasi-quotation to save some typing; we'll look at quasi-quotation in the next section.

Listing 6.1 shows a static method that's decorated with the `[Meta]` attribute and that accepts an AST expression. This is all you need to create a meta-method.

When you have a meta-method, you can call it like a regular method:

```
verify ( 1 == 2 )
```

A note about the code in this chapter

In this chapter, I will show the compiler manipulation code in Boo and provide several examples in C#. Boo is more suited to writing code for compiler manipulation, but most languages will do.

We'll discuss code management (IDEs, compilation, and the like) in chapter 10 (which focuses on UIs) and in chapter 12 (on managing DSL code).

If you want to use an IDE for the code in this chapter, you will need to use Sharp Develop (http://www.icsharpcode.net/OpenSource/SD/).

The code in this chapter was compiled using Boo 0.9.2 and Sharp Develop 3.1.0.4977.

Because Boo supports method invocations without parentheses, you can also call it in the following fashion:

```
verify 1 == 2
```

When the compiler sees a call to a meta-method, it doesn't emit code to call the meta-method at runtime. Instead, the meta-method is executed during compilation. The compiler passes the meta-method the AST of the arguments of the method code (including anonymous blocks), and then we replace this method on the AST with the result of calling the meta-method. Figure 6.3 shows the transformation that is caused by the meta-method.

This process is similar to text-substitution macros in C and C++ (and even more like Lisp and Scheme macros, if you're familiar with them), but this not mere text pre-processing. It's actual code that runs during compilation and outputs any code it wants back into the compilation process. Another difference is that we're dealing directly with the compiler's AST, not just copying lines of text.

A lot of people seem to have a hard time grasping this distinction. The compiler will ask you, at compilation time, what kind of transformation you want to do on the code. It then takes the results of the transformation (the method's return value, which is an AST expression) and replace the method call with the returned expression.

Note the difference between a method returning a value at runtime and what meta-methods are doing. The return value from a meta-method is an AST expression that is replacing the method call. When the compiler emits the final IL, it is the returned expression that will end up in the compiled DLL, not the method call.

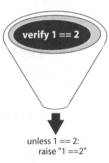

The idea of code running at compilation time and modifying the compiled output is the main hurdle to understanding how you can modify the Boo language. I suggest taking a look at the compiled output with Reflector—it usually help clear things up. Figure 6.3 also shows the transformation happening at compile time.

The Boo code in listing 6.1 can also be translated to the C# shown in listing 6.2. This version shows what happens under the covers, and it's a bit more explicit about what is going on. Both method implementations have exactly the same semantics.

Figure 6.3 The code transformation caused by the `verify` meta-method

---

Listing 6.2   A C# implementation of the `verify` method

```
[Meta]
public static UnlessStatement verify(Expression expr)
{
    UnlessStatement unless = new UnlessStatement();
    unless.Condition = expr.Clone();
    RaiseStatement raise = new RaiseStatement();
    raise.Exception = new StringLiteralExpression(expr.ToCodeString());
    unless.Statements.Add(raise);
    return unless;
}
```

We've used meta-methods before, when we implemented the when keyword for the Scheduling DSL, in chapter 3. Meta-methods are often used in DSLs. When you run into the limits of what the compiler offers out of the box, meta-methods are your next best option.

It's important that you come to grips with the idea of AST manipulation; this is the key to what we'll discuss in the rest of the chapter. Further on in this chapter, we'll talk about AST macros and AST attributes, both of which are similar to meta-methods, and rightfully so. They take the same AST manipulation approach, but they're used differently and generally have more power at their disposal.

But before we get to them, we should take a look at quasi-quotation and why it's useful.

6.3 Quasi-quotation

You've already seen quasi-quotation in the verify method (listing 6.1). Quasi-quotation is a way to use the compiler's existing facilities to translate text into code. But in this case, instead of translating text to code, the compiler is translating the original text into code that produces the code. Confusing, isn't it? It will be easier to look at some examples.

Let's say you wanted to create the AST for a trivial if statement. The code that you want to generate looks like this:

```
if date.Today.Day == 1:
    print "first of month"
```

Remember the AST diagrams you have seen so far? Let's see what it takes to generate the AST for this statement. We'd need all the code in listing 6.3 to make this work.

Listing 6.3 Generating the AST for a trivial if statement

```
ifStmt = IfStatement(
    Condition: BinaryExpression(
        Operator: BinaryOperatorType.Equality,
        Left: AstUtil.CreateReferenceExpression("date.Today.Day"),
        Right: IntegerLiteralExpression(1)
        ))
write = MethodInvocationExpression(
        Target:
      AstUtil.CreateReferenceExpression("System.Console.WriteLine")
    )
write.Arguments.Add( StringLiteralExpression('first of month') )
ifStmt.TrueBlock = Block()
ifStmt.TrueBlock.Add(
    write
)
```

If you're like me, you're looking at this code and thinking that programming suddenly seems a lot harder than it used to be. In truth, though, it's not much different than working with the XML or HTML DOM, which you're likely already familiar with. If you've ever done any work using System.CodeDOM, for that matter, the code in listing 6.3 should be instantly familiar to you. Nevertheless, if you've ever done any work with any type of DOM, you'll know that it's extremely tedious. It's easy to get lost in the details when you have even slightly complex scenarios.

You likely won't need to write much AST—usually just wrappers and the like—but this is probably the most tedious and annoying part of having to deal with the compiler. For that reason, we have quasi-quotation, which allows us to produce the AST we want without the pain.

The 15 lines of code in listing 6.3 can be written in 4 lines by using quasi-quotation, as shown in listing 6.4.

> **Listing 6.4   Generating the AST of a trivial `if` statement by using quasi-quotation**

```
ifStmt = [|
        if date.Today.Day == 1:
                System.Console.WriteLine("first of month")
|]
```

Listing 6.4 produces the exact same results as listing 6.3. When the compiler encounters this code, it does the usual parsing of the code, but instead of outputting the IL instructions that would execute the code, it outputs the code to build the required AST, much in the same way we did in listing 6.3.

The fun part is that you aren't limited to generating the AST code statically; you can also generate it dynamically. You can use `$variable` to refer to an external variable or `$(variable.SomeValue)` to refer to a more complex expression, and they will be injected into the generated AST building code. Let's look at an example.

Let's say you want to generate code that will output the date that this code was compiled. You could do it with the code in listing 6.5.

> **Listing 6.5   Generating code that outputs date this code was compiled**

```
currentDate = date.Today.ToString()
whenThisCodeWasCompiled = [|
        System.Console.WriteLine( $currentDate );
|]
```

I believe this is the cue for a light-bulb-over-the-head moment. You aren't limited to using strings to pass to quasi-quotation blocks; you can use anything that's directly translatable to AST. Listing 6.6 shows a more interesting example, if not a particularly useful one.

> **Listing 6.6   Composing AST using quasi-quotation**

```
if compilingOnMono:
    createConnection = [|
        Mono.Data.Sqlite.SqliteConnection()
    |]
else:
    createConnection = [|
```

```
        System.Data.Sqlite.SqliteConnection()
    |]
connectToDatabase = [|
using con = $createConnection():
    con.ConnectionString = GetConnectionString()
    con.Open();
        # make use of the opened connection...
|]
```

Consider using this code when you want to generate conditional code. As shown in listing 6.6, we choose, at compile time, which library to use to connect to a database, based on the platform we're running on. Different code will be generated for each platform. This will make those things a piece of cake.

Does this mean that we're limited to building in Boo?

No, it doesn't. The Boo AST is composed of standard CLR classes, and it can be used from any CLR language. As such, you can use any CLS-compliant language to interact with the Boo compiler. I have quite a few Boo DSLs in use right now that use C# to manipulate the AST.

But Boo does have facilities to make AST manipulation easier, quasi-quotation being chief among them. You'll have to decide for yourself what is easier for you.

You can also use the $() syntax directly, as in listing 6.7.

Listing 6.7 Using complex expressions in quasi-quotation

```
whenThisCodeWasCompiled = [|
        System.Console.WriteLine( $( date.Now ) );
|]
```

We'll make heavy use of this technique as we get more involved with AST manipulations.

Now, let's see how we can use this knowledge to do some really interesting things.

6.4 AST macros

Meta-methods and AST macros differ in several ways:

- An AST macro has full access to the compiler context and the full AST of the code, and it can collaborate with other macros, compiler steps, and AST attributes to produce the final result. A meta-method can only affect what was passed to it via its parameters. Meta-methods can produce the same results as AST macros, but not as easily.
- An AST macro can't return values, but a meta-method can.
- An AST macro is exposed by importing its namespace; a meta-method must be referenced by namespace and class. This is a minor difference.

Let's look at a simple example—a macro that will unroll a loop.

Generating blocks with quasi-quotation and macros

When we're using quasi-quotation, we're using the standard Boo parser and compiler to generate the AST code. This is great, because it means that we can use quasi-quotation to generate any type of AST node that we can write on our own (classes, namespaces, properties, method, statements, and expressions). But it means that when the compiler is parsing the code inside the quasi-quotation, it must consider that you can put any type of AST node there.

This means that when the compiler encounters the following piece of code, it will output an error:

```
block = [|
        val = 15
        if val == 16:
            return
|]
```

Here the parser believes that we're starting with field declarations because a quasi-quotation can be anything. It can be a class declaration, a method with global parameters, a single expression, or a set of statements. Because of that, the parser needs to guess what the context is. In this particular edge case, the compiler gets it wrong, and we need to help it figure it out.

The problem in the previous example is that we're parsing field declarations (which means that we are in a class declaration context), and then we have an `if` statement in the middle of that class declaration. This is obviously not allowed, and it causes the compiler error.

Here's a simple workaround to avoid this problem:

```
code = [|
        block:
            val = 15
            if val  == 16:
                    return
|]
block = code.Body
```

Adding `block` in this fashion has forced the parser to consider the previous code as a macro statement, which means it's inside a method where `if` statements are allowed. We're only interested in the content of the block, so we extract the block of code from the macro statement that we fooled the parser into returning.

6.4.1   The unroll macro

Listing 6.8 shows the code using the macro, and listing 6.9 shows the results of compiling this code.

Listing 6.8   Using the unroll macro

```
unroll i, 5:
      print i
```

Listing 6.9   The compiled output of the `unroll` macro

```
i = 0
print i
i = 1
print i
i = 2
print i
i = 3
print i
i = 4
print i
```

Now look at listing 6. 10, which shows the code for the unroll macro.

Listing 6.10   The `unroll` macro

```
# Create a class for the macro. The class name is
# meaningful: [macro name]Macro allows us to later refer
# to the macro using [macro name].
# Note that we inherit from AbstractAstMacro
class UnrollMacro(AbstractAstMacro):

    # Perform the compiler manipulation.
    # The compiler hands us a macro statement, and we have
    # to return a statement that will replace it.
    override def Expand(macro as MacroStatement) as Statement:

        # Define a block of code
        block = Block()

        # Extract the second parameter value
        end = cast(IntegerLiteralExpression, macro.Arguments[1]).Value

        for i in range(end):
            # Create assignment statement using the block: trick
            # and add it to the output
            assignmentStatement = [|
                block:
                    $(macro.Arguments[0]) = $i
            |].Body
            block.Add(assignmentStatement)

            # Add the original contents of the macro
            # to the output
            block.Add(macro.Body)

        return block
```

We'll go over listing 6.10 in detail, because AST macros can be confusing the first time you encounter them. AST macros are capable of modifying the compiler object model, causing it to generate different code than what is written in the code file.

First, we define a class that inherits from `AbstractAstMacro`, and then we override the `Expand()` method. When the compiler encounters a macro in the source code, it instantiates an instance of the macro class, calls the `Expand()` method (passing the

> **The macro class versus the macro statement**
>
> It's important to make a distinction between a class that inherits from Abstract-AstMacro (a macro class) and one that inherits from MacroStatement (a macro statement).
>
> The first is the class that implements logic to provide a compile-time transformation. The second is part of the compiler object model, and it's passed to the macro class as an argument for the transformation.

macro statement as an argument), and replaces the original macro statement with the output of the call to Expand().

The MacroStatement argument that the compiler passes to the macro class contains both the arguments (the parameters passed after the call to the macro) and the block (the piece of code that's inside the macro statement).

In the case of the unroll macro, we take the second argument to the macro and extract it from the compiler object model. Then we run a for loop, and in each iteration we perform four basic actions:

- Generate an assignment of the current value to the first argument to the macro
- Generate a call to the macro body
- Add both statements to the output code
- Return the output of the code to the compiler, which will replace the Macro-Statement that was in the code

Note that you can return a null from the Expand() method, in which case the node will be completely removed. This is useful in various advanced scenarios, as we'll see when we discuss correlated macros in section 6.4.5.

6.4.2 *Building macros with the MacroMacro*

The Boo compiler can do a lot of stuff for us, so it should come as no surprise that it can help us with building macros. The MacroMacro is an extension to the compiler that makes it simpler to write macros. You don't need to have a class, inherit from AbstractAstMacro, override methods, and so on. All you need to do is write the code to handle the macro transformation.

Let's write the unroll macro again, this time using the MacroMacro. Listing 6.11 contains the code.

Listing 6.11   Using the MacroMacro to write the UnrollMacro

```
# Using the MacroMacro, we don't need a class,
# just to define what we want the macro to do
macro Unroll2:

    # extract the second parameter value
    end = cast(IntegerLiteralExpression, Unroll2.Arguments[1]).Value
```

```
for i in range(end):
    # create assignment statement, using the block:
    # trick and add it to
    # the output
    statement = [|
        block:
            $(Unroll2.Arguments[0]) = $i
    |].Body
    yield statement

    # add the original contents of the macro
    # to the output
    yield Unroll2.Body
```

As you can see, the main differences between this and listing 6.10 is that the Macro-Macro removes the need to create a class. We can also yield the statements directly, instead of gathering them and outputting them in a single batch. Inside the macro block, we can refer to the macro statement using the macro's name. This means that whenever you see Unroll2 inside the macro in listing 6.11, it refers to the Macro-Statement instance that's passed in to the macro implementation (the MacroMacro creates a MacroStatement variable named Unroll2 behind the scenes).

From the point of view of the code, we've been using macros throughout the book. I just didn't tell you about them until now. Let's take a look at the most common macro:

```
print "hello there, I am a macro"
```

Print will translate to calls to Console.WriteLine. Let's take a look at the slightly simplified version of this implementation in listing 6.12.

Listing 6.12 Boo's print macro code

```
# This is a helper method that's useful for all sorts of "write line"
# type macros, such as print, debug, warn, etc.
# It accepts the macro and two method invocation expressions: one for
# outputting text and the second for outputting text and a line break.
# This method will take the arguments of the macro and print them all.
def expandPrintMacro(macro as MacroStatement,
                     write as Expression,
                     writeLine as Expression):
    # If the macro is empty, output an empty line
    if len(macro.Arguments) == 0:
        return [| $writeLine() |]

    # Create a block of code that will contain the output
    # methods that will be generated
    block = Block()
    # -1 in Boo's lists means the last element
    last = macro.Arguments[-1]
    for arg in macro.Arguments:
        if arg is last: break
        # Add method call to output a single macro argument
        block.Add([| $write($arg) |].withLexicalInfoFrom(arg))
```

```
        block.Add([| $write(' ') |])
    # Output the last macro argument with a line break
    block.Add([| $writeLine($last) |].withLexicalInfoFrom(last))
    return block

# The macro, which does a simple redirect
macro print:
    return expandPrintMacro(print,
                [| System.Console.Write |],
                [| System.Console.WriteLine |])
```

Note that the macro will direct you to the `expandPrintMacro` method. This method is also used elsewhere, such as in the debug macro, to do most of the work.

> **Lexical info**
>
> You'll note that we're using the `withLexicalInfoFrom(arg)` extension method in listing 6.12. This is a nice way of setting the `LexicalInfo` property of the node.
>
> *Lexical info* is the compiler's term for the location this source code came from, and it's important for things like error reporting and debugging. We're going to do a lot of code transformations, and it's easy to lose lexical info along the way.
>
> Keeping track of the lexical info is simply a matter of carrying it around, either by using `withLexicalInfoFrom(arg)` or by setting the `LexicalInfo` property directly. Put simply, whenever we make any sort of transformation, we must also include the original code's lexical info in the transformation output.
>
> Without lexical info, the compiler couldn't provide the location for an error. Imagine the compiler giving you the following error: "Missing ; at file: unknown, line: unknown, column: unknown." This is why keeping the lexical info around is important.

The `print` macro also passes two methods to the `expandPrintMacro()` helper method: `Write` and `WriteLine`. Those use quasi-quotation again to make it easier to refer to elements in the code. The interesting part, and what makes Boo easy to work with, is that we can still take advantage of things like overloading when we're rewriting the AST. The method resolution happens at a later stage, which makes our work a lot simpler.

The `expandPrintMacro()` method checks whether we passed any arguments to the macro. If we did, it will output all of them using the `write()` method and output the last one using `writeLine()`.

This explanation of how the `print` macro works took a lot more text than the macro itself, which I consider a good thing. We'll take a peek at another well-known macro, the `using` macro, and then we'll write one of our own.

6.4.3 Analyzing the using macro

In C#, `using` is a language keyword. In Boo, it's a macro, and it has a tad more functionality. Take a look at listing 6.13, which makes use of Boo's `using` statement.

Listing 6.13   The using statement in Boo, with multiple parameters

```
using file = File.Create("myFile.txt"),  reader = StreamWriter(file):
        reader.WriteLine("something")
```

You can specify multiple disposables in Boo's using macro, which often saves nested scoping. When the Boo compiler sees the code in listing 6.13, it attempts to find a macro for any unknown keywords it finds. It will only generate an error if it can't find a matching macro.

The compiler finds relevant macros by searching the imported namespaces. Boo has no problem if several macros have the same name in different namespaces (though there may be some confusion on the part of the user).

The macro in listing 6.13 will generate the AST shown in figure 6.4. This is the MacroStatement instance that the using macro implementation will get. As you'll notice, it's split into two major parts: the Arguments collection contains everything that was written after the macro name, and the Block contains all the code that was written within this macro.

At compilation time, the compiler will create a new instance of the macro class and pass it the MacroStatement object. It will also replace the macro statement with the output that was returned from the macro. If this sounds familiar, that's because it's precisely the way meta-methods work.

Listing 6.14 shows the implementation of the using macro.

Listing 6.14   The using macro's implementation

```
macro using:
    # Get the content of the using statement
    expansion = using.Body
    # Iterate over all the macro expressions in reverse order
    for expression as Expression in reversed(using.Arguments):
        # Create a temporary variable and assign it the
        # current expression.
        temp = ReferenceExpression(_
                context.GetUniqueName("using", "disposable"))
        assignment = [|
                    $temp = $expression as System.IDisposable
                |].withLexicalInfoFrom(expression)

        # Create a try/ensure block, with the current expansion, and
        # place it in the expansion variable, so it will be wrapped
```

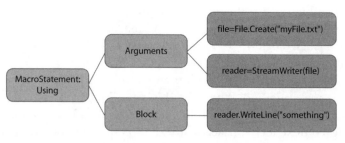

Figure 6.4   A simplified AST representation of a using macro statement

```
    # by the next macro argument
    expansion = [|
        $assignment
        try:
            $expansion
        ensure:
            if $temp is not null:
                $temp.Dispose()
                $temp = null
    |]

return expansion
```

In listing 6.14, we gain access to the MacroStatement using the macro name—in this case, using. Then we assign the using.Body to the expansion variable.

Once that's done, we iterate over the argument collection in reverse order. On each iteration, we create a new try ... ensure statement (the Boo equivalent for C#'s try ... finally) and dispose of the argument properly in the ensure block. We then take the content of the expansion variable and place it inside the try block. We set the newly created try ... ensure statement as the new value of the expansion variable, which we carry forward to the next iteration.

The end result of the code in listing 6.14 is shown in listing 6.15.

Listing 6.15   The code outputted by the using macro

```
__using2__ = ((file = File.Create('myFile.txt')) as System.IDisposable)
try:
    __using1__ = ((reader = StreamWriter(file)) as System.IDisposable)
    try:
        reader.WriteLine()
    ensure:
        if __using1__ is not null:
            __using1__.Dispose()
            __using1__ = null
ensure:
    if __using2__ is not null:
        __using2__.Dispose()
        __using2__ = null
```

I'm sure you'll agree that this isn't pretty code—not with all those underscores and variable names that differ only by a numeral. But it's what the compiler generates, and you won't usually see it. I should note that this isn't code in the style of Form1.Designer.cs. This code is generated by the compiler; it's always regenerated during compilation and never sees the light of day, nor is it saved.

You can see, in the second try block, the code that we originally placed in the using block: in the ensure block we dispose of the reader safely. The inner try block is wrapped in another try block, which disposes of the file safely.

Now, if you go back to listing 6.14, you'll see that we're making use of a strange Context.GetUniqueName() method. Where did this come from?

The availability of the context is one of the main differences between macros and meta-methods. The context lets you access the entire state of the compiler. This means you can call the `GetUniqueName()` method, which lets you create unique variable names, but it also means that you can access more interesting things:

- Compiler services, which include such things as the Type System Service, Boo Code Builder, and Name Resolution Service
- The compilation unit—all the code being compiled at that moment
- The assemblies referenced by the compiled code
- The compiler parameters, which include the compiler pipeline, inputs, and other compilation options
- The errors and warnings collections

Those are useful for more advanced scenarios. But before we make use of them, we'll write a more complex macro, to see how it goes.

6.4.4 Building an SLA macro

Recently I needed to check how long particular operations took and to log warnings if the time violated the service level agreement (SLA)[1] for those operations. The code was in C#, and I couldn't think of any good way of doing this except by manually coding it over and over again. All the ideas I had for solving this problem were uglier than the manual coding, and I didn't want to complicate the code significantly. Let's see how we can handle this with Boo, shall we?

First, we need to define how we want the code using the SLA to look. Listing 6.16 contains the initial draft.

> **Listing 6.16 Initial syntax of a macro that logs SLA violations**

```
limitedTo 200ms:
    PerformLongOperation()
    whenExceeded:
        print "Took more than 200 ms!"
```

Let's start small by creating a macro that will print a warning if the time limit is exceeded. We should note that Boo has built-in support for time spans, so we can say `200ms` (which is equal to `TimeSpan.FromMilliseconds(200)`) and it will create a `TimeSpan` object with 200 milliseconds for us.

Listing 6.17 shows an initial implementation.

> **Listing 6.17 Initial implementation of the `limitedTo` macro**

```
macro limitedTo:

    # Get the expected duration from the macro arguments
    expectedDuration = limitedTo.Arguments[0]
    # Generate a unique variable name to hold the duration
    durationName = ReferenceExpression(Context.GetUniqueName("duration"))
    # Generate a unique variable name to hold the start time
    startName = ReferenceExpression(Context.GetUniqueName("start"))
```

---

[1] SLA (service level agreement) refers to the contracted delivery time of the service or its performance.

```
# Use quasi-quotation to generate the code to write
#a warning message
actionToPerform = [|
    block:
        print "took too long"
|].Body

# Generate the code to mark the start time, execute the code, get
# the total duration the code has run, and then execute the action
# required if the duration was more than the expected duration
block = [|
    block:
        $startName = date.Now
        $(limitedTo.Body)
        $durationName = date.Now - $startName
        if $durationName > $expectedDuration:
            $actionToPerform
|].Body

return block
```

We define the macro itself. Quasi-quotation is useful, but it has its limitations, so we use the `block:` trick to force the compiler to think that we're compiling a macro statement, from which we can extract the block of code that we're actually interested in.

Now, if we write this code, it will print "took too long":

```
limitedTo 200ms:
    PerformLongOperation()
```

We aren't done yet. We still need to implement the `whenExceeded` part, and this leads us to the idea of nested macros.

6.4.5 *Using nested macros*

When we talk about nested macros, we're talking about more than nesting a `print` macro in a `using` macro. Nested macros are two (or more) macros that work together to provide a feature. The `limitedTo` and `whenExceeded` macros in the previous section are good examples of nested macros.

Before we get to the implementation of nested macros, we need to understand how Boo processes macros. The code in listing 6.18 will produce the AST in figure 6.5.

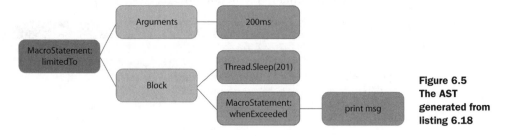

Figure 6.5
The AST
generated from
listing 6.18

Listing 6.18   Using the `limitedTo` and the nested `whenExceeded` macros

```
limitedTo 200ms:
    Thread.Sleep(201);
    whenExceeded:
            print "Took more than 200 ms!"
```

Macros are processed in a depth-first order, so the `whenExceeded` macro will be evaluated before the `limitedTo` macro. Keeping this in mind, we can now write the when-Exceeded macro, as shown in listing 6.19.

Listing 6.19   The implementation of the nested `whenExceeded` macro

```
macro limitedTo:
    macro whenExceeded:
            limitedTo["actionToPerform"] = whenExceeded.Block
```

The `whenExceeded` macro is decidedly simple. It merely puts the block of code that was under the `whenExceeded` macro in a well-known location in that `limitedTo` dictionary. This ability to annotate AST nodes is useful, because it allows different parts of the compilation process to communicate by adding information to the relevant node, as we did here.

To finish the implementation, we need to modify listing 6.17 and change the `actionToPerform` initialization as follows:

```
actionToPerform as Block = limitedTo["actionToPerform"]
```

Because `whenExceeded` is evaluated before `limitedTo`, we'll have the block of code that was passed to `whenExceeded` in the `limitedTo` dictionary by the time we execute the `limitedTo` macro. This pattern is common with nested macros: the nested macros pass their state to the parent macros, and the parent macros do all the work. The only thing we need to do now is add some error handling and we're ready to go.

Correlated macros

What would happen if we didn't want to nest the `whenExceeded` macro? What if we wanted this code instead:

```
limitedTo 200ms:
    Thread.Sleep(201);
whenExceeded:
    print "Took more than 200 ms!"
```

This looks like a language feature, similar to the `try ... except` statement. There's no nesting, and the `limitedTo` macro is evaluated before the `whenExceeded` macro. We use the `limitedTo` macro to find the `whenExceeded` macro (by going to the parent node and finding the next node, which is the `whenExceeded` macro) and move the `limitedTo` state to it.

Because `whenExceeded` is the macro that's evaluated last, it will be in charge of producing the final code. This is a simple extension of what we did with the nested macros.

One thing that's worth remembering is that quasi-quotation doesn't generally work with macros; you won't be able to use a macro inside a quasi-quotation expression. Usually, you can unpack them manually and it's rarely a bother.

Macros are one of the key extensibility points of the compiler. They can be used inside a method or inside a class definition (to modify fields, methods, and properties),[2] but they can't modify the class itself. You will occasionally want to do this, and there's a solution for that: AST attributes.

6.5   *AST attributes*

An AST attribute applies the same concepts that we've looked at so far, but it does so on a grander scale. Instead of dealing with a few parameters and maybe a block of code, you can use an AST attribute anywhere you can use a typical attribute. The difference between an AST attribute and a standard attribute is that AST attributes take an active part in the compilation process.

We've already covered the basics of AST manipulation, so we'll go directly to the code, and then discuss how it works. Listing 6.20 shows an example of adding post conditions on the class level that apply to all the class's methods.

Listing 6.20   Sample usage of an AST attribute

```
[Ensure(name is not null)]
class Customer:

    name as string

    def constructor(name as string):
        self.name = name

    def SetName(newName as string):
        name = newName
```

This attribute ensures that if we call the `Customer.SetName` method with a `null`, it will throw an exception.

But what does it take to make this happen? Not much, as it turns out. Take a look at listing 6.21.

Listing 6.21   Implementing an AST attribute

```
# AST attributes inherit from AbstractAstAttribute
class EnsureAttribute(AbstractAstAttribute):
    # expr is the expression that we were supplied by the compiler
    # during the compilation process
    expr as Expression
    # Store the expression in a field
    def constructor(expr as Expression):
        self.expr = expr
```

---

[2] For more information about using macros for changing class definitions, see the "Boo 0.9—Introducing Type Member Macros" entry in the Bamboozled blog: http://blogs.codehaus.org/people/bamboo/archives/001750_boo_09_introducing_type_member_macros.html.

```
# Make the changes that we want
def Apply(target as Node):

    # Cast the target to a ClassDefinition and
    # start iterating over all its members.
    type as ClassDefinition = target

    for member in type.Members:
        method = member as Method
        # We do not support properties to
        # keep the example short
        continue if method is null

        # If the member is a method, modify
        # it to include a try/ensure block, which
        # asserts that the expression must
        # be true. Then override the method body with
        # this new implementation.
        methodBody = method.Body

        method.Body = [|
            try:
                $ methodBody
            ensure:
                assert $expr
        |]
```

We first inherit from `AbstractAstAttribute`; this is the key. We can accept expressions in the constructor, which is helpful, because we can use them to pass the rule that we want to validate.

The bulk of the work is done in the `Apply` method, which is called on the node that the attribute was decorating. We assume that this is a class definition node and start iterating over all its members. If the type member is a method (which includes constructors and destructors), we apply our transformation.

The transformation in this example is simple. We take all the code in the method and wrap it up in a `try ... ensure` block. When the `ensure` block is run, we `assert` that that expression is valid.

In short, we got the node the attribute was decorating, we applied a simple transformation, and we're done. Vidi, vicissitude, vici—I saw, I transformed, I conquered (pardon my Latin).

We can apply AST attributes to almost anything in Boo: classes, methods, properties, enums, parameters, fields, and so on. Boo has several interesting AST attributes, as listed in table 6.1.

AST attributes are a great way to package functionality, particularly for avoiding repetitive or sensitive coding. Implementing the Singleton pattern, the Disposable pattern, or validation post conditions are all good examples.

However good AST attributes are, they only apply to a single node. This can be useful when you want specialized behavior, but it's a pain when you want to apply some cross-cutting concerns, such as adding a method to all classes in a project or changing the default base class.

Table 6.1 Interesting attributes in Boo

Attribute	Description	Sample
[property]	Applies to fields and will generate a property from a field.	```[property(Name)]``` ```name as string```
[required]	Applies to parameters and will verify that a non-null reference was passed to the method.	```def Foo([required] obj):``` ``` pass```
[required(arg!= 0)]	Applies to parameters and will verify that the parameter matches the given constraint.	```def Foo([required] i as int):``` ``` pass```

[default]	Applies to parameters and will set the parameter to a default value if null was passed.	```def Foo([default("novice")]```
		``` level as string):```
		``` pass```

[once]	Applies to methods and properties. It will ensure that a method only executes once; any future call to this method will get the cached value.	```[once]```
		```def ExpensiveCall():```
		``` pass```

[singleton]	Applies to classes and ensures the correct implementation of the Singleton pattern.	```[singleton]```
		```class MySingleton:```
		``` pass```

As you probably have guessed, Boo has a solution for that as well. Welcome to the world of compiler steps.

AST attributes with DSL

I have used AST attributes with a DSL several times. Mostly, it was to supply additional functionality to methods that were defined in the DSL or to specific parameters of those arguments.

Here's a trivial example:

```
[HtmlEncode]
def OutputFile( \
      [requires(File.Exists(file)] file as string ):

      return File.ReadAllText(file)
```

6.6   *Compiler steps*

At the beginning of this chapter, we looked at the compiler pipeline and saw that it was composed of a lot of steps executed in order to create the final executable assembly. Most modern compilers work in this fashion,[3] but most modern compilers don't

---

[3]   I have quite a bit of respect for older compilers, which had to do everything in a single pass. There was some amazing coding involved in them.

boast an extensible architecture. Because Boo does have an extensible compiler architecture, you shouldn't be surprised that you can extend the compiler pipeline as well.

6.6.1 Compiler structure

Let's look again at how the compiler is structured. Figure 6.6 shows a list of compiler steps, along with a custom step that you can write and inject into the compiler pipeline. But what, I hear you asking, is a compiler step in the first place? That's a good question. A *compiler step* is a class that implements `ICompilerStep` and is registered on the compiler pipeline. When a compiler step is run, it has the chance to inspect and modify the AST of the current compilation. The entire Boo compiler is implemented using a set of compiler steps, which should give you an idea of how powerful compiler steps can be.

We can do anything we want in a compiler step. I've seen some interesting compiler steps that do the following things:

- Introduce an implicit base class for any code that isn't already in a class
- Transform unknown references to calls to a parameters collection
- Modify the `if` statement to have clearer semantics for the domain at hand (to be done with caution)
- Extend the compiler naming convention so it will automatically translate `apply_discount` to `ApplyDiscount`
- Perform code analysis (imagine FxCop integrated into the compiler)
- Perform compile-time code generation, doing things like inspecting the structure of a database and creating code that matches that structure

As you can imagine, this is a powerful technique, and it's useful when you want to build a more complex DSL.

Up until now, everything that we built could be executed directly by the compiler, because we used the well-known extension paths. Compiler steps are a bit different; you need to add them to the compiler pipeline explicitly.

There are two ways to do that. The first involves creating your own pipeline and inserting the compiler step into the list of steps in the appropriate location. Then you can ask the compiler to use that custom pipeline. The second approach involves setting up the compiler context yourself, and directly modifying the pipeline.

We'll see both approaches shortly. First, though, because implicit base classes are so useful, let's take a look at how we can implement them.

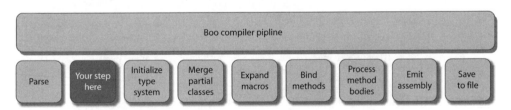

Figure 6.6   The structure of the Boo compiler pipeline, shown with a custom step

TIP   The Rhino DSL project already contains a generic implementation of the implicit base class compiler step, and the `DslFactory` introduced in chapter 2 makes it easy to use. The example in section 6.6.2 shows how to build a simple compiler step. I suggest you take advantage of the Rhino DSL project for such common operations. The steps included in Rhino DSL are much more robust than the simple implementation that we will build shortly.

6.6.2   *Building the implicit base class compiler step*

The first thing we need to do when we create an implicit base class is create the base class. Listing 6.22 contains a trivial example. Instead of using one of the DSLs that we introduced in chapter 4, we will use a trivial DSL. In this case, we want to talk only about the mechanics of modifying the compiler, not about a specific DSL.

> **Listing 6.22   A trivial base class for a trivial DSL**

```
abstract class MyDsl:
    [getter(Name)]
    name as string
    abstract def Build():
        pass
```

Listing 6.23 contains the compiler step to perform the transformation from a free-standing script to one with an implicit base class.

> **Listing 6.23   A compiler step for creating implicit base classes**

```
# Inheriting from AbstractTransformerCompilerStep gives us a lot of
# convenience methods
class MyDslAsImplicitBaseClassStep(AbstractTransformerCompilerStep):

    # This is the method that the compiler pipeline will execute
    override def Run():
        # The Visitor pattern makes it easy to pick and choose
        # what we want to process
        super.Visit(CompileUnit)

    # Choose to process all the modules
    override def OnModule(node as Module):
        # Use quasi-quotation to generate a class definition
        # with all the code that was in the module inside it.
        # Use the same name as the module and inherit from MyDsl
        baseClass = [|
            class $(node.Name) (MyDsl):
                override def Build():
                    $(node.Globals)
        |]
        # Clear the module's globals and add the newly
        # created class to the node's members.
        node.Globals = Block()
        node.Members.Add(baseClass)
```

We start off by inheriting from the `AbstractTransformerCompilerStep` class, which makes it easier to surgically get the information we want by overriding the appropriate `On[NodeType]` method and transforming only that node.

In this case, we call `Visit(CompileUnit)` when the compiler step is executed. This uses the Visitor pattern to walk through the entire AST node and call the appropriate methods, which makes navigating the AST much easier than it would be otherwise.

In the `OnModule()` method, we create a new class that inherits from the `MyDsl` class. We take the contents of the module's `Globals` section and stick it in the `Build()` method of the newly created class. We also give the class the module name. This is usually the name of the file that originated this module.

Finally, we clear the module's `Globals` section and add the new class to the module's members.

Now we need to understand how to plug this into the compiler. That also turns out to be fairly uncomplicated. We start by creating a new pipeline that incorporates our new compiler step, as shown in listing 6.24.

> **Listing 6.24   A compiler pipeline that incorporates our custom steps**

```
class WithMyDslStep(CompileToFile):
    def constructor():
        super()
        Insert( 1, MyDslAsImplicitBaseClassStep() )
```

This compiler pipeline will add our new compiler step as the second step in the pipeline. The first step in the pipeline is the parsing of the code and the building of the AST, and we want to get the code directly after that.

Now let's compile this code. We can do it from the command line, because the compiler accepts a parameter that sets the compiler pipeline. Here's how it's done:

```
booc "-p:WithMyDslStep, MyDsl" -r:MyDsl.dll -type:library test.boo
```

Assuming that the test.boo file contains this line,

```
name = "testing  implicit base class"
```

we'll get a library that contains a single type, test. If you examine this type in .NET Reflector, you'll see that its `Build()` method contains the code that was in the file, and that the name variable is set to the text "testing implicit base class".

Where to register the compiler step?

In general, the earlier that you can execute your compiler step, the better off you'll be. The code you move or create will still need to go through all the other compiler steps for successful compilation.

You want the code that you add to benefit from full compiler processing, so it's best to add the compiler step as early as possible.

TIP   .NET Reflector is a tool that allows you to decompile IL to source code. You can find out more at http://www.red-gate.com/products/reflector/.

When you're building a DSL, though, you'll usually want to control the compilation process yourself, and not run it from the command line. For that, you need to handle the compilation programmatically, which listing 6.25 demonstrates.

Listing 6.25   Adding a compiler step to a pipeline and compiling programmatically

```
compiler = BooCompiler();
compiler.Parameters.Pipeline = new CompileToFile();
AddInputs(compiler.Parameters) # Add files to be compiled
compiler.Parameters.Pipeline.Insert(1, MyDslAsImplicitBaseClassStep() )
compilerContext = compiler.Run()
```

The `DslFactory` and `DslEngine` in the Rhino DSL project already handle most of this, so we'll usually not need to deal with setting the pipeline or building the compiler context manually. Knowing how to do both is important, but for building DSLs I would recommend using Rhino DSL instead of writing all of that yourself.

6.7   *Summary*

In this chapter, you've seen most of the extensibility mechanisms of Boo, both from the language perspective and in terms of the compiler's extensibility features. You have seen how to use the language to extend the syntax so you can expose a readable DSL to your end users.

Meta-methods, AST macros, AST attributes, and compiler steps compose a rich set of extension points into which you can hook your own code and modify the language to fit the domain that you're working on at the moment. But those aren't the only tools you have available when you build a language; the standard features of the Boo language (covered in chapter 2) make for a flexible syntax that can easily be made more readable. You can often build full-fledged DSLs without dipping into the more advanced features of compiler extensibility.

You've also seen that features such as quasi-quotation make extending the compiler a simple matter. It's not much harder to extend the compiler without using quasi-quotation, but this is somewhat tedious. Using quasi-quotation also requires far less knowledge about the AST, because you can utilize the compiler to build the AST. This isn't entirely a good thing, though, and I encourage you to learn more about the AST and how to work with it. All abstractions are leaky, and it's good to understand how to plug the leaks on your own. An easy way to do this is to look at the code that Boo generates for quasi-quotations using .NET Reflector. You'll see the AST building code that way.

So far, we've dealt only with the mechanics of extending the language. The features we've explored are powerful, but we're still missing something: how to take the language extensibility features and build a real-world DSL. There is much more to that than extending the language. Concerns such as ease of use, readability, maintainability, versioning, documentation, and testing all need to be considered when you design and implement a DSL.

We've also talked a bit about how Rhino DSL can take care of a lot of the common things that we need to do. I keep saying that we'll get to that in a bit. The next chapter is dedicated to exploring what we can shuffle off for Rhino DSL to handle.

DSL infrastructure
with Rhino DSL

By now, you've heard about Rhino DSL several times. I keep saying that it's a library that makes building DSLs easier, but I've never gone into the details. This chapter will address that omission.

We'll go over Rhino DSL in detail and see what it has to offer and under what circumstances you might want to roll your own DSL infrastructure instead. This chapter isn't intended to replace API documentation; it's intended to review what a DSL infrastructure should offer and how Rhino DSL measures up.

To be clear, you don't need to use Rhino DSL to build DSLs in Boo. Rhino DSL is merely an aggregation of idioms that I have found useful across many DSL examples.

7.1 *Understanding a DSL infrastructure*

Before we get into Rhino DSL, let's consider what we want from a DSL infrastructure, and why we need one in the first place. There is a set of problems that we need to deal with and resolve in order to build production-quality DSLs, including the following:

- Dealing with the compiler directly is awkward. It involves a fair amount of work, which needs to be done for each DSL you build. Many DSL implementations share common idioms (as discussed in chapters 4 and 5), and there is little sense in duplicating them all over the place.
- Compiling scripts time after time is inefficient. Caching reduces compilation costs, but caching comes with its own set of problems. To begin with, you need to perform cache invalidation and recompile scripts that have been changed.
- Compiling each script individually is costly in terms of performance. Compilation costs can be significantly reduced if you compile many files at once, instead of doing them one by one. This also helps to reduce the number of loaded assemblies in the AppDomain, which reduces memory consumption.

None of those problems are particularly difficult to resolve. Rhino DSL does so, and it's a tiny library (not even two thousand lines of code, at the time of writing).

A DSL infrastructure also needs to be able to handle some of the things that we talked about in chapter 5, such as ordering of DSLs and managing which are run and when, for example.

Here are the main requirements that a DSL infrastructure should meet:

- Codify common DSL idioms so you don't have to keep rewriting them
- Handle caching of DSL scripts
- Abstract the compiler bootstrapping
- Batch compile DSLs
- Manage ordering and script discovery
- Not harm the DSL's extensibility

Rhino DSL is the result of several years' experience building DSLs and dealing with these issues. It isn't a masterpiece of programming, but it can save you a lot of time. I suggest that you use Rhino DSL instead of rolling your own infrastructure, at least while you are getting started building DSLs.

Rhino DSL is an active project

Rhino DSL is updated regularly. Most of these updates are either bug fixes or enhancements to support the more advanced scenarios (which are less generically applicable).

As a result, this chapter covers most of Rhino DSL, but it doesn't cover everything. I don't cover the parts that are of interest only to a small minority of language implementers.

Before we get into the nitty gritty details, we should take an overall look at the structure of Rhino DSL.

7.2   *The structure of Rhino DSL*

Rhino DSL is composed of two important classes, both of which you've probably familiarized yourself with by now: `DslEngine` and `DslFactory`. You can see both of them in figure 7.1.

The `DslFactory` is the external facing interface, used by clients of the DSL, and it uses the `DslEngine` to perform all the DSL-specific work. The `DslEngine` is an abstract class that DSL authors are expected to derive from. It provides the standard services out of the box, but it allows you to override most of them as needed. Both classes provide most of the infrastructure services that we've talked about so far in this chapter.

There are implementations for `IDslEngineStorage` and `IDslEngineCache` as well, which deal with less common scenarios. We'll look at them in detail later in this chapter.

Aside from those classes, Rhino DSL includes a few others that codify common DSL idioms (implicit base class, script references, and so on).

The end result of using Rhino DSL is that you can get a DSL out the door quickly and extend it as your needs grow.

Let's focus on each class in turn, starting with the `DslFactory`.

7.2.1   *The DslFactory*

The `DslFactory` contains all the DSL infrastructure logic that's common to all DSLs, regardless of their implementation. There isn't much of that, though. The `DslFactory` mainly contains logic for managing the DSL engines, handling batch compilations, and performing cache invalidation.

Listing 7.1 shows a typical usage of a `DslFactory`.

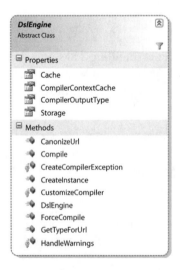

Figure 7.1   The structure of `DslEngine` and `DslFactory`

Listing 7.1 Using the `DslFactory`

```
// This should happen once in the application
DslFactory factory = new DslFactory();
factory.Register<MyDslBaseClass>(new MyDslEngine());
// Use the factory to create DSL instances
MyDslBaseClass dsl = factory.Create<MyDslBaseClass>("my_dsl_name");
dsl.Execute();
```

As you can see in the code comments, you're supposed to create the `DslFactory` once, and *only once*. The `DslFactory` also manages the compilation cache for each `DslEngine`, so keeping only one of those around ensures that you don't recompile unnecessarily.

Then the `DslEngine` instances, along with their associated implicit base classes, are registered in the factory, and then you can request an instance by name.

At that point, the `DslFactory` asks the `DslEngine` to compile the script (it's more complex than that, but we'll discuss it in section 7.4), create an instance of it, and then return it to the caller.

Orchestrating the DSL engine is the main job of the DSL factory, so this is a good time to look at DSL engines.

7.2.2 *The DslEngine*

The `DslEngine` class is where most of the action happens. It's structured so you can override specific functionality without having to take on too big a burden. The `DslEngine` class contains the default (and most common) implementation, and it performs most of its work in virtual methods, so you can override and modify the behavior at specific points.

The most important extension point, which we've already seen, is the `CustomizeCompiler` method. This method allows us to modify the compiler pipeline, modify the compiler parameters, and in general set up the compiler infrastructure that we want.

Listing 7.2 shows a typical use of `CustomizeCompiler`.

Listing 7.2 Using the `CustomizeCompiler` method to add the implicit base class

```
// Customize the compiler for the Authorization DSL
protected override void CustomizeCompiler(
    BooCompiler compiler,
    CompilerPipeline pipeline,
    Uri[] urls)
{
    // The compiler should allow late-bound semantics
    compiler.Parameters.Ducky = true;
    pipeline.Insert(1,
        new ImplicitBaseClassCompilerStep(
        // The base type
            typeof(AuthorizationRule),
        // The method to override
            "CheckAuthorization",
```

```
        // Import the following namespaces
            "BDSLiB.Authorization"));
    pipeline.Insert(2, new AutoReferenceFilesCompilerStep());
}
```

As you can see, this code does three things:

1. It tell the compiler to use late-bound semantics if it can't use early-bound ones (this is what `Ducky = true` means).
2. It registers the `ImplicitBaseClassCompilerStep` as the second step on the pipeline (the first step is parsing the code into the AST).
3. It registers the `AutoReferenceFilesCompilerStep` as the third step on the pipeline, which will support script references.

With that, our job of writing the DSL is more or less done. We may need to do some additional things in the implicit base class, or introduce an AST macro or attribute, but the main work in creating our DSL is done.

Table 7.1 lists the other methods that you can override to provide additional functionality for your DSL. Those are less commonly used, though.

Other extension points relate to the `DslEngine` local cache, change notifications when a script is changed, the location where the scripts are stored, and so on. In order to keep those concerns outside the code that builds the DSLs, they are split into two interfaces: `IDslEngineStorage` and `IDslEngineCache`.

`IDslEngineStorage` handles everything that relates to the storage of scripts: enumerating them, sending notifications on changes, and retrieving script content from storage. The default implementation of `IDslEngineStorage` is `FileSystemDslEngine-Storage`, which is what we've used so far.

`IDslEngineCache` holds the compilation results of scripts. Its default implementation is an in-memory cache linking each script URL (the path to the actual script file) to the compiled script type generated from that script, but an interesting extension of the cache would be a persistent cache that would allow you to compile the script once and keep the compilation result around, surviving application restarts, until the script is changed.

Figure 7.2 shows the class diagrams of `IDslEngineStorage` and `IDslEngineCache`.

Table 7.1 The less-common extension points that the `DslEngine` provides

Method	Purpose	Notes
Compile	Allows you to completely modify the compilation process	Generally it's better to use the `CustomizeCompiler` method.
CreateCompilerException	Handles compilation errors and adds additional information or guidance	The default implementation throws an exception with the full compiler output.
CreateInstance	Creates an instance of the DSL	This is useful if you want to create a DSL instance by using a special factory, or by using an IoC container.

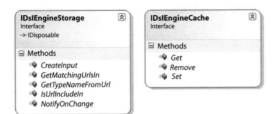

Figure 7.2 The `IDslEngineStorage` and `IDslEngineCache` class diagrams

Although overriding `CustomizeCompiler` usually works, let's see a more complex example of extending `IDslEngineStorage` to create a script storage system based on an XML file.

7.2.3 Creating a custom IDslEngineStorage

For this example, we aren't interested in the language of the DSL; we're interested in its surroundings. We'll create a DSL system whose scripts aren't located on a filesystem, but in an XML file instead.

NOTE Storing the scripts in an XML file is the simplest way to show the full range of the DSL extensibility, but more interesting applications would use source control-based script storage, or database storage. Unfortunately, those approaches are significantly more complex, and aren't appropriate as simple examples.

We'll take the Authorization DSL and make it store its scripts in an XML file. Listing 7.3 shows the structure of that XML storage file.

Listing 7.3   The XML storage file for the Authorization DSL

```xml
<?xml version="1.0" encoding="utf-8" ?>
<authorizationRules>
  <rule operation="/account/login" name="administrators can always login">
    <![CDATA[
if Principal.IsInRole("Administrators"):
  Allow("Administrators can always log in")
  return
]]>
  </rule>
  <rule operation="/account/login" name="work hours">
    <![CDATA[
if date.Now.Hour < 9 or date.Now.Hour > 17:
  Deny("Cannot log in outside of business hours, 09:00 - 17:00")
]]>
  </rule>
</authorizationRules>
```

Now that we have the structure of the XML file, let's analyze the `XmlFileDslEngine-Storage` class. Listing 7.4 shows the code for the class, minus some methods that we'll examine in the following discussion.

Listing 7.4   The `XmlFileDslEngineStorage` class

```
public class XmlFileDslEngineStorage : IDslEngineStorage
{
    private readonly XmlDocument xdoc;

    public XmlFileDslEngineStorage(string pathToXmlFile)
    {
        xdoc = new XmlDocument();
        xdoc.Load(pathToXmlFile);
    }

    public void NotifyOnChange(IEnumerable<string> urls,
                                          Action<string> action)
    {
        // Not supporting this
    }

    public string GetTypeNameFromUrl(string url)
    {
        return url;
    }

    public void Dispose()
    {
        // Nothing to do here
    }

    public string[] GetMatchingUrlsIn(string parentPath, ref string url)
    {
        // Discussed later (shown in listing 7.5)
    }

    public ICompilerInput CreateInput(string url)
    {
        // Discussed later (shown in listing 7.6)
    }

    public bool IsUrlIncludedIn(string[] urls,
                                string parentPath,
                                string url)
    {
        // Discussed later (shown in listing 7.7)
    }
}
```

The `NotifyOnChange` method should call the action delegate when any of the URLs that were passed have changed, but we aren't supporting this, so we'll ignore it. A more thorough implementation would watch the XML file for changes and autoload on change, but that isn't necessary for our example.

The `GetTypeNameFromUrl` method is useful for cases where the type name and the URL are different. This is the single case where the `DslEngine` and the `IDslEngine-Storage` need to work in concert.

Now let's look at the methods we ignored in listing 7.4. Listing 7.5 shows the `Get-MatchingUrlsIn` method.

Listing 7.5   The `GetMatchingUrlsIn` method implementation

```
public string[] GetMatchingUrlsIn(string parentPath, ref string url)
{
    List<string> ruleNames = new List<string>();
    foreach (XmlNode node in xdoc.SelectNodes("/authorizationRules/rule"))
    {
        if (node.Attributes["operation"].Value == url)
            ruleNames.Add(node.Attributes["name"].Value);
    }
    if (ruleNames.Count > 0)
        url = ruleNames[0];
    return ruleNames.ToArray();
}
```

There's nothing particularly interesting here, except that the URL that was passed in is a reference parameter. It gets set to the first rule name we find, but why? Doing so gives us the canonized URL. This is a common problem with paths, because there are many ways to refer to the same file. The canonized format is the one that is returned by the `IDslEngineStorage` and is ensured to be included in the returned URLs. Otherwise, we might run into an issue where we pass a URL in, get a list of matching URLs from the method, but can't figure out which URL is the one matching our original one.

In this case, the original URL is the operation name, but the canonized URL is the name of the rule. The URL goes in with the value "/account/login" and comes out with the value "administrators can always login".

Listing 7.6 shows the `CreateInput` method, which extracts the code from the XML document.

Listing 7.6   The `CreateInput` method

```
public ICompilerInput CreateInput(string url)
{
    string xpath = string.Format(
            "/authorizationRules/rule[@name='{0}']/text()", url);
    string text = xdoc.SelectSingleNode(xpath).Value;
    return new StringInput(url, text);
}
```

In this method, we extract the content of the rule and return a `StringInput` with the URL of the rule as the name, and the text of the rule as the context. This will ensure that if there are errors in the script, we'll get good error messages back, with a pointer to the right location.

Last (and probably also least), listing 7.7 shows the `IsUrlIncludedIn` method.

Listing 7.7   The `IsUrlIncludedIn` method

```
public bool IsUrlIncludedIn(string[] urls, string parentPath, string url)
{
    return urls.Length != 0;
}
```

This is a trivial implementation, but the method is important. In batching scenarios (discussed further in section 7.4), it's common to do a batch compilation of the whole directory, even if the script that you're searching for isn't there. This is simply an optimization—the directory was accessed, so it might as well be compiled, because other scripts from that directory are likely to be accessed soon. To avoid that scenario, the `IsUrlIncludedIn` method checks that the batch to be compiled contains the script we want to execute.

That's it for our XML-based storage. Now we need to hook it up to the DSL engine. Listing 7.8 shows the code for this.

Listing 7.8   Integrating `XmlFileDslEngineStorage` with the DSL engine

```
public class AuthorizationDslEngine : DslEngine
{
    public AuthorizationDslEngine()
    {
        Storage = new XmlFileDslEngineStorage(
                    @"Authorization/AuthorizationRules.xml");
    }

    // implementation ...
}
```

As you can see, all it involves is setting the proper implementation in the constructor. We can now run all our code, and it would work against the XML file.

The names of the scripts are also important, since those will be the class names generated for those scripts. Now consider figure 7.3, which shows the compiled output of a few Authorization DSL scripts.

As you can see, we have some strangely named classes. This is valid from the CLR perspective, but not from the perspective of most programming languages. It works, but it's amusing.

Prefer file-based solutions

Although it's good that we have the option to store scripts in other mediums, I strongly recommend that you keep to the tried and true method of storing scripts in the filesystem. This offers a couple of important advantages over the other approaches.

First and foremost, it makes it easy to put the scripts in source control and perform all the usual source-control actions on them (such as diffing changes in scripts or merging a development branch into the production branch).

Second, we can *debug* scripts. I haven't discussed it so far, but debugging scripts is just an F11 key away. But this doesn't work unless the scripts are compiled from the filesystem. Otherwise, the debugger has no real way to find the script's source code.

The source-control advantage is the more critical consideration, in my opinion. I strongly prefer to be able to make use of source control without having to jump through hoops, and I have never seen anything that works better than simple text files in a folder hierarchy. It's the simplest solution, and it's also the best.

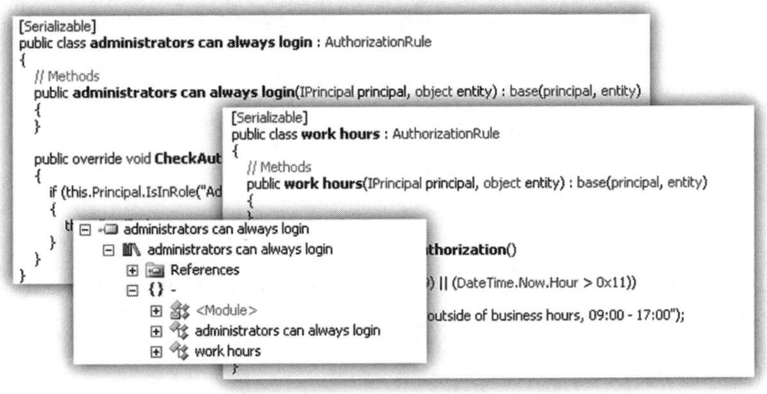

Figure 7.3   The application of the law of unintended consequences: our authorization rules in Reflector

Anyway, we have a whole library to explore yet. Let's jump directly into the DSL idioms that we get from Rhino DSL.

7.3   *Codifying DSL idioms*

Most DSL idioms are widely useful across many types of DSLs. The Implicit Base Class pattern, for example, is useful for nearly all DSLs. But after covering the common ground, most DSLs take wildly differing paths.

Rhino DSL contains six reusable idioms (at the time of this writing, at least). You're probably familiar with most of them by now:

- `ImplicitBaseClassCompilerStep`
- `AutoReferenceFilesCompilerStep`
- `AutoImportCompilerStep`
- `UseSymbolsStep`
- `UnderscoreNamingConventionsToPascalCaseCompilerStep`
- `GeneratePropertyMacro`

These six common idioms are the ones I've found most useful across many DSL implementations. Let's look at them each in turn.

7.3.1   *ImplicitBaseClassCompilerStep*

The good old Implicit Base Class is codified as `ImplicitBaseClassCompilerStep`. We need to insert it into the pipeline (preferably in the second position), and it will move all the code not inside a class into an overridden method in the implicit base class.

Listing 7.9 shows a sample use of this class, taken from the Authorization DSL code.

```
pipeline.Insert(1,
        new ImplicitBaseClassCompilerStep(
        // the base type
            typeof(AuthorizationRule),
        // the method to override
            "CheckAuthorization",
        // import the following namespaces
            "BDSLiB.Authorization"));
```

In addition to specifying the base type and the method to move the code to, we can specify namespaces that we want to auto-import.

7.3.2 *AutoReferenceFilesCompilerStep*

`AutoReferenceFilesCompilerStep` supports script references, which we talked about in chapter 5. This class just needs registration in the pipeline to work. Again, it's best placed near the start of the pipeline.

The code to make this happen is trivial:

```
pipeline.Insert(2, new AutoReferenceFilesCompilerStep());
```

Once that's done, the following syntax will cause the referenced script to be compiled and then referenced on the fly:

```
import file from AnotherScript.boo
```

7.3.3 *AutoImportCompilerStep*

Auto-import support is usually handled by the `ImplicitBaseClassCompilerStep`, but you can also configure it separately, using `AutoImportCompilerStep`. Listing 7.10 shows how to use this compiler step.

```
compiler.Parameters.References.Add(typeof(XmlDocument).Assembly);
pipeline.Insert(1, new AutoImportCompilerStep(
                "System.Xml",
                "System.Xml.XPath"));
```

You should note that this is a two-stage process. You need to add a reference to the relevant assembly (which is done on the first line of listing 7.10) and then you add the auto-import compiler step and pass it the namespaces that will automatically be imported to all compiled files.

7.3.4 *UseSymbolsStep*

The symbols compiler step is codified as `UseSymbolsStep`. Symbols represent a nicer, more fluent way of handling string literals.

Consider this snippet,

```
send_to "administrator"
```

versus this one:

```
send_to @administrator
```

UseSymbolsStep will convert all identifiers starting with @ to string literals. The difference between the two approaches is syntactic only, but this is often important when you want to make certain parts of a DSL clearer. The @identifier approach makes a clear distinction between strings that you pass and elements of the language.

As you've probably figured out already, UseSymbolsStep repeats the usage pattern we've seen so far:

> **Getting even better syntax**
>
> Boo allows you to have a far more natural syntax, like this:
>
> ```
> send_to administrator
> ```
>
> This will work, but it requires special treatment: an AST macro or compiler step with more context than a generic step offers. A compiler step that transforms all unknown references to strings is easy to write, but it tends to produce ambiguous errors, so I suggest creating one only after careful consideration.

```
pipeline.Insert(2, new UseSymbolsStep());
```

Like the other compilers steps, it should be registered at the beginning of the pipeline. Usually I recommend clustering all our compiler steps one after another, directly after the parsing step.

7.3.5 UnderscoreNamingConventionsToPascalCaseCompilerStep

The CLR has well-defined naming conventions, and deviations like send_to are annoying. At the same time, send_to is easier to read in DSL code than SendTo. If only there were a way to resolve this automatically ...

Luckily, we have such a way: UnderscoreNamingConventionsToPascalCaseCompilerStep can automatically translate send_to to SendTo. This compiler step will automatically make this transformation for any member call that contains an underscore. Because I never use underscores in my applications, this works fine for me. You may have to decide on extending UnderscoreNamingConventionsToPascalCaseCompilerStep to understand your convention if you're using underscores in method or property names.

The process for registering this compiler step is a bit different than all the rest. Unlike the previous steps, we don't want this one to run as soon as possible. Quite the reverse—we want it to run as late as possible, which means before we start to process the method bodies.

As a result, we register it using the following snippet:

```
pipeline.InsertBefore(
    typeof (ProcessMethodBodiesWithDuckTyping),
new UnderscoreNamingConventionsToPascalCaseCompilerStep());
```

We haven't used it so far, but we'll make use of it the next time we create a language.

That's it for compiler steps.

7.3.6   *GeneratePropertyMacro*

We have one last thing to explore, the `GeneratePropertyMacro`. It allows us to take a snippet like this,

```
operation "/account/login"
```

and turn it into a property that will return the parameters we called.

Enabling its use is simple, as you can see in listing 7.11.

Listing 7.11   Using the `GeneratePropertyMacro`

```
public class OperationMacro : GeneratePropertyMacro
{
      public OperationMacro()
          : base("Operation")
      {

      }
}
```

We create a class that inherits from `GeneratePropertyMacro`, and we specify in the constructor the property name it needs to generate. The name of the derived class is important, because it's the name we'll use in the DSL to refer to this macro (without the `Macro` suffix).

Those six common idioms are useful across many DSL implementations. For advanced DSL, you will likely want to add your own custom steps and macros to the mix, and we discussed many of those options in chapter 4. But as you can see, you get quite a bit with what's "in the box," so to speak.

Now that we are done discussing what idioms Rhino DSL offers, we need to cover the caching and batch compilation infrastructure. More specifically, we have to understand how they work and why they work as they do.

7.4   *Batch compilation and compilation caches*

Compiling code is a costly process, and when you're creating a DSL, you have to consider ways to reduce this cost. We already talked a bit about that in previous chapters. Now we'll look at the design of Rhino DSL's compilation process, and at why it was built in such a way.

To save on compilation costs, we introduce a cache (and cache invalidation policy) so we only compile a script once. But assuming that we have many scripts, we're still going to pay the compilation cost many times over.

NOTE   Compiling each script individually will also create many small assemblies. The general recommendation for .NET applications is to prefer a few large assemblies over many small assemblies. Batching helps us reduce the number of assemblies that we compile.

You might wish that you could compile everything once, instead of performing many small compilations. The problem with that, though, is that you run into issues with compilation time when you have large numbers of scripts.

The best solution is a compromise. We want some batching in our compilation, but we don't want to compile everything at once and pay the high cost of a large compilation.

NOTE We'll assume here that we're talking about scripts that reside on the file-system. For scripts stored elsewhere, the concepts are similar, but the implementation depends on the concept of hierarchy in the selected storage mechanism.

When we get a request to execute a certain script, we perform the following operations:

1 Check if the script has already been compiled and exists in the cache.
2 If it's in the cache, instantiate and return the new instance, and we're done.
3 If it isn't in the cache, compile all the scripts in the script directory.
4 Register all the scripts in the cache.
5 Instantiate the compiled script and return the new instance.

The key here is in step number 3. Instead of compiling only the script we're interested in, we compile all the scripts in the current directory and register them in the cache. This means that we pay the compilation cost once per directory. It also means that we have bigger (and fewer) assemblies. We can now rely on the natural organization of the filesystem to limit the number of scripts in a directory to a reasonable number.

Because we usually place scripts on the filesystem according to some logic, and because we usually access them according to the same logic, this turns out to be a pretty good heuristic to detect which scripts we should compile.

Cache invalidation puts a tiny wrinkle in this pretty scenario, though. When a script changes, we remove it from the cache, but we also note that this is a script that we have already compiled. When a new request comes for this script, we won't find it in the cache, but we *will* find it in the list of files that were compiled and then changed. As a result, we won't perform a batch compilation in this scenario; we'll compile only the current script. The logic is simple: if we had to recompile the script, we already performed a batch compilation on its directory, so we don't need to compile the entire directory again. The end result is a tiny assembly that contains the compiled type from the script that was changed.

This process isn't my own idea. ASP.NET operates in a similar way when it compiles ASPX files. I used the same ideas when the time came to build the compilation and caching infrastructure of Rhino DSL.

This just about wraps things up for Rhino DSL (it's a tiny library, remember?). We just have one final topic to cover: handling external dependencies and integration with external factories.

7.5 *Supplying external dependencies to our DSL*

Although the default approach of creating new instances of the DSL using the default constructor is fine for simple cases, it gets tricky for more complex situations. For complex DSLs, we need access to the application's services and infrastructure.

In most applications, this is handled by using either a static gateway (a static class that provides the given service) or by using dependency injection (passing the services to the instance using the constructor or settable properties).

The advantage of static gateways is that the DSL can call them. Listing 7.12 shows an Authorization DSL that makes additional calls to the Authorization static gateway to perform its work.

Listing 7.12   An Authorization DSL script that calls back to the Authorization gateway

```
canApprove = Authorization.IsAllowed(Principal, "/order/approve")
canDispatch = Authorization.IsAllowed(Principal, "/order/dispatch")

if canApprove and canDispatch:
    return Allow("Can both approve and dispatch")
else:
    return Deny("Cannot both approve and dispatch")
```

This is easy to build, but I dislike this approach. It tends to make testing awkward (we'll discuss DSL testing in the next chapter). I much prefer to use dependency injection.

Depending on the infrastructure of our application, we have different ways of handling external dependencies, but the built-in option is to pass the parameters to the constructor. That's what we did when we built the Quote-Generation DSL, as you can see in listing 7.13.

Listing 7.13   Passing parameters to the Quote-Generation DSL instance

```
QuoteGeneratorRule rule = dslFactory.Create<QuoteGeneratorRule>(url,
                      new RequirementsInformation(200,"Vacation"));
rule.Evaluate();
```

Listing 7.13 shows the bare-bones approach to dependency injection, but we may want to use a more advanced technique. The advanced options all essentially amount to overriding the `DslEngine` `CreateInstance` method and modifying how we create an instance of our DSL.

Listing 7.14 shows how we could create an instance of a DSL by routing its creation through an IoC container (such as Windsor or StructureMap).

Listing 7.14   Routing DSL creation through an IoC container

```
public override object CreateInstance(Type type,
    params object[] parametersForConstructor)
{
    return container.CreateInstance(type);
}
```

Now all the DSL dependencies can be satisfied by the container, instead of having to be manually supplied.

NOTE The `type` we created in listing 7.14 was not previously registered in the container (we just compiled it, after all). The IoC container needs to support creating instances of unregistered types, but most of them do.

Note that although it works, directly using the application services from the DSL is an approach you should consider carefully. IoC containers aren't often written with an eye toward their use in DSLs, and they may allow leakage of programming concerns into the language.

It's generally better to handle the application services inside the DSL base class, and then to expose methods that properly match the style of the DSL. This also helps significantly when you need to create a new version of the DSL, and you need to change those services. If you have a facade layer, your job is that much easier. We'll talk about this more in chapter 9.

7.6 *Summary*

In this chapter, we looked at the requirements of a DSL infrastructure and saw how they're implemented by Rhino DSL. We looked at caching and batching, and at how those work together to produce a well-performing system.

We explored the extensibility options that Rhino DSL offers and we wrote a DSL engine storage class that could load scripts from an XML file, as an example of how to deal with non-filesystem-based storage (databases, source control, and so on). And last, but not least, we discussed the issue of providing dependencies to our DSL scripts.

This chapter is short, but it provides a thorough grounding in the underlying infrastructure that we build upon, as well as outlining the design requirements that have led to building it in this fashion.

With this knowledge, we can now start managing DSLs in real-world applications. We'll look next at how we can integrate our DSLs with test-driven development practices and test both the DSL implementations and the DSLs themselves.

Testing DSLs 8

The reasons for creating testable systems have been debated elsewhere for years, so we won't go over them again here. It's well accepted that testable and tested systems have lower maintainability costs, are easier to change and grow, and generally are more effective in the long run. I have a high regard for testability, and I consider it a first-level concern in any application or system that I build.

Unlike most systems, a DSL isn't a closed environment. DSLs are built explicitly to enable greater openness in the environment. It's almost guaranteed that your DSL will be used in ways that you can't predict. To ensure that you can grow the language as needs change, you need to know what can be done with your language in the first place, and ensure that you have tests to cover all those scenarios.

8.1 Building testable DSLs

It's *hard* to find breaking changes (or regression bugs) in a language. We tend to ignore the possibility of bugs at the language level, so it's doubly hard to track them down.

> **Testability, regressions, and design**
>
> So far in this book, I have ignored the effect of testability on the design of a system. Ask any test-driven development (TDD) advocate, and they'll tell you that the ability to run the tests against the application to find regressions is a secondary benefit compared to the impact on the design that using a TDD approach will have.
>
> *I* can certainly attest to that. Building a DSL in a TDD manner, with tests covering all your corners, will give you a language design that's much more cohesive. Such a language will be much easier to evolve as time goes on.

Regression tests help identify this sort of bug by ensuring that all the scenarios your language supports are covered. Users may still find ways to use the language that you didn't anticipate—ways that your future releases may break—but regression testing reduces that risk by a wide margin. DSLs are usually focused on specific scenarios, so you can be fairly certain that you can cover the potential uses. This gives you a system that can be worked on without fear of breaking existing DSL scripts.

Before we try to figure out what we need to test, let's review the typical structure for a DSL, as shown in figure 8.1.

The syntax, API, and model compose the language of the DSL, and the engine is responsible for performing the actions and returning results. Note that, in this context, the engine isn't the class that inherits from `DslEngine`. It's the generic concept, referring to the part of the application that does the work, such as the part of the Quote-Generation DSL that takes the generated quotes and does something with them.

Given that there are four distinct parts of the DSL, it shouldn't come as a surprise that we test the DSL by testing each of those areas individually, and finally creating a set of integration tests for the whole DSL.

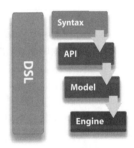

Figure 8.1   A typical structure for a DSL

8.2   *Creating tests for a DSL*

The Message-Routing DSL that we created in chapter 5 routes messages to the appropriate handlers. Listing 8.1 shows a simple scenario using this DSL.

Listing 8.1   A simple example using the Message-Routing DSL

```
HandleWith RoutingTestHandler:
    lines = []
    return NewOrderMessage( 15,  "NewOrder", lines.ToArray(OrderLine) )
```

When I start to test a DSL, I like to write tests similar to the one in listing 8.2.

Listing 8.2   The first DSL test usually verifies that the script compiles

```
[Test]
public void CanCompile()
{
    DslFactory dslFactory = new DslFactory();
    dslFactory.Register<RoutingBase>(new RoutingDslEngine());
    RoutingBase routing =
            dslFactory.Create<RoutingBase>(@"Routing\simple.boo");
    Assert.IsNotNull(routing);
}
```

This may not seem like a interesting test, but it's a good place to start. It checks that the simplest scenario, compiling the script, will work. As a matter of fact, I create a CanCompile() test for each of the features I build into the language.

> ### Rhino DSL and testability
> One of the design principles for Rhino DSL is that it *must* be testable, and easily so. As such, most of the internal structure is built in such a way that it's easily replaceable. This principle allows you to replace the infrastructure when you write your own tests, and it makes it easier to separate dependencies.

I am using basic tests, such as CanCompile(), to go from a rough idea about the syntax and user experience of the language to a language implementation that can be successfully compiled (but not necessarily run or do anything interesting).

Once we have a test that shows that our syntax works and can be successfully compiled, we can start working on the more interesting tests ...

8.2.1   Testing the syntax

What do I mean when I talk about testing the syntax? Didn't we test that with the Can-Compile() test? Well, not really.

When I talk about testing the syntax, I don't mean simply verifying that it compiles successfully. We need to make sure the syntax we created has been compiled into the correct output. The CanCompile() test is only the first step in that direction.

> ### Testing syntax in external DSLs
> In general, when you hear someone talking about testing the syntax of a DSL, they're talking about testing whether they can parse the textual DSL into an AST, whether the AST is valid, and so on. This is a critical stage for external DSLs, but not one you'll usually have to deal with in internal DSLs.
>
> By building on a host language, we can delegate all of those issues to the host language compiler. Our syntax tests for internal DSLs run at a higher level—we test that our syntax will execute as expected, not that it's parsed correctly.

Take a look at listing 8.1 for a moment. What's going on there? If you recall from chapter 5, the compiler will translate the code in listing 8.1 to code similar to what you see in listing 8.3.

Listing 8.3   C# representation of the compiled script in listing 8.1

```
public class Simple : RoutingBase
{
    public override void Route()
    {
        this.HandleWith(typeof(RoutingTestHandler), delegate
        {
            return new NewOrderMessage( 15,   "NewOrder", new OrderLine[0] )
        ;
        });
    }
}
```

We want to test that this translation has happened successfully, so we need to write a test for it. But how can we do this?

Interaction-based testing for syntax

Interaction-based testing is a common approach to testing DSLs. It is particularly useful for testing the syntax of a DSL in isolation.

It may seem strange to use interaction-based testing to test the syntax of a language, but it makes sense when you think about what we're trying to test. We're testing that the syntax we created interacts with the rest of the DSL infrastructure correctly. The easiest way to test *that* is through interaction testing.

In general, I use Rhino Mocks to handle interaction-based testing. However, I don't want to introduce any concepts that aren't directly tied to the subject at hand, so we'll create mock objects manually, instead of using Rhino Mocks.

We need some way to know whether the HandleWith method is called with the appropriate values when we call Route(). To do this, we'll take advantage of the implicit aspect of the implicit base class and replace the base class for the Message-Routing DSL with a testable implementation. This will allow us to override the HandleWith method and verify that it was called as expected.

We'll start by creating a derived class of RoutingBase that will capture the calls to HandleWith, instead of doing something useful with them. The StubbedRoutingBase class is shown in listing 8.4.

Listing 8.4   A routing base class that captures the values for calls to HandleWith

```
public abstract class StubbedRoutingBase  : RoutingBase
{
    public Type HandlerType;
    public MessageTransformer Transformer;
```

```
public override void HandleWith(
        Type handlerType,
        MessageTransformer transformer)
{
    this.HandlerType = handlerType;
    this.Transformer = transformer;
}
}
```

Now that we have this base class, we need to set things up in such a way that when we create the DSL instance, the base class will be `StubbedRoutingBase`, instead of `RoutinBase`. We can do this by deriving from `RoutingDslEngine` and replacing the implicit base class that's used. Listing 8.5 shows how it can be done.

Listing 8.5   Replacing the implicit base class with a stubbed class

```
public class RoutingDslEngine : DslEngine
{
    protected override void CustomizeCompiler(
        BooCompiler compiler,
        CompilerPipeline pipeline,
        string[] urls)
    {
        // The compiler should allow late-bound semantics
        compiler.Parameters.Ducky = true;
        pipeline.Insert(1,
                        new AnonymousBaseClassCompilerStep(
                                // the base type
                                BaseType,
                                // the method to override
                                "Route",
                                // import the following namespaces
                                "BDSLiB.MessageRouting.Handlers",
                                "BDSLiB.MessageRouting.Messages"));
    }

    protected virtual Type BaseType
    {
    get { return typeof (RoutingBase); }
    }
}

public class StubbedRoutingDslEngine : RoutingDslEngine
{
    // Uses the stubbed version instead of the real one
    protected override Type BaseType
    {
        get
        {
            return typeof(StubbedRoutingBase);
        }
    }
}
```

In this listing, we extract the `BaseType` into a virtual property, which we can override and change in the `StubbedRoutingDslEngine`. I find this to be an elegant approach.

Now that we've laid down the groundwork, let's create a full test case for syntax using this approach. Listing 8.6 shows all the details.

Listing 8.6 Testing that the proper values are passed to `HandleWith`

```
[Test]
public void WillCallHandlesWith_WithRouteTestHandler_WhenRouteCalled()
{
    const IQuackFu msg = null;

    dslFactory.Register<StubbedRoutingBase>(new StubbedRoutingDslEngine());

    var routing = dslFactory.Create<StubbedRoutingBase>(
                                        @"Routing\simple.boo");

    routing.Initialize(msg);

    routing.Route();

    Assert.AreEqual(typeof (RoutingTestHandler), routing.HandlerType);

    Assert.IsInstanceOfType(
        typeof(NewOrderMessage),
        routing.Transformer()
        );
}
```

First, we register the stubbed version of the DSL in the `DslFactory`, and then we ask the factory to create an instance of the script using the stubbed version. We execute the DSL, and then we can inspect the values captured in the `StubbedRoutingBase` when `HandleWith` is called.

NOTE In the sample code for this chapter, you will find a test called `WillCallHandlesWithRouteTestHandlerWhenRouteCalled_UsingRhino Mocks`, which demonstrates how you can use Rhino Mocks to test your DSL syntax.

Note that the last line of this test executes the delegate that received from the script to test that it produces the expected response (a type of `NewOrderMessage`, in this case).

What does this test do for us? It ensures that the syntax in listing 8.1 produces the expected response when the script is executed.

This is an important step, but it's only the first in the chain. Now that we can test that we're creating compilable scripts and that the syntax of the language is correct, we need to move up the ladder and start testing the API that we expose to the script.

8.2.2 Testing the DSL API

What exactly *is* a DSL API? In general, it's any API that was written specifically for a DSL. The methods and properties of the implicit base class are an obvious candidate (if they aren't directly part of the DSL syntax, such as `RoutingBase.HandleWith` in our case).

Because the Message-Routing API has little API surface area worth talking about, we'll use the Authorization DSL as our example for testing the API. Figure 8.2 shows the class diagram for the Authorization DSL's base class.

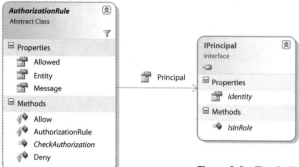

Figure 8.2   The Authorization DSL class diagram

As you can see in figure 8.2, there are several API calls exposed to the DSL. `Allow()` and `Deny()` come to mind immediately, and `Principal.IsInRole()` is also important, though in a secondary manner (see sidebar on the difference between the DSL API and the model). I consider those to be the DSL API because they're standard API calls that we explicitly defined as part of our DSL.

The rules we follow for the API are different than those we follow when we write the rest of the application. We have to put much more focus on language orientation for those calls. The DSL API is here to be used by the DSL, not by other code, so making the API calls easier to use trumps other concerns. For example, in the case of the Authorization DSL, we could have provided a method such as `Authorized(bool isAuthorized)`, but instead we created two separate methods, `Allow()` and `Deny()`, to make it clearer for the users of the DSL.

The difference between the DSL API and the model

In figure 8.1, we distinguished between the DSL API and the model. But what is the difference between the two?

A DSL API is an API built specifically to be consumed by the DSL, whereas the application model, which the DSL often shares, is a more general concept describing how the application itself is built.

The domain model of the application is composed of entities and services that work together to perform the application's tasks. This domain model isn't designed first and foremost to be consumed by the DSL. You may find that it's suitable for the DSL and make use of it, but that isn't its main purpose.

A DSL API, however, is intended specifically for the DSL. You can create DSL API facades on top of existing models to supply better semantics for what you intend to do.

When you test your DSL, there is no need to test the model. The model is used by the DSL but isn't part of it. The tests for the model should have been created when the model was created.

Once you've identified your DSL API, how do you test it? My personal preference (and recommendation) is that you should test the API without using the DSL at all. This goes back to testing in isolation. You're testing the API, not the interaction of the API and the DSL (which was tested with syntax tests). This has the side benefit of ensuring that the API is also usable outside the DSL you're currently building, which is important, because you'll probably want to reuse the API in your tests, if not in a different DSL altogether (see section 8.3.2 on creating the Testing DSL).

To test your DSL API without using the DSL infrastructure, you use standard testing techniques. Listing 8.7 shows how you can test that the `Allow()` and `Deny()` methods perform their duties appropriately.

Listing 8.7 Testing the `Allow()` and `Deny()` methods

```
// Pretends to be a DSL that allows access
public class AllowAccess : AuthorizationRule
{
    public override void CheckAuthorization()
    {
        Allow("just a test");
    }
}

// Pretends to be a DSL that has no opinion on the matter
public class AbstainFromVoting : AuthorizationRule
{
    public override void CheckAuthorization()
    {
    }
}

// Pretends to be a DSL that denies access
public class DenyAccess : AuthorizationRule
{
    public override void CheckAuthorization()
    {
        Deny("just a test");
    }
}

[Test]
public void WhenAllowCalled_WillSetAllowedToTrue()
{
    AllowAccess allowAccess = new AllowAccess(null, null);
    allowAccess.CheckAuthorization();

    Assert.IsTrue(allowAccess.Allowed.Value);
    Assert.AreEqual("just a test", allowAccess.Message);
}

[Test]
public void WhenAllowOrDenyAreNotCalled_AllowHasNoValye()
{
    AbstainFromVoting allowAccess = new AbstainFromVoting(null, null);
```

```
    allowAccess.CheckAuthorization();

    Assert.IsNull(allowAccess.Allowed);
}

[Test]
public void WhenDenyCalled_WillSetAllowedToFalse()
{
    DenyAccess allowAccess = new DenyAccess(null, null);
    allowAccess.CheckAuthorization();

    Assert.IsFalse(allowAccess.Allowed.Value);
    Assert.AreEqual("just a test", allowAccess.Message);
}
```

In this example, we start by defining a few classes that behave in a known manner regarding the methods we want to test (`Allow()` and `Deny()`). Once we have those, it's a simple matter to write tests to ensure that `Allow()` and `Deny()` behave the way we expect them to. This is a fairly trivial example, but it allows us to explore the approach without undue complexity.

The next step would be to test the model, but we're not going to do that. The model is used by the DSL, but it isn't part of it, so it's tested the same way you would test the rest of your application. Therefore, it's time to test the engine ...

8.2.3   *Testing the DSL engine*

When I talk about the *DSL engine* in this context, I'm referring to the code that manages and uses the DSL, not classes derived from the `DslEngine` class. The DSL engine is responsible for coordinating the use of the DSL scripts.

For example, the `Authorization` class in the Authorization DSL, which manages the authorization rules, is a DSL engine. That class consumes DSL scripts, but it isn't part of the DSL—it's a gateway into the DSL, nothing more. The DSL engine will often contain more complex interactions between the application and the DSL scripts.

Because the engine is usually a consumer of DSL instances, you have several choices when creating test cases for the engine. You can perform a cross-cutting test, which would involve the DSL, or test the interaction of the engine with DSL instances that you provide to it externally. Because I generally want to test the engine's behavior in invalid scenarios (with a DSL script that can't be compiled, for example), I tend to choose the first approach.

Listing 8.8 shows a few sample tests for the `Authorization` class. These tests exercise the entire stack: the syntax, the API, and the DSL engine.

Listing 8.8   Testing the `Authorization` class

```
[TestFixture]
public class AuthorizationEngineTest
{
    private GenericPrincipal principal;

    [SetUp]
    public void Setup()
```

```
{
    Authorization.Initialize(@"Auth/AuthorizationRules.xml");
    principal = new GenericPrincipal(new GenericIdentity("foo"),
                            new string[]{"Administrators"});
}

[Test]
public void WillNotAllowOperationThatDoesNotExists()
{
    bool? allowed = Authorization.IsAllowed(
                                principal, "/user/signUp");
    Assert.IsFalse(allowed.Value);
}

/// <summary>
/// One of the rules for /account/login is that administrators
/// can always log in
/// </summary>
[Test]
public void WillAllowAdministratorToLogIn()
{
    bool? allowed = Authorization.IsAllowed(
                                principal, "/account/login");
    Assert.IsTrue(allowed.Value);
}

[Test]
public void CanGetMessageAboutWhyLoginIsAllowed()
{
    string whyAllowed = Authorization.WhyAllowed(
                                principal, "/account/login");
    Assert.AreEqual("Administrators can always log in",
                        whyAllowed);
}
}
```

As you can see, there's nothing particularly unique here. We define a set of rules in the AuthorizationRules.xml files and then use the Authorization class to verify that we get the expected result from the class. This is an important test case, because it validates that all the separate pieces are working together appropriately.

I would also add tests to check the order in which the Authorization DSL engine executes the scripts and how the engine handles errors in compiling the scripts and exceptions when running them. I would also test any additional logic in the class, but now we're firmly in the realm of unit testing, and this isn't the book to read about that.

TIP   For information on unit testing, you should take a look at *The Art of Unit Testing*, by Roy Osherove (http://www.manning.com/osherove/). Another good book is *xUnit Test Patterns*, by Gerard Meszaros (http://xunitpatterns.com/).

So far, we've talked about testing each component in isolation, and using some overarching tests to ensure that the entire package works. We've tested the syntax, the API, and the engine, and I've explained why we aren't going to test the model in our DSL tests. That covers everything in figure 8.1.

But we haven't yet talked about testing the DSL scripts themselves.

8.3 Testing the DSL scripts

Considering the typical scenarios for using a DSL (providing a policy, defining rules, making decisions, driving the application, and so on), you need to have tests in place to verify that the scripts do what you think they do. In fact, *because* DSLs are used to define high-level application behavior, it's essential to be aware of what the scripts are doing and protect ourselves from accidental changes.

We'll explore two ways to do this, using standard unit tests and creating a full-blown secondary testing DSL to test our primary DSL.

8.3.1 Testing DSL scripts using standard unit testing

One of the more important things to remember when dealing with Boo-based DSLs is that the output of those DSLs is IL (Intermediate Language, the CLR assembly language). This means that this output has all the standard advantages and disadvantages of other IL-based languages.

For example, when testing a DSL script, you can reference the resulting assembly and write a test case directly against it, just as you would with any other .NET assembly. Usually, you can safely utilize the implicit base class as a way to test the behavior of the scripts you build. This offers a nearly no-cost approach to building tests.

Let's take the Quote-Generation DSL as our example and write a test to verify that the script in listing 8.9 works as expected.

Listing 8.9   Simple script for the Quote-Generation DSL

```
specification @vacations:
    requires @scheduling_work
    requires @external_connections

specification @scheduling_work:
    return # Doesn't require anything
```

Listing 8.10 shows the unit tests required to verify this behavior.

Listing 8.10   Testing the DSL script in listing 8.9 using standard unit testing

```
[TestFixture]
public class QuoteGenerationTest
{
    private DslFactory dslFactory;

    // Set up the DSL factory appropriately
    [SetUp]
    public void SetUp()
    {
        dslFactory = new DslFactory();
        dslFactory.Register<QuoteGeneratorRule>(
```

```
                                    new QuoteGenerationDslEngine());
    }

    // Standard test to ensure we can compile the script
    [Test]
    public void CanCompile()
    {
        QuoteGeneratorRule rule =
                    dslFactory.Create<QuoteGeneratorRule>(
            @"Quotes/simple.boo",
            new RequirementsInformation(200, "vacations"));
        Assert.IsNotNull(rule);
    }

    // Positive test, to ensure that we add the correct information
    // to the system when we match the requirements of the current
    // evaluation
    [Test]
    public void Vacations_Requirements ()
    {
        QuoteGeneratorRule rule =
                    dslFactory.Create<QuoteGeneratorRule>(
            @"Quotes/simple.boo",
            new RequirementsInformation(200, "vacations"));
        rule.Evaluate();

        SystemModule module = rule.Modules[0];
        Assert.AreEqual("vacations", module.Name);
        Assert.AreEqual(2, module.Requirements.Count);
        Assert.AreEqual("scheduling_work", module.Requirements[0]);
        Assert.AreEqual("external_connections",
                                        module.Requirements[1]);
    }

    // Negative test, to verify that we aren't blindly doing
    // things without regard to the current context
    [Test]
    public void WhenUsingSchedulingWork_HasNoRequirements()
    {
        QuoteGeneratorRule rule =
                    dslFactory.Create<QuoteGeneratorRule>(
            @"Quotes/simple.boo",
            new RequirementsInformation(200, "scheduling_work"));
        rule.Evaluate();

        Assert.AreEqual(0, rule.Modules[0].Requirements.Count);

    }
}
```

In this test, we use the DslFactory to create an instance of the DSL and then execute it against a known state. Then we make assertions against the expected output from the known state.

This test doesn't do anything special—these are standard methods for unit testing—but there is something disturbing in this approach to testing. The code we're trying to test is exactly 5 lines long; the test is over 45 lines of code.

There is some repetitive code in the test that could perhaps be abstracted out, but I tend to be careful with abstractions in tests. They often affect the clarity of the test. And although I am willing to accept a certain disparity in the number of lines between production and test code, I think that when the disparity is measured in thousands of percent, it's time to consider another testing approach.

8.3.2 *Creating the Testing DSL*

The main reason there's such a disparity between the DSL script and the code to test it is that the DSL is explicitly designed to express information in a concise (yet readable) form. When we try to test the DSL script with C# code, we have to deal with well-abstracted code using relatively few abstractions, so it's no wonder there's a big disparity in the amount of code.

Clearly we need a different approach. This being a book about DSL, my solution is to introduce another DSL, a Testing DSL, that will allow us to handle this at a higher level.

Don't we need a testing DSL to test the Testing DSL?

If we create a Testing DSL to test the primary DSL, don't we also need another testing DSL to test the Testing DSL? Taken to the obvious conclusion, that would require a third testing DSL to test the second testing DSL used to test the first testing DSL, and so on, ad infinitum. Who watches the watchers? Do we need an infinite series of testing DSLs?

Fortunately, we don't need recursive testing DSLs. We only need one testing DSL for each DSL we're testing. We'll use the old idea of double-entry booking to ensure that we're getting the right results.

The chance of having complementing bugs in both DSLs is small, so we'll use each DSL to verify the other when we're testing. A bug in the testing DSL would manifest itself because there wouldn't be a matching bug in the primary DSL.

We'll use the same approach in building the Testing DSL as we'd use for any DSL. We first need to consider what kind of syntax we want to use, in order to test that. Look back at the script in listing 8.9 and consider what kind of syntax would express the tests in the clearest possible manner.

We also need to identify the common things we'll want to test. Judging by the tests in listing 8.10, we'll generally want to assert on the expected values from the script under various starting conditions.

Listing 8.11 shows the initial syntax for the Testing DSL.

Listing 8.11 Testing DSL syntax for Quote-Generation DSL scripts

```
script "quotes/simple.boo"

with @vacations:
    should_require @scheduling_work
```

```
    should_require @external_connections

with @scheduling_work:
    should_have_no_requirements
```

Let's try to build that. We'll start with the implicit base class, using the same techniques we applied when building the DSL itself.

> **DSL building tip**
>
> A good first step when building a DSL is to take all the keywords in the language you're building and create matching methods for them that take a delegate as a parameter. You can then use anonymous blocks to define your syntax.
>
> This is a low-cost approach, and it allows you to choose more complex options for building the syntax (such as macros or compiler steps) later on.

We'll first look at the structure of the implicit base class in listing 8.12. Then we'll inspect the keyword methods in detail.

Listing 8.12 Implicit base class for testing Quote-Generation DSL scripts

```
/// <summary>
/// Implicit base class for testing the Quote-Generation scripts.
/// </summary>
public abstract class TestQuoteGeneratorBase
{
    private DslFactory dslFactory;
    private QuoteGeneratorRule ruleUnderTest;
    private string currentModuleName;

    protected TestQuoteGeneratorBase()
    {
        ruleUnderTest = null;
        dslFactory = new DslFactory();
        dslFactory.Register<QuoteGeneratorRule>(
                    new QuoteGenerationDslEngine());
    }

    /// <summary>
    /// The script we're currently testing
    /// </summary>
    public abstract string Script { get; }

    // removed: with
    // removed: should_require
    // removed: should_have_no_requirements

    public abstract void Test();
}
```

There is only one thing worth special attention in listing 8.12: the abstract property called `Script` holds the path to the current script. This will be mapped to the script declaration in the Testing DSL using a property macro (property macros are discussed in chapter 7).

Now that we have the overall structure, let's take a deeper look at the language key-words. We'll start with the `with` keyword, in listing 8.13.

Listing 8.13   The implementation of the `with` keyword

```
/// <summary>
/// A keyword
/// The scenario that we're testing.
/// Execute the script and then test its state.
/// </summary>
/// <param name="moduleName">The module name we're using
/// as the starting requirement</param>
/// <param name="action">Action that verified the state under the
/// specified module</param>
public void with(string moduleName, Action action)
{
    Assert.IsNotEmpty(Script, "No script was specified for testing");

    ruleUnderTest = dslFactory.Create<QuoteGeneratorRule>(
        Script,
        new RequirementsInformation(0, moduleName));
    ruleUnderTest.Evaluate();

    currentModuleName = moduleName;

    action();
}
```

In listing 8.13, we create and execute the specified DSL and then use the last parame-ter of the `with` method, which is a delegate that contains the actions to verify the cur-rent state.

Listing 8.14 shows one of the verification keywords, `should_require`. The imple-mentation of `should_have_no_requirements` is similar, so I won't show it.

Listing 8.14   The implementation of one of the verification keywords in our Testing DSL

```
/// <summary>
/// A keyword
/// Expect to find the specified module as required for the current module
/// </summary>
public void should_require(string requiredModule)
{
    // Search for the appropriate module
    SystemModule module = ruleUnderTest.Modules.Find(
        delegate(SystemModule m)
    {
        return m.Name == currentModuleName;
    });
    // Fail if not found
    if (module == null)
    {
        Assert.Fail("Expected to have module: " +
                    currentModuleName +
                    " but could not find it in the registered modules");
    }
```

```
    // Search for the expected requirement
    foreach (string requirement in module.Requirements)
    {
        if (requirement == requiredModule)
            return;
    }
    // Not found, we fail the test
    Assert.Fail(currentModuleName +
            " should have a requirement on " +
        requiredModule +
        " but didn't.");
}
```

We use methods like `should_have_no_requirements` and `should_require` to abstract the verification process, which gives us a high-level language to express the tests. This approach significantly reduces the amount of effort required to test DSL scripts.

We're not done yet

A word of caution. The Testing DSL created here can test only a limited set of scenarios. If you want to test a script with logic in it, you need to extend it. For example, what we have so far couldn't test the following script:

```
specification @vacations:
    requires @scheduling_work
    requires @external_connections if UserCount > 50
```

Extending the Testing DSL to support this is easy enough, but I'll leave that as an exercise for you (the solution is in the sample code). If you'd like a hint, this is the syntax I used:

```
script "quotes/WithLogic.boo"
with @vacations, UserCount=51:
    should_require @scheduling_work
    should_require @external_connections
with @vacations, UserCount=49:
    should_require @scheduling_work
    should_not_require @external_connections
```

Now that we've built the Testing DSL, are we done? Not quite. We still have to figure out how to execute it. Listing 8.15 shows one way of doing this.

Listing 8.15 Manually executing the Testing DSL

```
[TestFixture]
public class TestQuoteGenerationTest
{
    private DslFactory dslFactory;

    [SetUp]
    public void SetUp()
    {
        dslFactory = new DslFactory();
        dslFactory.Register<TestQuoteGeneratorBase>(
```

```
                            new TestQuoteGenerationDslEngine());
    }

    [Test]
    public void CanExecute_KnownGood()
    {
        TestQuoteGeneratorBase test =
                dslFactory.Create<TestQuoteGeneratorBase>(
                        @"QuoteGenTest.Scripts/simple.boo");
        test.Test();
    }
}
```

Although this will work, I don't like this method much. It has too much friction in it. You'd have to write a separate test for each test script. Much worse, if there's an error in the test, this manual execution doesn't point out the reason for the failure; it points to a line, which you'd then have to go and read, as opposed to reading the name of the test.

A better method is to integrate the Testing DSL with the unit-testing framework.

8.4   *Integrating with a testing framework*

When we're talking about integrating the Testing DSL scripts with a unit-testing framework, we generally want the following:

- To use standard tools to run the tests
- To get pass or fail notification for each separate test
- To have meaningful names for the tests

Ideally, we could drop Testing DSL scripts in a tests directory, run the tests, and get all the results back.

Probably the simplest approach is to write a simple script that would generate the explicit tests from the Testing DSL scripts on the filesystem. Adding this script as a precompile step would ensure that we get the simple experience we're looking for. This approach is used by Boo itself in some of its tests, and it is extremely simple to implement.

But this approach isn't always suitable. For example, consider the syntax we have for testing:

```
with @vacations:
    # ...
with @scheduling_work:
    # ...
```

We have two distinct tests here that happen to reside in a single file. We could split them so there's only one test per file, but that's an annoying requirement, particularly if we have three or four such tests with a few lines in each. What I'd like is to have the test figure out that each with keyword is a separate test.

As it turns out, it's pretty easy to make this happen. Most unit-testing frameworks have some sort of extensibility mechanism that allows you to plug into them. In my experience, the easiest unit-testing framework to extend is xUnit.NET, so that's what we'll use.

Listing 8.16 shows a trivial implementation of a test using xUnit. You can take a look at the xUnit homepage for further information: http://xunit.codeplex.com.

Listing 8.16 Sample test using xUnit

```
public class DemoOfTestUsingXUnit
{
    [Fact]
    public void OnePlusOneEqualTwo()
    {
        Assert.Equal(2, 1+1);
    }
}
```

Before we can start extending xUnit, we need to make sure we have a way to differentiate between the different tests in a single file. We'll do this by defining with as a unit test. What do I mean by that? Figure 8.3 shows the transformation I have in mind.

We'll take each with section and turn it into its own method, which will allow us to treat them separately.

NOTE Because this chapter presents two radically different ways to unit test a DSL, this chapter's code is split into two parts: /Chapter8 contains the code for sections 8.1 through 8.3, and /Chapter8.UnitTestIntegration contains the source code for section 8.4 through the end of the chapter.

If you look at figure 8.3 closely, you'll notice that we now have a WithModule() instead of the with. This helps us avoid naming collisions. After renaming the with() method to WithModule(), all we have to do is create a method each and every time with is used. We can do this with a macro, as shown in listing 8.17.

```
with @vacations:
    should_require @scheduling_work
    should_require @external_connections

with @scheduling_work:
    should_have_no_requirements
```

```
public class Simple(TestQuoteGenerationBase):

    def with_vacations:
        WithModule @vacations:
            should_require @scheduling_work
            should_require

    def with_scheduling_work:
        WithModule @scheduling_work:
            should_have_no_requirements
```

Figure 8.3 The transformation from the test script to multiple tests

Listing 8.17 A macro that moves a with block to its own method

```
/// <summary>
/// Move the content of a with block to a separate method
/// and call the WithModule method.
/// </summary>
public class WithMacro : AbstractAstMacro
```

```
{
    public override Statement Expand(MacroStatement macro)
    {
        // Create a call to WithModule method
        var mie = new MethodInvocationExpression(macro.LexicalInfo,
            new ReferenceExpression("WithModule"));
        // with the arguments that we were passed
        mie.Arguments.Extend(macro.Arguments);
        // as well as the block that we have there.
        mie.Arguments.Add(new BlockExpression(macro.Block));

        // Create a new method. Note that the method "name"
        // is the content of the with block. This is allowed by
        // the CLR, but not by most languages.
        var method = new Method(macro.ToCodeString());
        // Add the call to the WithModule to the new method.
        method.Body.Add(mie);

        // Find the parent class definition
        var classDefinition = (ClassDefinition) macro.GetAncestor(
                NodeType.ClassDefinition);
        // Add the new method to the class definition
        classDefinition.Members.Add(method);

        // Remove all the code that was where this macro used to be
        return null;
    }
}
```

During compilation, whenever the compiler encounters a `with` block, it will call the `WithMacro` code. When that happens, this code will create a new method whose name is the content of the `with` block, and move all the code in the `with` block to the method, removing it from its original location. It also translates the `with` block to a call to the newly renamed `WithModule` method.

With this new macro in place, compiling the script in listing 8.11 will produce the output in listing 8.18 (translated to pseudo C# to make it easier to understand).

Listing 8.18   The result of compiling listing 8.11 with the `WithMacro` macro

```
public class Simple : TestQuoteGeneratorBase
{
    public void with 'scheduling_work':
    should_have_no_requirements()
();

    public void with 'vacations':
    should_require('scheduling_work')
    should_require('external_connections')
();

    public override string Script { get { ... } }
}
```

The method names aren't a mistake; we have a method name with all sorts of interesting characters in it such as spaces, line breaks, and even parentheses. It doesn't make sense as C# code, but it *does* make sense as IL code, which is what I translated listing 8.18 from. This is one way to ensure that tests will *never* have misleading names.

Now that we have each individual test set up as its own method, we can integrate the tests into xUnit fairly easily. Listing 8.19 shows the most relevant piece for integrating with the unit-testing framework.

Listing 8.19 Integrating our DSL with xUnit

```
public class DslFactAttribute : FactAttribute
{
    private readonly string path;

    public DslFactAttribute(string path)
    {
        this.path = path;
    }

    protected override IEnumerable<ITestCommand>
                      EnumerateTestCommands(MethodInfo method)
    {
        DslFactory dslFactory = new DslFactory();
        dslFactory.Register<TestQuoteGeneratorBase>(
                new TestQuoteGenerationDslEngine());

        TestQuoteGeneratorBase test =
                        slFactory.Create<TestQuoteGeneratorBase>(path);
        Type dslType = test.GetType();

        BindingFlags flags = BindingFlags.DeclaredOnly |
            BindingFlags.Public |
            BindingFlags.Instance;

        foreach (MethodInfo info in
                                dslType.GetMethods(flags))
        {
            if (info.Name.StartsWith("with"))
            {
                yield return new DslRunnerTestCommand(
                                                dslType, info);
            }
        }
    }
}
```

This code is straightforward. We accept a path in the constructor for the script we want to test. When the time comes to find all the relevant tests, we create an instance of the script and find all the test methods (those that start with `with`). We then wrap them in `DslRunnerTestCommand`, which will be used to execute the test.

The `DslRunnerTestCommand` class is shown in listing 8.20.

Listing 8.20   `DslRunnerTestCommand` can execute a specific test in the DSL

```
public class DslRunnerTestCommand : ITestCommand
{
    private readonly MethodInfo testToRun;
    private readonly Type dslType;

    public DslRunnerTestCommand(Type dslType, MethodInfo testToRun)
    {
        this.dslType = dslType;
        this.testToRun = testToRun;
    }

    public MethodResult Execute(object ignored)
    {
        object instance = Activator.CreateInstance(dslType);
        return new TestCommand(testToRun).Execute(instance);
    }

    public string Name
    {
        get { return testToRun.Name; }
    }
}
```

We need a specialized test command to control which object the test is executed on. In this case, we pass the DSL type in the constructor, instantiate it during execution, and then hand off the rest of the test to the xUnit framework.

All we have left to do is use `DslFact` to tell the unit-testing framework how to find our tests, which is shown in listing 8.21.

Listing 8.21   Using `DslFact` to let xUnit find our tests

```
public class UsingUnitTestingIntegration
{
    [DslFact("QuoteGenTest.Scripts/simple.boo")]
    public void Simple()
    {
    }

    [DslFact("QuoteGenTest.Scripts/WithLogic.boo")]
    public void WithLogic()
    {
    }
}
```

What about integrating with other unit-testing frameworks?

All the major unit-testing frameworks have *some* extensibility mechanism that you can use. Personally, I think that xUnit is the simplest framework to extend, which is why I chose it to demonstrate the integration. Integrating with other frameworks isn't significantly more complicated, but it does require more moving parts.

What did this integration with the unit-testing framework give us? Here is the result of a failing test:

```
1) with 'vacations', 49:
        should_require('scheduling_work')
        should_require('external_connections')
 : AssertionException : vacations should have a requirement on
     external_connections but didn't.
```

Compare that to the output we'd have gotten using the approach we took in listing 8.15. This approach gives us a much clearer error, and it's that much easier to understand what is going on and fix it.

Note that you still have to write a dummy test for each script you want to test. To improve on this, you could change `DslFact` so it will handle a directory instead of a single file. This would let you drop test scripts into a directory, and they would immediately be picked up by the unit-testing framework.

8.5 Taking testing further

We've looked at testing DSLs, but you could use DSLs to take testing further, by building a DSL to test your application, or by building testing into your language.

8.5.1 Building an application-testing DSL

Something that deserves a bit of attention is using testing DSLs not to test another DSL, but to test your application. This is an offshoot of automation DSLs, targeted specifically at testing applications.

The Fit testing tool (http://fit.c2.com/wiki.cgi?IntroductionToFit) can be used to let the customer build acceptance tests without understanding the code, and a testing DSL could be used for similar purposes. Frankly, having used Fit in the past, I find it significantly easier to build a DSL to express those concepts, rather than to use Fit fixtures for the task.

There isn't anything special in such an application-testing DSL; you can use the same tools and approaches as when building any DSL.

8.5.2 Mandatory testing

There is one approach to testing that we haven't talked about: mandatory testing as part of the language itself.

Imagine that when you create an instance of a script, the DSL engine looks for a matching test script (for example, the work-scheduling-specs.boo script would match to the work-scheduling-specs.test test). This test script would be compiled and executed the first time you request the primary script. That would ensure that your scripts are tested and working—a missing or failed test would stop the primary script from running.

There are problems with this approach. Tests might require a special environment, or take a while to run, or modify the state of the system in unacceptable ways for production, and so on. But it would be a good approach to use during development and staging. It would give you more motivation to write tests for your DSL scripts.

> **NOTE**   This approach to mandatory testing is just an idea at the moment. I haven't tried implementing it in a real project yet. The technical challenges of implementing such a system are nil, but the implications on the workflow and the ease of use of such a system are unknown. On the surface, checked exceptions are great. In practice, they're very cumbersome. This is why I have only toyed with the idea so far.

8.6   *Summary*

Testing is a big topic, and it can significantly improve the quality of software that we write. This chapter has covered several approaches for testing DSLs, but I strongly recommend reading more about unit testing if you aren't already familiar with the concepts and their application.

We covered quite a few topics in this chapter. We saw how to test each area of a DSL in isolation, and how to test the language as a whole. Having a layer of tests for the language itself is critically important—you need it the moment you make a change to the language. That layer of tests is your safety net. In the next chapter, we'll look at how to safely version a DSL, and having a solid foundation of regression tests is a baseline requirement for successfully doing so.

Beyond testing the language itself, we've also seen how to test the language artifacts: the DSL scripts. We started with executing DSL scripts in our unit tests, moved on to building a Testing DSL to test the primary DSL, and finished up by integrating the Testing DSL into a unit-testing framework, which provides better error messages and allows us to have the unit tests automatically pick up new test scripts as we write them.

With that solid foundation of tests under our feet, we can move on to the next stage in our DSL lifetime, version 2.0. Let's look at how to deal with that.

Versioning DSLs

Versioning refers to creating a second version of a language (or a product) that's compatible with the previous version. Code and other artifacts from the previous version can either run on the new version or there is a well-defined process for moving from one version to the next.

The development of the second version is a critical point in the lifecycle of any language. At that point, you no longer have a blank slate to draw upon; you need to take into account the existing investments in the previous version as well. The alternative would be to stop with a single release, or to abandon all the time and money invested in the previous version. These aren't choices most people would make.

In this chapter, we'll lay the foundations we need to create the versioning story for our DSLs. After that, we'll touch on several different approaches to versioning a language.

Many of the approaches that we'll discuss in this chapter are applicable to existing languages, but these approaches and techniques are most effective if they're used when you initially design and build the language. I strongly suggest that, even for small languages, you take the time to consider the versioning strategy you'll apply.

9.1   *Starting from a stable origin*

The obvious first step in any versioning scenario is to determine where things are right now. In order to make sure that the next version can accommodate the current version, you need to know what the state of the current version *is*. For example, if you want your next version to support existing scripts, you need to know what can be done with the language as it is now. This isn't the obviously redundant step that it may appear to be at first glance.

Trying to reverse engineer language syntax from its implementation is challenging. It's possible, for sure, but *hard*. The main hurdle is that a language is usually flexible in its input, and two people will often express the same thing in different ways.

You need some sort of baseline to ensure that you understand how the language is used. In general, I like to have this baseline in two forms:

- *Executable form*—This consists of unit and integration tests that use the language features. These tests allow you to see how various elements of the language are used in context. The tests we discussed in chapter 8 will do nicely here, and they'll ensure that we also have a regression test suite for the next version.

- *Documentation*—Although tests are my preferred method of diving into a code base, additional documentation will give you the complete picture, so you don't have to piece it together. This is particularly important when you want a cohesive picture of how all elements of the language play together. We'll discuss how best to approach writing documentation for a DSL in chapter 11.

With both tests and documentation in place, you'll have a good understanding of how the language is supposed to behave, and you can go on to extend and change it from a well-known position, rather than blindly.

Once you know where you are, you need to figure out where you're going, what kind of changes you need to make, and what their implications will be on the versioning story.

The lone language developer

You might think that versioning isn't an issue for languages that are written by and for a single developer, but this is most certainly not the case. There are always at least two people on any project: the developer who writes the code, and the developer who reads it. Even if they're the same physical person, they're looking at the code at different times.

Even if you wrote the code, you can't count on being able to remember and understand all the implications and use cases six months from now. I've made that mistake several times in the past, and it resulted in a lot of delay.

9.2 Planning a DSL versioning story

A DSL *versioning story* defines the overall approach you take to versioning the DSL over time—what versioning strategies you employ and what versioning guarantees you give to DSL users.

In chapters 3 and 5, we defined the parts that a DSL is composed of:

- *Engine*—The code that executes the DSL script and processes the results
- *Model and API*—The data and operations exposed to the DSL
- *Syntax*—The syntax of the language
- *Environment*—The execution environment of the DSL

When we talk about versioning a DSL, we're talking about making a change to one of those parts (or all of them), while maintaining some desired level of compatibility with the previous version. We'll examine each of them and look at the implications of each type of change.

9.2.1 Implications of modifying the DSL engine

There are several ways to modify the DSL engine.

The best scenario from a versioning perspective is a nonfunctional change, which means the behavior of the engine remains the same in all cases; the change is focused on internal behavior, optimizations, and the like. Any change in observable behavior is a bug, so there can't be any compatibility issues.

A functional change is when you've made some sort of change to the behavior of the engine. In this situation, you need to determine the implications of this change on existing DSL scripts.

In many cases, functional changes to the engine are safe changes to make. The engine is responsible for processing the results of executing the DSL, so the DSL will rarely be affected by this change. By the time the engine is running, the DSL has completed.

But there is one scenario in which a change in the engine can cause compatibility issues for the DSL. Restricting the legal values or operations that a DSL specifies can cause a DSL to fail, because formerly valid values may no longer be valid.

Listing 9.1 shows a valid snippet of a Quote-Generation DSL script.

> **Versioning means worrying about *intended* consequences**
>
> Although it's entirely possible for a change to cause unforeseen incompatibilities with previously written DSL scripts and code, that isn't something that I care about when I am talking about versioning strategies.
>
> If I make a change that has an unforeseen compatibility issue, what I have is a bug, and this should be caught using the regression test suite. Versioning, on the other hand, deals with how one can mitigate the issue of *planned* incompatibilities.

Listing 9.1   A snippet from a Quote-Generation DSL script

```
specification @vacations:
    requires @scheduling_work
    requires @external_connections
```

Let's say that you changed the engine to only allow a single requirement for each specified model; this previously valid snippet would become illegal.

We need more information about the reasons for this change to decide how to deal with this issue, so we'll defer dealing with this for now and move to dealing with changes in the model and the API.

9.2.2   *Implications of modifying the DSL API and model*

The API and the model exposed to the DSL compose a large part of the syntax that the DSL has. This means your existing investment in building a clear API and a rich model can be used directly in the DSL, which will save you quite a bit of time.

There is a problem with exposing the application's core API and model to the DSL: any change you make in the core API has to be tested with regard to how it will affect the DSL. In effect, the DSL becomes yet another client of the code, with all the usual implications that has on creating public APIs, worrying about versioning conflicts, and so on.

I don't expect you to be surprised that I recommend against directly exposing the API and model that are used in the application to the DSL. What I recommend is creating a facade layer between the two—you expose the application concepts that you need to use in the DSL only through a facade. This approach simplifies versioning, because changing the core API will not affect DSL scripts created previously. All the changes stop at the facade layer, which remains static. This allows parallel development of both the DSL and the model, without worrying about versioning issues between the two. What makes for nice, fluent, readable code doesn't necessarily make for good DSL syntax, so separating the two is useful even if you haven't reached the point where you're considering versioning concerns.

Versioning an external DSL

The problem with versioning an internal DSL is that there isn't usually a formal definition of the syntax. Most of the tools for building external DSLs work by building on a formal syntax definition, which is usually in the form of BNF (Backus-Naur Form, a language for formally defining a language syntax) or syntax derivative.

When you have a formal syntax definition, it's quite easy to create a diff between versions 1.0 and 2.0 of the language, and see what the syntactic differences between the two are. This is something you need to do yourself when building an internal DSL.

But syntax is a small part of versioning a DSL. The model, API, behavior, and application integration are all parts of the versioning story, and they all require the versioning approach that's outlined in this chapter.

WARNING Remember the client audience for your DSL. If you make a change to your DSL, you need to communicate that to the users of the DSL and ensure that they understand what changed, why, and how they should move forward in working with the DSL. This can be a much greater challenge than the mere technical problems you'll run into.

At the same time, I don't like having to start with a facade when I have a one-to-one relationship between the facade and the model. I like to use what I call a lazy facade approach: use the real objects until I run into the first situation where the needs of the DSL and the needs of the application diverge, and create the facade at that point.

This approach is often useful when you're starting development, because it frees you from maintaining a facade when the code and the DSL are both under active development.

Now let's consider the effect of changing the syntax.

9.2.3 *Implications of modifying the DSL syntax*

Modifying the syntax is generally what comes to mind when people think about versioning a DSL. This seems to be the most obvious place where incompatibilities may occur, after all.

Indeed, this *is* a troublesome spot, which requires careful attention to detail (and a robust regression test suite). We'll look at how to deal with it in detail when we discuss versioning strategies in section 9.4. There are quite a few tools that can help us deal with this issue.

That's about it from the point of view of changes that can affect the DSL. But we should consider one other thing that may change over time and that can certainly cause incompatibilities down the road—the DSL environment.

9.2.4 *Implications of modifying the DSL environment*

The DSL environment is as much a part of the DSL as its syntax, but it's easy to forget that. So easy, in fact, that I forgot to include it in the first draft of this chapter. We talked about the DSL environment in chapter 5. It includes everything from the naming convention, to the script ordering, to where you execute each DSL script.

Let's look at an example system where a DSL is used to provide additional business behavior. The DSL scripts are located in the following hierarchy:

```
▲ Account
  ▲ Create
      Generate Account Id.boo
      Send New Account Greeting.boo
  ▲ Delete
      Send Goodbye Note.boo
  ▲ Update
▲ Order
  ▲ Create
      Generate Order Id.boo
  ▲ Delete
  ▲ Update
```

As you can see, this system uses the filesystem structure to associate an event to the script that should run when that event fires. It has been humming along nicely, and the client is happy. Along comes version 2.0 of the DSL, and we know that we haven't touched any of the DSL code, so we can safely expect to run all the application tests and have them work. Except, version 2.0 renamed Account to Client, and we haven't made the same modification to the DSL directory. I'll leave you to guess what happens.

Or consider modifying the way the Authorization DSL determines the ordering of rules for a particular action. That can wreak havoc with the system, but it's unlikely to cause a problem with the DSL itself, or to reveal itself in any test that verifies the behavior of a single script.

If you want to detect such issues, you need to have a good regression test suite. Incidentally, that's our next topic.

9.3   *Building a regression test suite*

If you want to have a good versioning story, you need to have a good regression test suite. If you don't have one yet, you need to build one before you start working on the next version. Otherwise, you have no real way to know whether your changes are safe or not.

A regression test suite should include the following:

- Tests for the engine
- Tests for the API and model that are exposed to the DSL
- Tests for the syntax
- Tests that verify that the conventions used are kept

This regression test suite is usually the product of developing your DSL in a test-driven manner, or even by testing all the aspects of the DSL after you have built it.

It's important that these tests be automated, and that any breaking test should raise a compatibility alert, because such alerts mean that you're no longer compatible with the previous version.

In addition, the best-case scenario is to have test cases for each of the scripts you have created for the DSL. You can incorporate all of those tests into your regression test suite, and be very confident that you will be able to detect compatibility issues between versions.

Failing that, you can create a set of regression tests that mimic common functionality in the existing scripts. Those tests are full integration tests of the entire DSL implementation, and they should exercise as many of the supported language features as possible.

With a regression test suite in place, you can start making modifications to your DSL, knowing that if any compatibility issues arise, you will be alerted to them. The question is how to *deal* with them.

9.4 *Choosing a versioning strategy*

By now, you've probably realized that versioning is neither easy nor simple. It takes both time and effort to ensure that your DSL remains consistent from one version to the next. As such, you need to carefully consider whether the changes are worth the cost.

If you have a DSL that's in limited distribution with a limited number of scripts and a well-known (and small) number of users, you may decide that it isn't worth taking the time to have a formal versioning strategy, and just deal with any issues when they pop up. In most cases, however, you will care about making the migration to the next version easy. You can use the following strategies to manage your DSL versioning story:

- Abandon ship
- Single shot
- Additive change
- Tower of Babel
- Adapter
- Great migration

We will discuss them in turn here and then spend section 9.5 applying the theory with real code and examples.

9.4.1 *Abandon-ship strategy*

The abandon-ship strategy is also known as, "Versioning? We don't need no stinking versioning." It's extremely simple. You don't do any sort of versioning. Any problems with scripts as a result of updating the DSL are considered to be bugs in the scripts and are fixed there.

What this usually means is that after modifying the DSL, you test all your existing scripts and update them as necessary. For many scenarios, this is the preferred approach, because it has the best return on investment.

This isn't applicable if you have a large number of scripts, or if you need to support scripts that you don't control. If, for example, you used the DSL to allow other teams, business experts, or even third parties to extend your application, it isn't applicable.

9.4.2 *Single-shot strategy*

The single-shot strategy is also known as, "You've got only one shot at making this work, so make it work *right!*" In this case, you only have one chance to build the DSL. Once you've built it and people have started using it, no changes of any sort can be made to the DSL.

As a versioning strategy, it has the benefits of being ironclad; you *know* that you won't have any compatibility issues. But it leaves a lot to be desired in terms of allowing you to deal with changing requirements and the need to update your software. I would rarely call this a viable approach. I would seek a better alternative.

9.4.3   *Additive-change strategy*

The additive-change strategy is the most common approach, by far, to handling language versioning—all the mainstream languages (C#, C++, Java, and so on) use this strategy to maintain backward compatibility. By using this model, you can ensure that if the code was correct in a previous version, it's correct for any future version.

You can ensure this in two ways:

- Run a full regression suite for all supported scenarios and never allow a change to break them. If there's a scenario that users are using and that isn't in the regression suite, you might get a compatibility error, but you could treat that as a bug and fix it (and then add the scenario to the regression suite).
- Only ever perform additive changes. If you only ever add new things to the language, and never remove anything, you'll greatly reduce the chances of creating breaking changes.

Version numbering

One way of handling versioning is to ensure backward compatibility within a major version of the software, but not guaranteeing backward compatibility between major versions. For example, if you have version 1.0, revisions 1.1, 1.5, and 1.8 are all backward compatible. But version 2.0 isn't necessarily backward compatible with the 1.x versions.

This version-numbering system is widely used and is easy to follow. It has the advantage of making it clear what expectations you have for backward compatibility. It also provides a guideline for features. If you can't provide a new feature without breaking backward compatibility, that feature will have to wait until the next major version. If you can provide it without breaking backward compatibility, it can go into the next revision (1.1, for example).

This approach has its limits. Over time, it adds significantly to the complexity of the language, on both implementation and usage fronts. Sooner or later, the point of diminishing returns is reached, and further progress is extremely difficult. There is little doubt that Java, for example, has either reached this point or is near it. Most of the new language features that pop up in the Java world aren't based on Java, but on other languages (such as JRuby and Groovy) running on the JVM. C++, interestingly enough, has not reached this point, even though it's significantly older.

You probably don't have the same use case as Java, so you can push it further if you choose, but this is a major issue with this approach, and you need some way of handling it eventually.

The additive-change strategy is the recommended approach for starting out, because although it adds some complexity, it takes time for that to become onerous. Only when you have a radical change or have hit the ceiling of complexity do you need to look at other strategies to deal with versioning.

9.4.4 Tower of Babel strategy

The Tower of Babel strategy deals with the versioning problem head on, instead of avoiding dealing with it. This approach is applicable for radical changes; if you have lesser changes to make, you should prefer the additive-change strategy.

Broadly, this approach consists of never modifying a released version of a DSL. Once you ship version 1.0, it's frozen and can't be changed. When you

Figure 9.1   Handling versioning using the Tower of Babel strategy

build version 2.0, you start from a copy of version 1.0 and modify it until you get to shipping version 2.0, at which point it's frozen. Then you work on a copy of version 2.0 until you ship 3.0. And so on. Figure 9.1 illustrates this approach.

This closely follows the way a source control system works, with each version representing a parallel branch. It also ensures that scripts that worked in the past will continue to work in the future; you won't be burdened with the heavy weight of backward compatibility concerns.

Unlike the additive-change strategy, you aren't limited to additive changes between versions; each version is free to have breaking changes from the previous one. All versions of the DSL exist concurrently, and each script contains the version of the DSL that it was written against. When you execute a script, you choose the appropriate version of the language based on the DSL version that the script was written to.

Using the Tower of Babel strategy does pose a problem. Because several versions of the DSL may be in use at the same time, you need to select which version of the DSL you'll execute for a given DSL script.

IDENTIFYING SCRIPT VERSIONS

There are various ways to identify which DSL version a particular script is written for, but I like to use extensions for this purpose. Here are a few examples:

- *some-dsl-script.quote-generator*—A quote-generator DSL, version 1.0
- *some-dsl-script.quote-generator-2*—A quote-generator DSL, version 2.0
- *some-dsl-script.quote-generator-3*—A quote-generator DSL, version 3.0

When you want to execute a particular script, you can check the extension and select the appropriate version of the DSL factory to create an instance of the script.

Another approach is to encode the version using a folder-hierarchy convention:

```
▲ 📁 Quote-generator
  ▲ 📁 1.0
      📄 some-dsl-script
  ▲ 📁 2.0
      📄 some-dsl-script
  ▲ 📁 3.0
      📄 some-dsl-script
```

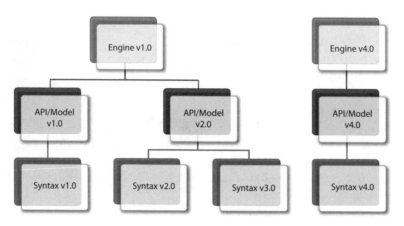

Figure 9.2   The copy-on-change alternative to the Tower of Babel strategy

There are probably other approaches that you could use, but these make the most sense and they're easier to implement in most scenarios. They're also the ones that make the most sense from the end user's perspective, because they clearly identify the script's version.

There is one big disadvantage to this Tower of Babel strategy. It makes code duplication a design choice.

CODE DUPLICATION

Code duplication is considered harmful for many reasons. Chief among them is that when you make a change in a code base that has duplicate code (such as when fixing a bug) you need to make the modification in several places.

A variation on the Tower of Babel strategy is to only create a copy of the code you're modifying (the copy-on-change approach). In this case, you'll end up with the situation depicted in figure 9.2.

I want to emphasize that both alternatives are valid design choices, because you literally freeze a version (or parts of a version). You aren't employing copy and paste as a reuse technique.

But this approach still makes me feel somewhat uncomfortable. A better approach is still waiting to be discovered …

9.4.5   *Adapter strategy*

The adapter strategy is just what it sounds like. Instead of duplicating the entire language code for each version, you create adapters between the existing version and the new version. When you make a breaking change in the language, you change the processing for the current version of the language so it preserves the same behavior as in the previous version, but it uses the new version of the engine and model. This approach is applicable for radical changes; again, if you're making non-radical changes, you should prefer the additive-change strategy.

As you can see in figure 9.3, an old version of the language consists of the syntax and an adapter to the current version. This is another common approach used by mainstream languages (check out the nearest C++ compiler switches).

This strategy has the following workflow:

- Modify the existing language to meet the new requirements.
- Take the existing regression tests for version 1.0 and create an adapter that will satisfy them.

The version 1.0 language is now a new DSL for mapping between the version 1.0 and 2.0 syntaxes. You can build it the same way you'd build any DSL. You just need to keep in mind that the purpose is to adapt, not to do anything else.

This adaptation can be done at runtime or at compilation time.

Adapting a DSL version at runtime mostly consists of modifying the API and model facade for version 1.0 to map calls and concepts to the API and model of version 2.0. This is simple to do in most cases, as shown in figure 9.4.

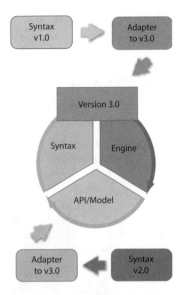

Figure 9.3 The adapter strategy consists of keeping the existing behavior as a facade and adapting it to match the next version.

Figure 9.4
Adapting DSL
versions at runtime

In general, runtime adaptation is the preferred approach, but it isn't always possible (usually, when you have drastic changes between versions). In that case, you need to consider using an adapter implementation that works during compilation. This lets you modify the output more directly and produce a syntax that looks like version 1.0 but that works directly against version 2.0 of the DSL, as illustrated in figure 9.5. This tends to be more work than the runtime adaptation approach, but it offers more options.

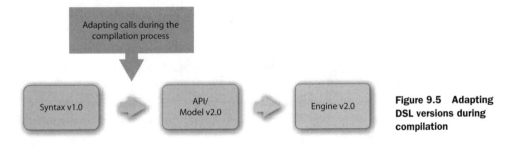

Figure 9.5 Adapting
DSL versions during
compilation

We've now looked at how to make a new version of the engine accept scripts written for the old version, but we've only briefly touched on going in the other direction: changing old scripts to match the new version of the DSL.

9.4.6   *The great-migration strategy*

We discussed the possibility of updating all your scripts to match the new DSL version (the abandon-ship strategy, in section 9.4.1), but that's only practical if you can update all the scripts. This often isn't possible, but there is another way of handling this: automatic updates.

> **Migrations**
>
> The database world faces a similar problem of change management and versioning. Some of the strategies that were developed to deal with the problem are similar to those discussed here (the additive-change strategy is a common approach).
>
> One of the more interesting strategies developed for databases is the migration. A migration describes the differences between two database versions, allowing you to move between any two versions by applying the differences to the database.
>
> In essence, the great-migration strategy is an application of the same idea, of automatically moving a DSL script from one version to another. If you choose this approach for versioning, I strongly recommend that you come up with a way to describe the differences between DSL versions and have an engine apply them to the script.
>
> Implementing this is beyond the scope of this book, but I'll point you to Boo's quasi-quotation and the BooPrinter compiler step, which will allow you to parse a file into an AST, change the AST, and then print the AST back to Boo code.

Imagine having a migration wizard that automatically updates scripts from one DSL version to the next. This would allow you to update even a large number of scripts quickly, and you could offer it to third parties so that they could update their scripts before deploying the new DSL version. This is a good solution, because it allows you to keep forging forward with the DSL, without being hindered by backward-compatibility concerns.

Unfortunately, this approach also has its own set of issues:

- Developing a migration wizard that can handle real-world DSL usage can be complex.
- You need some way to ensure that the before and after behavior of scripts is consistent. For example, you might also need to update tests during the migration process.
- Automatic migration means automatic code generation, and that's rarely a good way of getting concise, easy-to-read and understand code. It can be done, but it's not easy.

My favorite approach for handling this is to parse the version 1.0 DSL script into an AST, adapt it to the version 2.0 approach, and save it.

The major difference between this approach and the adapter strategy (shown in section 9.4.5) is that migrations will explicitly move you to the new version, whereas, with an adapter, you keep the old syntax around, so for version 3.0 you would need to map version 1.0 concepts to version 3.0 concepts. I find it easier when there's only a single version boundary to bridge.

Because this is a common use case for adding graphical interfaces on top of textual DSLs, I'll not go over the technique here, but rather point you to section 10.4 in chapter 10. We'll talk about persisting in-memory DSL models to a file.

And that's quite enough theory. It's time to see how those versioning strategies are used.

9.5 Applying versioning strategies

Before we start applying versioning strategies, let's look at what we're going to change.

We'll create a new version of the Quote-Generation DSL, adding the following features:

- A set of new operations: minimum memory and minimum CPU counts
- An explanation for the `requires` operation

Listing 9.2 shows an example script that uses the current version of the DSL.

> **Listing 9.2 A script using the current version of the Quote-Generation DSL**

```
specification @vacations:
    requires @scheduling_work
    requires @external_connections

specification @salary:
    users_per_machine 150

specification @taxes:
    users_per_machine 50

specification @pension:
    same_machine_as @health_insurance
```

We'll start by adding new operations.

9.5.1 Managing safe, additive changes

Adding a new operation is generally a safe change, because you don't modify the language; you merely extend it. Anything that used to work will continue to work.

The requirement is to support operations that specify minimum memory and minimum CPU counts. As usual, we start by considering the desired syntax. The simplest and most elegant solution for the problem is this (new syntax is shown in bold):

```
specification @taxes:
    users_per_machine 50
```

```
min_memory 2048
min_cpu_count 2
```

This is a clear indication of what we want, so we'll go with this approach. We'll implement this change in small steps.

The first step is to run all the tests for the Quote-Generation DSL, and ensure they all pass. Next, we can start defining the test scripts. Listing 9.3 shows them.

Listing 9.3   Test scripts for the new changes in the Quote-Generation DSL

```
# UsingMinCpu.boo
specification @taxes:
    users_per_machine 50
    min_cpu_count 2

# UsingMinMemory.boo
specification @taxes:
    users_per_machine 50
    min_memory 2048
```

Now we can write the tests for the script in listing 9.3, as shown in listing 9.4.

Listing 9.4   Tests for the new functionality in the Quote-Generation DSL

```
[Test]
public void Can_specify_min_memory()
{
    var rule = dslFactory.Create<QuoteGeneratorRule>(
        @"Quotes/UsingMinMemory.boo",
        new RequirementsInformation(49, "taxes"));
    rule.Evaluate();
    Assert.AreEqual(2048, rule.Modules[0].MinMemory);
}

[Test]
public void Can_specify_min_cpu_count()
{
    var rule = dslFactory.Create<QuoteGeneratorRule>(
        @"Quotes/UsingMinCpu.boo",
        new RequirementsInformation(49, "taxes"));
    rule.Evaluate();
    Assert.AreEqual(2, rule.Modules[0].MinCpuCount);
}
```

Now that we have the tests, we can start implementing the changes. We first add the `MinCpuCount` and `MinMemory` properties to the Quote-Generation DSL's `System-Module`, as shown in listing 9.5.

Listing 9.5   Additions to the Quote-Generation DSL's implicit base class

```
// on QuoteGeneratorRule.cs
public void min_memory(int minMemory)
{
    currentModule.MinMemory = minMemory;
}
```

```
public void min_cpu_count(int minCpuCount)
{
    currentModule.MinCpuCount = minCpuCount;
}
```

Now we can run all the tests to ensure that the new and old functionality both work and that we haven't got any regressions.

As you can imagine, the chance of introducing a breaking change using this approach is small if you're careful to make only additions, never modifications, to the code. If you do need to modify existing code to support the new functionality, keep it to a minimum and have tests in place to ensure that the observed behavior of the code isn't changed.

The change here was easy to make in a safe way, but not all changes are like that. Let's look at a change that requires modifying behavior in a way that results in a breaking change.

9.5.2 *Handling required breaking change*

In version 1.0 of the Quote-Generation DSL, the code in listing 9.6 is valid.

> **Listing 9.6 Valid version 1.0 Quote-Generation DSL script**

```
specification @vacations:
    requires @scheduling_work
    requires @external_connections
```

When starting to work with the Quote-Generation DSL for real, though, we discover a problem: it isn't clear why a particular module is required. Trying to figure out why certain modules were required in certain configurations increases costs for the organization. We decide to request a reason, in the form of a human-readable string, when requiring a module. This will make it clear why a certain module is required, without any extensive debugging or effort. The benefits of better audit information are worth the costs associated with updating all the rules.

We want something similar to listing 9.7.

> **Listing 9.7 Adding explanations to the Quote-Generation DSL**

```
specification @vacations:
    requires @scheduling_work, "We need to schedule vacations as well"
    requires @external_connections, "Needed in order to reserve places"
```

This is a easy change. Listing 9.8 shows the test for this feature.

> **Listing 9.8 Test that verifies explanation is attached to a requirement**

```
[Test]
public void Can_specify_a_reasoning_for_requiring_a_module()
{
    var rule = dslFactory.Create<QuoteGeneratorRule>(
        @"Quotes/WithRequiresExplanation.boo",
        new RequirementsInformation(49, "vacations"));
```

```
rule.Evaluate();

Assert.AreEqual("We need to schedule vacations as well",
    rule.Modules[0].RequirementsExplanations["scheduling_work"]);
Assert.AreEqual("Needed in order to reserve places",
    rule.Modules[0].RequirementsExplanations["external_connections"]);
}
```

The implementation is just as simple. Adding a `RequirementsExplanations` dictionary to the `SystemModule` and modifying the `requires()` method is shown in listing 9.9.

Listing 9.9   The modification to support explanations for required modules

```
public void requires(string moduleName, string explanation)
{
    currentModule.Requirements.Add(moduleName);
    currentModule.RequirementsExplanations.Add(moduleName, explanation);
}
```

That only took a few minutes, and we're done. We need to update the tests as well, but once that's done, we're ready to release it to user testing. Right?

Well, it's not that simple. Here's a bug report that this change would cause:

```
Boo.Lang.Compiler.CompilerError : simple.boo(2,5): BCE0017:
Boo.Lang.Compiler.CompilerError: The best overload for the method
BDSLiB.QuoteGeneration.QuoteGeneratorRule.requires(string, string)' is not
 compatible with the argument list '(string)'.
```

And that bug is not alone. The issue is that there's no association between the compiler error and the action that the user needs to take. We need better error handling.

We have an existing infrastructure in the .NET platform for handling such scenarios. It's called `System.ObsoleteAttribute`. We can use it as shown in listing 9.10.

Listing 9.10   Using the `Obsolete` attribute in your DSL

```
[Obsolete("use requires(moduleName, explanation) instead", true)]
public void requires(string moduleName)
{
    throw new NotSupportedException();
}
```

Here's the result from trying to execute an old version of the scripts:

```
BCE0144: Boo.Lang.Compiler.CompilerError:
'BDSLiB.QuoteGeneration.QuoteGeneratorRule.requires(string)' is obsolete.
use requires(moduleName, explanation) instead
```

This is a good, low-cost approach, but although this is much better than the original error, we can do better.

What we'll do is create a meta-method that matches the old `requires()` signature, and generate a compiler error or a warning with context about the issue. Listing 9.11 shows such an example.

Listing 9.11   Generating context-sensitive compiler errors

```
[Meta]
public static Expression requires(Expression moduleName)
{
    var message = @"
Requiring a module without supplying an explanation is not allowed.
Please use the following syntax:
'requires " + moduleName + "', '" + moduleName +
@" is required because...";
    CompilerContext.Current.Errors.Add(
            new CompilerError(moduleName.LexicalInfo, message));

    // Map to the correct call, by output call to
    // requires(string, string), which is useful if I want a warning
    // not an error
    return new MethodInvocationExpression
    {
        Target = new ReferenceExpression("requires"),
        Arguments = new ExpressionCollection
        {
            moduleName,
            new StringLiteralExpression("No explanation specified")
        }
    };
}
```

Now, when we execute an invalid script on this system, we'll get the following error:

```
BCE0000: Boo.Lang.Compiler.CompilerError:
Requiring a module without supplying an explanation is not allowed.
Please use the following syntax:
'requires 'scheduling_work', 'scheduling_work' is required because...'
```

I think you'll agree that this is a much better error message to give to the user.

We have two different approaches for handling the deprecated requires signature. We can either completely fail to compile this by creating a compiler error, as we've seen in listing 9.11, or we can emit a warning about it. We can do this by modifying the code in listing 9.10—change the second attribute parameter to false. In listing 9.11, change Errors.Add(new CompilerError()) to Warnings.Add(new CompilerWarning(). We could also use [Obsolete] as a warning flag and forward the call to the new requires method overload at runtime. Or we could do the same using the Meta method.

We've given the user a much better error message, but what if there are 15,000 scripts to update? At this point, it's a business decision about whether or not to update all of those. A person would have to go over each and every one of them, reverse engineer those scripts, and figure the business reasoning behind them. That's a long and expensive process, and businesses will often abort the attempt. But the decision to go ahead with this or not should be driven by business considerations, not by technical ones.

Accommodating both options

In many cases, you'll need to accommodate both options, at least for a certain period of time. Using warnings instead of errors is a good way to start. You could add warning handling to the DSL environment (in the editor, for example).

You could also add logging to the DSL so you can track troublesome scripts and pinpoint scripts that haven't been converted. A crazy option would be to have the compiler email the script author a request to update the script whenever the script is compiled. This might motivate users to update their scripts, but I suggest moving far away before you load this into production.

We've discussed several examples of implementing versioning in our systems. Let's see how it's done in some real-world projects.

9.6   *DSL versioning in the real world*

In the real world, there are much harsher constraints than I have outlined so far. The DSL changes and business implications described in section 9.5.2 are only a few of the constraints you'll have to deal with when you release your DSL into the wild and need to support new versions. In this section, we'll look at the versioning strategies of three different DSLs, all of them used in the wild by third parties, and at how each has dealt with versioning over time.

9.6.1   *Versioning Brail*

Brail is a text-templating language based on Boo that's primarily used in MVC frameworks. Brail was born as a view engine for the Castle MonoRail MVC framework, and there is a version available for the ASP.NET MVC framework as well. The initial release of the language (then called Boo on Rails) was in July 2005. Since then, it has been actively developed, and new features and versions have come out at a regular pace.

Brail is used by a wide variety of people, for a large number of scripts, so any breaking changes in the language have significant implications for all users. Because of that, major efforts have been made to ensure that every feature of the language is covered with tests, and, as a general rule, a change that breaks the tests doesn't get into the language.

Over time, there have been a few cases where a change has broken functionality that people were relying on. They were treated as bugs, regression test cases were created, the bug was fixed, and Brail was re-released. In this case, backward compatibility is the Holy Grail. If there is a choice between a new feature and a breaking change, the new feature is dropped.

Not all languages are treated this way. Let's examine a different approach.

9.6.2   *Versioning Binsor*

Binsor has been around since September 2006. It's a configuration DSL for the popular IoC Castle Windsor container. In fact, it started life somewhere around March

2006, but it took a while for the idea to come to fruition. Binsor has been actively developed ever since, and has had several major releases since its inception.

One of the major differences between Brail and Binsor is that Binsor scripts tend to be far fewer in number than Brail templates. Where a typical application can have a minimum of a few dozen Brail templates (and I have seen applications with hundreds and thousands), most applications where Binsor is used have only a small number of Binsor scripts, typically one or two. As such, the effect of a breaking change is much less severe. It's feasible to modify the scripts if necessary.

The versioning approach for Binsor is much more lax than the one used for Brail, but that isn't to say that breaking changes are acceptable. Breaking changes are still a hassle to deal with, and they should be avoided. But given a good enough reason, breaking changes do and will occur. They tend to be small and focused to limit their effects, but they exist.

This is the middle road, and it works well when your next version has a high level of fidelity to the previous version. Now let's consider the case where there's a high level of change.

9.6.3 *Versioning Rhino ETL*

Rhino ETL is a project that started in July 2007. It aims to be a programmer-friendly extract-transform-load (ETL) tool. It's textual, concise, and rather nice, if I say so myself. The current version has two sets of APIs, so you can write client code in C# or use a DSL to gain additional clarity. The first version relied heavily on the DSL alone, and was not accessible outside the DSL.

Shortly after Rhino ETL was first released, several issues were identified that made it hard to deal with. These specifically related to the way you would debug scripts and the entire ETL process. There were also performance problems related to the way the project moved data around. These interesting problems necessitated the need for a new version.

A new model was chosen for the new version—one that was more performant and scalable—and the decision was made to ensure that the API would be accessible from both C# and the DSL. That caused significant issues for backward compatibility. Because of the youthfulness of the tool, it wasn't that much of a problem, but even if it had been, there was no easy way to reconcile the differences between the two models.

Listing 9.12 shows the original syntax of Rhino ETL, and listing 9.13 shows the current syntax. Both listings perform the same task.

Listing 9.12 The original syntax of Rhino ETL

```
import file from connections.retl

source UsersSource, Connection="Connection":
    Command: "SELECT Id, Name, Email FROM Users_Source"

transform SplitName:
    Row.FirstName = Row.Name.Split(char(' '))[0]
    Row.LastName = Row.Name.Split(char(' '))[1]
```

```
destination UsersDestination, Connection = "Connection":
    Command: """INSERT INTO Users_Destination
                (UserId, [First Name], [Last Name], Email)
                VALUES (@Id, @FirstName, @LastName, @Email)
            """
pipeline CopyUsers:
    UsersSource >> SplitName
    SplitName >> UsersDestination

target default:
    Execute("CopyUsers")
```

Listing 9.13 The current syntax of Rhino ETL

```
operation split_name:
    for row in rows:
        continue if row.Name is null
        row.FirstName = row.Name.Split()[0]
        row.LastName = row.Name.Split()[1]
        yield row

process UsersToPeople:
    input "test", Command = "SELECT id, name, email  FROM Users"
    split_name()
    output "test", Command = """
        INSERT INTO People (UserId, FirstName, LastName, Email)
        VALUES (@UserId, @FirstName, @LastName, @Email)
        """:
        row.UserId = row.Id
```

As you can see, there are significant differences between the two. I don't want to get into a comparison of the two models, but there are differences not just in the syntax, but in the ideas that they represent.

This is a good example of a situation when the abandon-ship strategy was used to the benefit of all. When there is a radical model change, it's much easier to start from a blank slate and end up with a DSL that closely represents the model rather trying to shoehorn one model into another.

If you have existing clients relying on the old behavior, it may be beneficial to retain the old system for a while, or to write an adapter from the old system to the new, but in general the old system should be retired as soon as is practical.

So far we've talked a lot about versioning scenarios, but we haven't touched on one important concept. *When* should we version?

9.7   *When to version*

A versioning boundary is the point at which you decide you need to start worrying about versioning. In general, there are two types of these boundaries that you should care about: the first one, and all the rest.

Until you reach the first cutoff point, you have no versioning concerns. After that point, which is typically associated with a 1.0 release of the software, you need to start considering versioning with each decision that you make.

At the same time, you don't need to care about the versioning of anything new that you create until you reach the next boundary. None of the changes you make from versions 1.0 to 2.0 have versioning implications until you've released 2.0. This is important when it comes to considering the regression suite. You shouldn't include tests there for new features—not until they have been released and instantly become regression tests that you must never break or change.

Deciding when to define a versioning boundary is important, and something that should be made explicit in the tests and the release process. Otherwise you might trigger regression bugs (typically of higher priority than standard bugs, and there is a lot more consideration involved before making a change to a regression test).

9.8 *Summary*

In this chapter, we looked at how to ensure the longevity of our languages and how to help them survive and prosper from one version to the next. Of particular importance are the tests and regression test suite, which ensure that existing behavior isn't changed in an incompatible way, breaking client scripts.

We also considered the implications of versioning on the design and implementation of DSLs. In particular, facades are important in separating the DSL from the application's model and API, allowing them to be developed independently. This separation goes a bit further than merely a facade. It can ensure that the DSL engine is usable even without the DSL.

This seems like a strange requirement, but it's an important one. You want to be able to modify the engine without modifying the DSL, and vice versa. In addition, you might want to have several dialects of the same language (typically several versions) based on the same engine. This tends to be difficult or impossible if there isn't a good degree of isolation between the two.

Finally, the DSL environment (evaluation order, invocation call sites, and naming conventions) and its implication on versioning are something that most people tend to forget about, until they find out how critical it is for the usage of the language.

We walked through several versioning strategies, from always starting fresh, to allowing no changes, to languages with multiple versions, and even automatic migration tools. We also applied a few of those strategies to the Quote-Generation DSL. Then we saw how real-world DSLs have dealt with the versioning problem, and how various constraints led to the different choices that were made.

Versioning is a big topic, and there isn't enough room in a single chapter to cover it all. Most of the guidance about versioning is directly applicable for APIs as well, and I strongly recommend referring to other sources to learn more about this topic. One interesting source is the *.NET Framework Standard Library Annotated Reference*, volume 1, by Brad Abrams (Addison Wesley Professional), where you can see how much attention was paid to versioning concerns.

At this point, we're surely ready to release our DSL to the world, right? Well, from the technical perspective, certainly. But we're still missing something: a bit of shine, a hint of polish. Creating a DSL is easy, but making it slick and professional is another matter. That's what we'll spend the next chapter discussing.

Creating a professional UI for a DSL

In this chapter

- Creating an IDE for your DSL
- Integrating an IDE into your application
- Displaying DSL execution
- DSL code generation

We've talked about building DSLs, structuring them, adding advanced language options to them, integrating them into our applications, creating unit tests, and even creating test languages. We even looked at versioning them after they were in production. We can create working DSLs, and quite useful ones, but creating a professional-level DSL takes a bit more. Sometimes it takes a *lot* more.

A professional DSL is composed of more than the language's code; it also includes the DSL environment, the tools that are provided, and the overall experience of using it. That generally means some sort of an IDE, and it also means a greater investment in the tooling that you provide.

The IDE is usually the least of your worries. It's the overall tooling that should concern you. For simple DSLs, you can get away with editing the language in

Notepad, and managing everything on your own. For more complex DSLs, you have to provide additional tool support to make the DSL easier to use.

We'll use the Quote-Generation DSL as our example for this chapter. This DSL is a rule engine, at its heart. This implies that we're going to have a lot of rules: 15,000 rules is a figure from one real-world quote-generation system. Even managing hundreds of rules is a challenge, and we need to consider that when we build the DSL. The approach we have right now, of keeping a set of files in a directory, obviously isn't going to scale to that level. The DSL could handle it, but the complexity of managing it is too cumbersome. And that's only considering the naming issues.

An additional problem we'll face is tracing. Suppose we don't like the quote we get for a certain scenario, and we need to understand how the DSL came up with it. We can't physically debug 15,000 scripts in any reasonable amount of time, so we need another way of handling that. Usually, this means tracing, which involves active cooperation from the DSL itself.

Furthermore, although the textual representation of a DSL has a lot of advantages (such as clarity, and the ability to use source control and grep), it's often advantageous to have a graphical representation as well. It can be clearer in some situations, it might help sell the DSL, or it could be used as a full-fledged editable view of the DSL.

Last, but not least, you might need to provide an IDE environment for your application, with syntax highlighting and code completion. We'll start with this topic first, because this is likely what you're most interested in.

10.1 Creating an IDE for a DSL

An IDE can make or break your DSL in terms of acceptance. Regardless of anything else, having an IDE available implies a high level of dedication to this DSL, and thus a high- quality product.

As it turns out, creating an IDE is not that difficult. We'll look at several off-the-shelf components, but before we do, take a look at figure 10.1. It shows a trivial implementation of syntax highlighting for the Quote-Generation DSL.

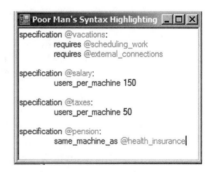

You probably won't be able to see the difference all that clearly in the figure, but the keywords have different syntax highlighting. It's easy to create basic effects like this, as the code in listing 10.1 shows, but the complexity grows significantly if you decide to roll your own IDE without using existing components.

Figure 10.1
Hand-rolled syntax highlighting

Listing 10.1   Implementing hand-rolled syntax highlighting

```
private void codeTextBox_TextChanged(object sender, EventArgs e)
{
    // Save current selection
```

```
int prevSelectionStart = codeTextBox.SelectionStart;
int prevSelectionLength = codeTextBox.SelectionLength;

// Reset coloring
codeTextBox.SelectionStart = 0;
codeTextBox.SelectionLength = codeTextBox.TextLength;
codeTextBox.SelectionColor = DefaultForeColor;

// Define keywords
var keyWords = new[] { "specification", "requires",
                       "users_per_machine", "same_machine_as" };
foreach (string keyWord in keyWords)
{
    // Match keywords using regex and color them
    MatchCollection matches = Regex.Matches(codeTextBox.Text, keyWord);
    foreach (Match match in matches)
    {
        codeTextBox.SelectionStart = match.Index;
        codeTextBox.SelectionLength = match.Length;
        codeTextBox.SelectionColor = Color.DarkOrchid;
    }
}

// Match references ( @name ) and color them
foreach (Match match in Regex.Matches(codeTextBox.Text, @"@[\w\d_]+"))
{
    codeTextBox.SelectionStart = match.Index;
    codeTextBox.SelectionLength = match.Length;
    codeTextBox.SelectionColor = Color.DarkSeaGreen;
}

// Find numbers and color them
foreach (Match match in Regex.Matches(codeTextBox.Text, @" \d+"))
{
    codeTextBox.SelectionStart = match.Index;
    codeTextBox.SelectionLength = match.Length;
    codeTextBox.SelectionColor = Color.DarkRed;
}

// Reset selection
codeTextBox.SelectionStart = prevSelectionStart;
codeTextBox.SelectionLength = prevSelectionLength;
}
```

I will say up front that the code in listing 10.1 suffers from multiple bugs, issues, and is generally not suited for anything but the simplest scenarios. Syntax highlighting can be done, but it generally suffers from far too much complexity to be useful.

I strongly suggest avoiding rolling your own components for this. The scope of the work is huge—much bigger than you would initially assume. You're far better off using an existing component, and you're probably already familiar with one called Visual Studio.

10.1.1 *Using Visual Studio as your DSL IDE*

Using Visual Studio as your DSL IDE seems ideal. It's a mature product with a lot of options and capabilities. With Visual Studio 2008, there is also the option of using

Visual Studio 2008 Shell, which allows you to plug your own language into the IDE. It's even freely redistributable, and you can create standalone applications that are based on Visual Studio (using isolated mode). For all intents and purposes, this seems like the ideal solution. But there are a few problems with this approach.

NOTE   Visual Studio 2010 promises much easier integration options, but I haven't had the chance to really take it for a spin, so I can't comment on how it compares with VS 2008 from the extensibility standpoint when adding a custom language.

First, Visual Studio isn't an embeddable solution. You can't add it as part of your own application. Second, and far more critical, the API that Visual Studio exposes is COM based (there is a managed API, but it's a thin wrapper) and it isn't friendly to use. In addition to that, Visual Studio assumes that if you host a language inside it you'll provide all the services that a language needs, and that's usually a far bigger task than you'll want to take on.

There are other issues, mostly related to the development and deployment of Visual Studio's language service, that make this more difficult than it might be. On the plus side, though, there's quite a lot of documentation on how to develop extensions for Visual Studio, and there are several screencasts on MSDN that can take you a long way.

There's also a project being developed that performs most of the work for you: Boo Lang Studio (http://codeplex.com/BooLangStudio) is an add-on for Visual Studio that provides Boo support in Visual Studio. It's an open source project, so you can take the code, modify it to fit your own language, and save a significant amount of time. The major detraction, from my point of view, is that you're forced into Visual Studio's way of working. You have an IDE in your hands, not an application that embeds a DSL editor. Depending on your needs, that might be exactly what you want, but I like having something that's lightweight in my hands. As we'll see in the rest of the chapter, creating a usable IDE for a DSL shouldn't take long. Using Visual Studio to do the same task takes an order of magnitude longer and is much more involved.

NOTE   As I write this, Boo Lang Studio hasn't been completed because of the difficulty of working with the Visual Studio API; it is currently waiting for the release of Visual Studio 2010 to see if developing a language service there will be easier.

Because of this issue, and the extensive information already available on Visual Studio, I won't discuss it further. If you're interested in this approach, though, you can start with the following two videos from MSDN and go from there:

- *How Do I: Create a Language Service?* http://msdn.microsoft.com/en-us/vstudio/bb851701.aspx
- *How Do I: Add Intellisense Functionality to My Language Service?* http://msdn.microsoft.com/en-us/vstudio/bb985513.aspx

If you choose to go with this approach, I strongly recommend using Boo Lang Studio as a base instead of starting from scratch.

If you don't like the full-blown Visual Studio approach, what other options are there?

10.1.2   *Using #develop as your DSL IDE*

Visual Studio isn't the only IDE that we can extend. We also have SharpDevelop (#develop).

#develop is an open source .NET IDE that provides a comparable experience to Visual Studio. Because #develop is built on .NET and doesn't have many years of legacy code behind it, it tends to be much easier to work with.

For example, setting up a new syntax highlighting scheme in Visual Studio involves building a lexer and parser. Setting up the same thing in #develop involves writing a simple (and readable) XML file. The Visual Studio approach is focused on providing maximum capabilities, whereas the #develop approach is focused on a low learning curve.

Like in Visual Studio, you can extend #develop to provide your own IDE experience. There's a free ebook, called *Dissecting a C# Application: Inside SharpDevelop*, that discusses the design and implementation of #develop in depth (available from http://damieng.com/blog/2007/11/08/dissecting-a-c-application-inside-sharpdevelop).

But again, building a complete IDE is something I'd like to avoid. #develop supports Boo natively, so you might be able to get away with providing #develop to your users as-is, perhaps with a customized syntax highlighting scheme (which is a simple XML file). But the scenario I want to focus on isn't building IDEs—it's integrating the DSL into your application. And for that, we don't need an IDE; we need an IDE component.

10.2   *Integrating an IDE with a DSL application*

The main difference between creating an IDE and integrating an IDE lies in the capabilities that you provide the user with. In the IDE scenario, you're providing the user with the tools to do development. In the integration scenario, you're allowing the user to work with the DSL.

This is an important difference, because it has big implications for your target audience. You would give an IDE to developers, but that isn't an appropriate tool to give to non-developers, and it doesn't demo as well as a tailored tool.

When you're working with code, syntax highlighting and code completion aren't something you want to build yourself, but there are existing packaged components that will do it for you. For example, the following IDE components can greatly ease creating an integrated editing experience inside your application:

- *Actipro SyntaxHighlighter*—On the commercial side, Actipro SyntaxHighlighter comes highly recommended. I haven't used it myself, but several people I trust have recommended it. It's available at http://www.actiprosoftware.com/Products/DotNet/WindowsForms/SyntaxEditor/Default.aspx.

- *#develop*—I have used #develop, and one of the nicer things about it is that you can extract pieces of the IDE and use them in your own application. In order to create an IDE for a DSL, you'll want to use the ICSharpCode.Text-Editor DLL, which contains the text editor and the baseline facilities to enable code completion.
- *AqiStar.TextBox*—For WPF applications, I can't say enough good things about AqiStar (http://www.aqistar.com/) text editor. It's similar to ICSharpCode.Text-Editor from the point of view of configuration (down to using the same XML syntax), it's simple to work with, and it provides all the features I require.

NOTE I will refer to the ICSharpCode.TextEditor component as #develop for the rest of this chapter. #develop is a .NET IDE that you can make use of in any .NET language, but more to the point, it comes prebuilt with support for Boo, which you can customize. #develop is open source and is provided under the LGPL license, so you can make use of it in commercial applications.

Listing 10.2 shows how you could use #develop to embed a syntax highlighting text-box into your application. Because #develop natively supports Boo, it's fairly easy to get the Boo syntax.

Listing 10.2 Embedding a Boo editor in our application

```
public class TextEditorForm : Form
{
    public TextEditorForm()
    {
        // Create a new text editor and add it to the form
        var editorControl = new TextEditorControl
        {
            Dock = DockStyle.Fill
        };
        Controls.Add(editorControl);
        // This controls how the editor handles indentation
        editorControl.Document.FormattingStrategy =
                new BooFormattingStrategy();
        // Set the syntax highlighting options
        editorControl.SetHighlighting("Boo");
    }
}

// This class was copied from #develop's Boo Binding
public class BooFormattingStrategy : DefaultFormattingStrategy
{
    // Disable the default way of handling lines
    public override void IndentLines(TextArea textArea, int begin, int end)
    {
    }

    // Indent the next line whenever the line ends with a colon
    protected override int SmartIndentLine(TextArea area, int line)
```

```
    {
        IDocument document = area.Document;
        LineSegment lineSegment = document.GetLineSegment(line - 1);
        if (document.GetText(lineSegment).EndsWith(":"))
        {
            LineSegment segment = document.GetLineSegment(line);
            string str = base.GetIndentation(area, line - 1)
                                    + Tab.GetIndentationString(document);
            document.Replace(segment.Offset, segment.Length, str
                    + document.GetText(segment));
            return str.Length;
        }
        return base.SmartIndentLine(area, line);
    }
}
```

The code in listing 10.2 is all you need. If you run this application, you'll get a working Boo editor that you can play around with, as shown in figure 10.2.

This is impressive, particularly when you consider that it takes less code to wire up the editor component than it took to (badly) handle syntax highlighting manually (in listing 10.1).

But this is still not enough. We have a Boo editor, but what we want is an editor for our DSL.

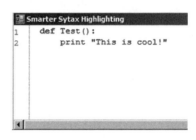

Figure 10.2   A standalone Boo editor

10.2.1   *Extending #develop highlighting for our DSLs*

I already mentioned that you can use XML to change the way the #develop TextEditor handles highlighting, so let's examine this in more depth.

Listing 10.3 shows a simplified version of the Boo language definition. (The full language definition is part of the #develop source code, and can also be found in the source code for this book.)

Listing 10.3   A simplified version of the Boo language definition

```xml
<?xml version="1.0"?>
<SyntaxDefinition name="Boo"
                  extensions=".boo">
  <Environment>
    <Default bold="false"
             italic="false"
             color="SystemColors.WindowText"
             bgcolor="SystemColors.Window" />
    <Selection bold="false"
               italic="false"
               color="SystemColors.HighlightText"
               bgcolor="SystemColors.Highlight" />
  </Environment>

  <Digits name="Digits"
          bold="false"
```

```
                italic="false"
                color="DarkBlue" />
    <RuleSets>
      <RuleSet ignorecase="false" >
        <Delimiters>
            &amp;&lt;&gt;~!@$%^*()-+=|\#/{}[]:;"' ,      .?
        </Delimiters>

        <Span name="LineComment"
              stopateol="true"
              bold="false"
              italic="false"
              color="Gray" >
          <Begin >#</Begin>
        </Span>

        <KeyWords name="JumpStatements"
                  bold="false"
                  italic="false"
                  color="Navy" >
          <Key word="break"/>
          <Key word="continue"/>
          <Key word="return"/>
          <Key word="yield"/>
          <Key word="goto" />
        </KeyWords>

      </RuleSet>
    </RuleSets>
</SyntaxDefinition>
```

Of particular interest in this listing is the way the syntax highlighting is defined. You
don't have to perform your own parsing; you can instead define the rules for parsing,
and #develop will figure out the parsing rules on its own.

For example, you can see how a LineComment is defined. That's how #develop
knows that # starts a line comment. Another example is defining keywords. All you
need to do is register them, and #develop will take it from there.

Armed with that knowledge, you can start extending the language definition to
support your own keywords. Doing so is as simple as adding the contents of listing 10.4
to the <RuleSet> element defined in the existing highlighting definition (in
listing 10.3).

Listing 10.4   Adding keywords to the language definition

```
<MarkFollowing markmarker="true"
               bold="false"
               italic="false"
               color="Purple">@</MarkFollowing>

<KeyWords name="DslKeywords"
          bold="false"
          italic="false"
          color="DarkOrange" >
```

```
    <Key word="specification"/>
    <Key word="users_per_machine"/>
    <Key word="requires"/>
    <Key word="same_machine_as"/>
</KeyWords>
```

When you do this, remember to change the language name, or you'll get naming collisions with the default Boo language. For example, I named my new language definition "dsl".

NOTE   When adding listing 10.4 to the existing Boo definition file (Boo.xshd), you need to place this code between the last `<MarkPrevious>` and the first `<KeyWords>` elements in the first ruleset in the file, in order to maintain the file schema.

The `<MarkFollowing>` tag is an interesting one. In listing 10.4, it paints all module references (such as @vacations) in purple. This tag will mark all non-delimiters (delimiters are specified in listing 10.3) following the at sign (@) with the appropriate color. It's surprisingly easy to plug everything together.

   To make the text editor recognize your language, you also need to modify listing 10.2 to register the new file. Listing 10.5 shows how to do this (replace the last line in the `TextEditorForm` constructor in listing 10.2 with the full text in listing 10.5). The results are shown in figure 10.3.

Listing 10.5   Registering the language definition and setting the highlighting strategy

```
HighlightingManager.Manager.AddSyntaxModeFileProvider(
    new FileSyntaxModeProvider(@"C:\Path\to\language\definition"));
//.. setup text editor
editorControl.SetHighlighting("dsl");
```

The full syntax definition is covered in depth in chapter 9 of *Dissecting a C# Application: Inside SharpDevelop*. I strongly suggest that you read it, and use the #develop forums, when creating UIs based on ICSharpCode.TextEditor.

   I hope that I have given you a sense of how easy it is to define the syntax highlighting rules and create a rich editor experience. Now let's look at code completion.

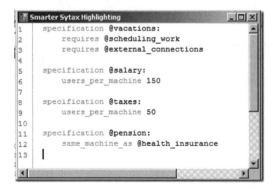

Figure 10.3   Custom keywords highlighting in action

10.2.2 *Adding code completion to our DSL*

Code completion is a killer feature that can make all the difference in using a language, but it's significantly more difficult to define than syntax highlighting rules. The main problem is that you need to deal with the current context.

Let's take a look at what code completion could do for the Quote-Generation DSL.

- On an empty line, show `specification`
- On a specification parameter, show all available modules
- On an empty line inside a specification block, show all actions (`requires`, `users_per_machine`, `same_machine_as`)
- On an action parameter, find appropriate values (available modules for the `requires` and `same_machine_as` actions, prespecified user counts for the `users_per_machine` action)

This doesn't even deal with code completion for the CLR API that we could use.

#develop offers the baseline facilities to deal with code completion, but the logic of deciding what goes where needs to be written, and you have to deal with it in some fashion. We will explore the facilities that #develop gives us for handling code completion in the following sections.

There are a couple of interesting infrastructure classes that we can make use of. First, there's the `CodeCompletionWindow`, which will display the members that the code completion code will suggest to the user. Next, there's the implementation of `ICompletionDataProvider`, which is how you provide #develop with the information to be displayed.

Listing 10.6 shows how you can hook up the code for code completion.

> ### You can't re-create Visual Studio in an hour
>
> The approach that I outline here will give you a functional IDE for a small cost. But if you're truly interested in a full-fledged IDE, rather than embedding DSL editing into the application, this isn't the approach you should take.
>
> Instead, you should focus on creating a language binding to either #develop or Visual Studio. Both already have base binding for Boo, which you can extend to map to your own language. But this is not a trivial task. Having the full Visual Studio experience will take a significant investment.

Listing 10.6 Hooking up the events to support code completion

```
private void RegisterCodeCompletionHandling()
{
    var textArea = editorControl.ActiveTextAreaControl.TextArea;
    textArea.KeyDown += delegate(object sender, KeyEventArgs e)
    {
        if (e.Control == false)
            return;
        if (e.KeyCode != Keys.Space)
            return;
```

```
            e.SuppressKeyPress = true;
            ShowCodeCompletion((char) e.KeyValue);
        };
}

private void ShowCodeCompletion(char value)
{
    ICompletionDataProvider completionDataProvider =
        new QuoteGenerationCodeCompletionProvider(intellisenseImageList);

    codeCompletionWindow = CodeCompletionWindow.ShowCompletionWindow(
        this, // The parent window for the completion window
        editorControl, // The text editor to show the window for
        "", // Filename - will be passed back to the provider
        completionDataProvider, // Provider to get the list of completions
        value // Key pressed - will be passed to the provider
        );
    if (codeCompletionWindow != null)
    {
        // ShowCompletionWindow can return null when the provider
        // returns an empty list
        codeCompletionWindow.Closed += CloseCodeCompletionWindow;
    }
}
```

The code in listing 10.6 registers to the KeyDown event and invokes code completion if Ctrl-Space is pressed. The ShowCodeCompletion() method is where we start to deal with the #develop code completion API.

We start by creating an instance of QuoteGenerationCodeCompletionProvider. This class is the heart of our code completion effort, and we'll discuss it shortly. For now, all you need to know is that it's where we decide what the user will be shown. Note that the intellisenseImageList is passed to the code completion provider so it can later show the list to the user using the code completion window. (Yes, the code completion provider and the code completion window work closely together.)

Next, we create the code completion window, which will call our code completion provider to check what needs to be done. The parameters for this should be fairly obvious.

Last, we register to close the window when needed.

That's about it for the common infrastructure. Now we need to start digging into QuoteGenerationCodeCompletionProvider. Figure 10.4 shows the interface that it implements. It has three properties:

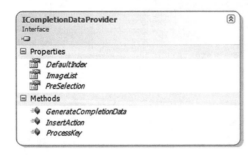

Figure 10.4   The ICompletionDataProvider is used by the #develop API to figure out how to show code completion information to the user.

- DefaultIndex—The index of the item you want to be selected in the list of suggestions you show the user.
- ImageList—The icons for the items in the list.
- PreSelection—This one is a bit complex to explain. Figure 10.5 shows an example of preselection.

Figure 10.5 How preselecting is presented to the user

Let's say that the user has invoked code completion and started to type. In the example in figure 10.5, the user typed "tos". The code completion provider has determined that a good match for that is the ToString method. The user selects that option and presses Enter.

At this point, inserting the text into the document would be a mistake, because it would result in foo.tosToString(), which is obviously not a desirable result. Preselection helps out by instructing #develop what should be included in the selection and what should be removed when the new code is inserted.

The ProcessKey method decides whether to continue with the code completion dialog or bring it to its conclusion. A typical implementation of that is shown in listing 10.7.

Listing 10.7 Deciding whether to continue code completion based on current character

```
public CompletionDataProviderKeyResult ProcessKey(char key)
{
    if (char.IsLetterOrDigit(key) || key == '_')
    {
        return CompletionDataProviderKeyResult.NormalKey;
    }
    return CompletionDataProviderKeyResult.InsertionKey;
}
```

In this case, if the user is typing a symbol (alphanumeric or underscore), code completion should continue; otherwise, it terminates the code completion and inserts the selected item.

The InsertAction() method decides where to place that selected item. A simple implementation of that is shown in listing 10.8.

Listing 10.8 Inserting code completion item into the document

```
/// <summary>
/// Called when an entry should be inserted. Forward to the insertion
/// action of the completion data.
/// </summary>
public bool InsertAction(
    ICompletionData data,
    TextArea textArea,
    int insertionOffset,
    char key)
{
    textArea.Caret.Position = textArea.Document.OffsetToPosition(
        Math.Min(insertionOffset, textArea.Document.TextLength)
        );
    return data.InsertAction(textArea, key);
}
```

In listing 10.8, we first find the appropriate place to insert the text (by changing the caret position based on the text offset) and then insert the data at that location by calling InsertAction.

So far, we've dealt only with the UI of code completion, and there's nothing that's particularly important for the application. Even this tiny API has a lot of functionality built in, and you can add a lot of capabilities to streamline the workflow using the options we've just looked through. You can find more information about creating a good user experience in the #develop book and in the #develop forums: http://community.sharpdevelop.net/forums/.

Let's now focus on the functionality of the code completion provider, rather than on the UI issues.

10.2.3 *Adding contextual code completion support for our DSL*

Regardless of the infrastructure that you use to implement it, a good code completion function is based on a simple question: from the current position of the caret (the term used in #develop to refer to the cursor position in the document), what are the possible valid options the user could write?

In order to implement this, we need to know two things. First, we need to know where we are in the text, and not only the caret position, but what this position means. Going back to the Quote-Generation example, are we at the beginning of an empty line? Are we at the end of a specification statement? Are we at the end of a requires statement? Once we know that, we need to look at the overall context to decide what the user's options are.

These two actions are completely independent of how you display the selections (whether by using #develop, integrating a commercial control, or using Visual Studio). We're going to look at them in the context of a specific tool (#develop), but the same approach is used with any tool. And with that said, let's get right to the task of figuring out the current context.

The basic approach is simple: we know the current caret position, and we have the text in the editor. Now we need to figure out what the current context is. This generally involves parsing the text and finding the node that matches the position of the caret. With Boo, we can invoke the BooParser.ParseString() method to get the abstract syntax tree (AST) of the code in question, which we can traverse to find the appropriate node.

This is a good solution for high-end needs, but for a simple scenario there's an even simpler solution. #develop has already parsed the code to display it properly, and it makes this information available to us. This way, we don't have to do any extra work. Another point in favor of the #develop approach is that it's already highly focused on displaying the items, whereas the Boo parser's approach is more focused on textual and processing needs.

The #develop parser isn't sophisticated, but as long as it fits your needs, you can get a long way fast with it. Listing 10.9 shows how to retrieve and use the parser information.

> **Listing 10.9 Getting the current context and making decisions based upon it**

```
public ICompletionData[] GenerateCompletionData(
                string fileName, TextArea textArea, char charTyped)
{
    TextWord prevNonWhitespaceTerm = FindPreviousWord(textArea);
    if (prevNonWhitespaceTerm == null)
        return EmptySuggestion(textArea.Caret);

    string name = prevNonWhitespaceTerm.Word;
    if (name == "specification" || name == "requires" ||
        name == "same_machine_as" || name == "@")
    {
        return ModulesSuggestions();
    }
    int temp;
    if (name == "users_per_machine" || int.TryParse(name, out temp))
    {
        return NumbersSuggestions();
    }
    return EmptySuggestion(textArea.Caret);
}

private static TextWord FindPreviousWord(TextArea textArea)
{
    LineSegment lineSegment =
                textArea.Document.GetLineSegment(textArea.Caret.Line);
    TextWord currentWord = lineSegment.GetWord(textArea.Caret.Column);
    if (currentWord == null && lineSegment.Words.Count > 0)
        currentWord = lineSegment.Words[lineSegment.Words.Count - 1];
    // We want the previous word, not the current one,
    // in order to make decisions on it.
    int currentIndex = lineSegment.Words.IndexOf(currentWord);
    if (currentIndex == -1)
        return null;

    return lineSegment.Words.GetRange(
            0,
            currentIndex)
                .FindLast(word => word.Word.Trim() != "");
}
```

The `FindPreviousWord()` method (or its more generic cousin, `FindRelevantExpression()`) is responsible for answering, "What is the current DSL context for the current caret position?" This method takes the text editor as an argument and uses the #develop API to find the current word. A *word*, in #develop terms, is a token that's being highlighted in a certain way.

We want the previous word, not the current one, because it's the previous word that will provide the context. For example, assume that we currently have this text in the editor:

```
specification [caret position]
```

If the user invokes code completion now, there is no current word, because it's positioned at the end of the line, so we go back to the previous one.

Another scenario is when we have this text in the editor:

```
specification @vac[caret position]
```

In this case, the current word is still empty, because it's positioned at the end of the line again, but we select the vac as the current word, back off one to the @, and return @ as the previous word.

The last condition occurs if the user invokes code completion when they're in the middle of a sentence, like this:

```
specification [caret position]@vac
```

Now the current word is the @, and we back off to specification, which is what we'll return.

The GenerateCompletionData() method makes the decisions. This method receives the current word and decides how to act. In more complex scenarios, we'd probably want to deal with the current context, such as what items are in scope, and GenerateCompletionData() can delegate the final decision about what to display to one of several functions, depending on the context.

If we're at the beginning of a line, we'll show the empty selection. If we're in a specification (or same_machine_as or requires), we'll show the modules collection. For users_per_machine or for a numeric, we'll display a list of predefined numbers. It's as simple as that. Grab the current context and make a decision about it.

Listing 10.10 shows the implementation of ModulesSelection() to show how it's done. In a real-world scenario, you would probably get the modules collection from a database or configuration file. Here, I've hard-coded the values.

Listing 10.10   Generating the code completion list

```
private ICompletionData[] ModulesSuggestions()
{
    return new ICompletionData[]
    {
        new DefaultCompletionData("@vacations", null, 2),
        new DefaultCompletionData("@external_connections", null, 2),
        new DefaultCompletionData("@salary", null, 2),
        new DefaultCompletionData("@pension", null, 2),
        new DefaultCompletionData("@scheduling_work", null, 2),
        new DefaultCompletionData("@health_insurance", null, 2),
        new DefaultCompletionData("@taxes", null, 2),
    };
}
```

The first parameter for DefaultCompletionData is the text that the user will see in the completion list, the second is an optional description, and the third is the image index from the image list we expose.

Figure 10.6 shows how everything comes together.

I want to point out again that this is an 80 percent solution. This can get you going and give you a good experience, but it has limits. When you reach those limits, you need to start working with the parser, or maybe use a more advanced text editor. But a more advanced solution will use the same approach of identifying the context and making a decision based upon that.

Syntax highlighting and code completion aren't the only options you have for creating professional-looking DSLs. You can also provide a graphical representation of a textual DSL.

```
10
11   specification @pension:
12       same_machine_as @health_insurance
13
14   specification
```

Figure 10.6   Showing off our new code completion support

10.3   *Creating a graphical representation for a textual DSL*

The idea of creating a graphical representation for a textual DSL seems nonsensical at first, but doing so can be useful. Consider class diagrams in Visual Studio, or having designer and code views of the same web page.

A common problem with graphical representations is that they are, by their very nature, a high-level form of communication. This makes them extremely useful when we want to talk at that high level, but not so helpful in many DSL scenarios, because they tend to hide too much.

Another common problem with graphical DSLs is the serialization format, which tends to cause severe issues with source control usage. It's hard or impossible to resolve merge conflict errors along the common development path.

But nothing helps sales as much as a pretty diagram, so we need to explore our options.

NOTE   I am not a designer, so I decided to build a functional design rather than a pretty one. This will demonstrate the principals of UIs and DSLs, but it shouldn't be taken as design advice.

10.3.1   *Displaying DSL execution*

The first thing to remember is that our DSLs are standard .NET code. That means we can use simple code to build the UI from the information that's given to us. Listing 10.11 shows the essential details.

Listing 10.11   Displaying the results of evaluating a quote-generation rule

```
private void VisualizeScript_Load(object sender, EventArgs e)
{
    var rule = factory.Create<QuoteGeneratorRule>(
        @" Scripts\QuoteGenerator\sample.boo",
        new RequirementsInformation(50,"vacations", "work_scheduling"));
    rule.Evaluate();
    foreach (var module in rule.Modules)
    {
        ListViewItem item = modulesListView.Items.Add(module.Name);
        item.Tag = module;
    }
}
```

```
private void modulesListView_SelectedIndexChanged(
                                object sender, EventArgs e)
{
    if(modulesListView.SelectedItems.Count==0)
        return;
    var module = (SystemModule)modulesListView.SelectedItems[0].Tag;

    requiresListView.Items.Clear();
    sameMachineAsListView.Items.Clear();

    foreach (var requirement in module.Requirements)
    {
        requiresListView.Items.Add(requirement);
    }

    foreach (var anotherModule in module.OnSameMachineWith)
    {
        sameMachineAsListView.Items.Add(anotherModule);
    }
}
```

In `VisualizeScript_Load`, we create a new instance of the DSL script, evaluate the rule with the rule state, and display all the valid modules. In `modulesListview_SelectedIndexChanged`, we extract additional information from the selected system module and display that to the user.

This is pretty trivial, but I've shown it for two reasons. The first is to remind you how simple it is to work with the DSL instance. The second is to demonstrate how you can visualize the *result* of executing a DSL script. Figure 10.7 shows the result in all its glory.

But, however useful seeing the results of executing the DSL might be, it doesn't help us visualize the DSL. Did you notice that only the `vacations` module is visible? That's because it's the only one that was selected by the rule. What happens when we want to show the user everything that this script can do? With the current implementation, we don't have any way of doing that. The code doesn't execute if the condition isn't met, and we can't know up front what all the conditions are.

This is a problem. Luckily, there are several solutions for that.

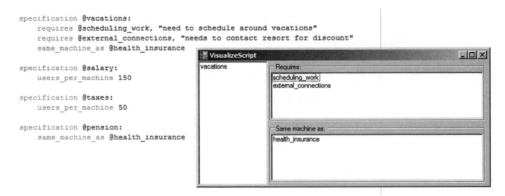

Figure 10.7   Showing the result of executing a quote-generation rule

10.3.2 *Creating a UI dialect*

The easiest way to extract the information from the DSL script without executing it is to create another backend language implementation for the same DSL syntax. One DSL implementation would be used for the execution and the second for UI purposes. Let's see what we need to do to get this running.

The first order of business is to investigate what part of the execution engine is causing us to see only the selected modules. Listing 10.12 shows the relevant code.

Listing 10.12 `QuoteGeneratorRule.specification` selects the module

```
public void specification(string moduleName, Action action)
{
   if (Array.IndexOf(information.RequestedModules, moduleName)==-1 &&
       Modules.Exists(module=> module.Name == moduleName) == false)
     return;

   currentModule = new SystemModule(moduleName);
   Modules.Add(currentModule);
   action();
}
```

As you can see, it's only the `if` statement that's causing issues for us. If we could somehow remove it, we'd get the UI that we want.

Listing 10.13 shows a derived implementation of `QuoteGeneratorRule`, meant specifically for the UI (with `specification()` made virtual).

Listing 10.13 Derived dialect for quote-generation rules user interface

```
public abstract class QuoteGeneratorRuleForUI : QuoteGeneratorRule
{
    protected QuoteGeneratorRuleForUI()
        // We don't care about the runtime values; they are unused
        : base(new RequirementsInformation(0))
    {
    }

    public override void specification(string moduleName, Action action)
    {
        currentModule = new SystemModule(moduleName);
        Modules.Add(currentModule);
        action();
    }
}
```

NOTE We also need to create a `DslEngine` implementation that can process `QuoteGeneratorForUI`. Using the same approach, I derived from `QuoteGenerationDslEngine` and changed the implicit base class. In the interest of brevity, I haven't included that here—you can check the implementation in the book's source code.

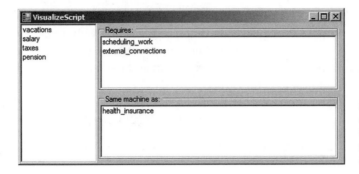

Figure 10.8   All the options, not just the ones that were selected by the rule evaluation of the current context

By changing the type of implicit base class (which is the DSL execution engine), we can get (from the same script) the results shown in figure 10.8. The code in listing 10.14 shows the updates required to make listing 10.11 support the new DSL dialect.

Listing 10.14   Selecting which rule implementation to create at runtime

```
private void VisualizeScript_Load(object sender, EventArgs e)
{
    QuoteGeneratorRule rule;
    // We can create either a rule that we can execute to get
    // an answer for the current state or a rule instance that
    // describes all the potential states
    if(GenerateRuleForUI)
    {
        rule = factory.Create<QuoteGeneratorRuleForUI>(
                @" Scripts\QuoteGenerator\sample.boo");
    }
    else
    {
        rule = factory.Create<QuoteGeneratorRule>(
            @" Scripts\QuoteGenerator\sample.boo",
            new RequirementsInformation(50,"vacations", "work_scheduling"));
    }
    // same as Listing 10.11
```

By performing a simple change, we were able to go from an opaque structure at runtime to a fully discoverable model at runtime. But not all DSLs will be as easy to modify; there will be cases where it is not possible to expose the DSL model so easily.

In those cases, you'll often be able to create a new DSL engine (implicit base class) that has the same API as the runtime execution engine. But the implementation would be focused on gathering the information required to deal with the UI.

This approach covers an even wider range of scenarios, but it's still not enough. The Authorization DSL is a good example of one that can't be treated this way. But there are ways of handling even this situation ...

10.3.3   *Treating code as data*

Extracting runtime information from our DSLs often won't be enough to build a graphical representation—we'll need to deal with things at a lower level than the

> ## The M language and the Oslo toolset
>
> The Oslo Modeling Language (M) is a language from Microsoft that's aimed at building DSLs. According to Microsoft, "'M' lets users write down how they want to structure and query their data using a textual syntax that is convenient to both author and reader" (http://msdn.microsoft.com/en-us/library/dd129519%28VS.85%29.aspx).
>
> The most relevant point for the purposes of this chapter is that M comes with a set of tools, including one called Quadrant, which can inspect an M grammar definition and provide the IDE UI for it.
>
> It's still early, and I have some doubts about the way it will turn out, but it's certainly something to keep an eye on. It is worth pointing out that, even in this state, M is intended for creating external DSLs, rather than internal ones. You can refer back to our discussion about the different DSL types in chapter 1 to see why I would much rather write an internal DSL than take on the challenge of writing an external one.

compiled code will give us. The distinction is clear when we compare declarative DSLs to imperative DSLs. We can't execute an imperative DSL the way we can a declarative DSL because that would perform the action, not just build the description of the desired action.

The Authorization DSL is a good example of this. Look at listing 10.15 for a reminder about how the Authorization DSL looks and behaves.

Listing 10.15   An Authorization DSL example

```
if Principal.IsInRole('Administrators'):
    Allow('Administrators can always log in')
    return

if Principal.IsInRole('Everyone'):
    Deny('We do not allow just anyone, you know')
    return
```

We can't take this syntax and deal with it at runtime in some fashion. The interesting part here is the condition in the `if` statement, not the structure we're building. How can we create a user interface on top of that?

At this point, we have to start dealing with the DSL as data, not as executable code. And we'll do it by utilizing the same approach that the compiler does. Say hello to the `BooParser` class. The `BooParser` will take a piece of text and return a graph (AST) that represents this text in Boo terms. This allows you to manually process the code and generate the UI that you want.

Let's take a look at how we can use the power of `BooParser` and some conventions to build a nice UI to manage the Authorization DSL. Once again, we're going to touch just the tip of the iceberg here, and we'll intentionally use the simplest approach to demonstrate the technique.

At the heart of this approach is the idea of pattern recognition. For example, in listing 10.15, we identify the pattern of allowing or disallowing by role. Once we have identified such a pattern, we can automatically recognize it and build the appropriate UI for it. Listing 10.16 shows the highlights of this approach.

Listing 10.16   Recognizing repeating patterns in the Authorization DSL

```
public class AuthorizationRulesParser
{
    public IEnumerable<Control> GetControlsFor(CompileUnit compileUnit)
    {
        if (compileUnit.Modules.Count != 1)
            throw new NotSupportedException(
                        "we support only a single file parsing");
        var module = compileUnit.Modules[0];
        foreach (var stmt in module.Globals.Statements)
        {
            var ifStatement = (stmt as IfStatement);
            if (ifStatement == null)
                throw new NotSupportedException(
                        "Only if statements are parsable by the UI");
            yield return GetControlFor(ifStatement);
        }
    }

    private Control GetControlFor(IfStatement statement)
    {
        var mie = statement.Condition as MethodInvocationExpression;
        if(mie != null &&
                ((ReferenceExpression)mie.Target).Name=="IsInRole")
        {
            //We recognize this pattern...
            return AllowByRoleControl(statement, mie);
        }
        throw new NotSupportedException("Could not understand...");
    }

    private Control AllowByRoleControl(IfStatement statement,
                                        MethodInvocationExpression mie)
    {
        var stmt = ((ExpressionStatement)statement.TrueBlock.Statements[0]);
        var action = (MethodInvocationExpression) stmt.Expression;
        return new AllowByRole
        {
            Role = ((StringLiteralExpression)mie.Arguments[0]).Value,
            Allow = ((ReferenceExpression)action.Target).Name=="Allow",
            Reason = ((StringLiteralExpression)action.Arguments[0]).Value
        };
    }
}
```

In `GetControlsFor(CompileUnit)`, we get the compile unit. This holds the parsed code AST (we only support a single file for this demonstration). We start by reading all the code in the `globals` section, which is where code that isn't in a method or a class is located. We go over it statement by statement, failing if we encounter a statement that is not an `if` statement.

> **How is this better than using XML?**
>
> We're doing all this hard work to go from the DSL code to the UI. Wouldn't it be easier to go with something XML-based instead of doing all this work?
>
> Not really, in my opinion. The major benefit of XML is that you don't have to write a parser, but aside from that, you're on your own. Using this approach, we don't need to write a parser; we use an existing one that already contains most of the ideas that we're dealing with.
>
> Trying to express concepts such as the `if` statement using XML is a lot of manual work. Doing the same with Boo is a matter of asking the parser for the AST. From there, the amount of work you have to do is more or less identical.
>
> The main problem is that we're trying to represent concepts that are difficult to deal with in nontextual form. The way we store them doesn't make a lot of difference.

When we find an `if` statement, we pass it to `GetControlFor(IfStatement)`. This class is responsible for doing the pattern recognition. In this example, we set it to recognize `if` statements where the condition is a method invocation for `IsInRole`. When we find that particular pattern, we call `AllowByRoleControl()`, which extracts the pertinent information from the AST and creates the appropriate control.

Listing 10.17 shows the setup code that uses the `AuthorizationRulesParser`.

Listing 10.17 Using the `AuthorizationRulesParser` to generate the UI

```
public partial class ViewAuthorizationRules : Form
{
    public ViewAuthorizationRules()
    {
    InitializeComponent();
    var compileUnit = BooParser.ParseString("test", @"

if Principal.IsInRole('Administrators'):
    Allow('Administrators can always log in')
    return

if Prinicpal.IsInRole('Everyone'):
    Deny('We do not allow just anyone, you know')
    return");

    var parser = new AuthorizationRulesParser();
    foreach (var control in
            parser.GetControlsFor(compileUnit).Reverse())
    {
        control.Dock=DockStyle.Top;
        Controls.Add(control);
    }
    }
}
```

We use the `BooParser.ParseString()` method to turn a piece of code into an AST, which we then pass to the `AuthorizationRulesParser()`. From there, it's pretty straightforward. We get all the controls from the rule parser and display them (in reverse order because of the way WinForm's `DockStyle.Top` works, to get the same ordering as in the text). The result is shown in figure 10.9.

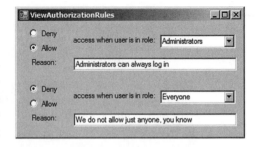

Figure 10.9   The UI representation for the Authorization DSL rules shown in listing 10.15

There isn't much to this approach, as you can see—only the pattern recognition and the specialized UI for each pattern. But although this is a cool demo, there are significant costs in pushing this to its ultimate limits. I would much rather have the textual version than this one. The textual version is richer, just as readable, and easier to work with. Of course, I am a developer, so I am *slightly* biased.

So far, we've seen only half of the solution. We've taken an existing script and displayed it. But how do we go the other way around? How can we get from figure 10.9 to the code in listing 10.15?

10.4   DSL code generation

We've taken DSL code, parsed it, and made it graphical. That was the hard part. The easy part is going the other way, from the abstract concept down to the DSL code.

At least, that's how it might seem at first. Let's take a look at our options for code generation and the benefits each approach buys us.

10.4.1   The CodeDOM provider for Boo

The CodeDOM API is the official API that the CLR provides for generating code without being dependant on a particular language. Using this API, we can build an AST and generate the code in a variety of languages, including Boo.

The Boo implementation of the CodeDOM API is located in Boo.Lang.CodeDOM.dll, and it's fairly complete. Using it is a good approach (if tedious) when you need to programmatically generate code artifacts.

> **Using BooParser versus executable code**
>
> Why bother with the parser when we could probably get the AST of the code at runtime and represent the same structure without all the parsing work? (We'll look at how to get the AST at runtime in chapter 12, section 12.3.3.)
>
> One major reason is that the parser is much more robust. A compilation error that would stop us in our tracks at runtime will still probably generate a usable AST that we can access with the parser. The ability to handle slightly off code is important for a tool that needs to accept code written by people. Error handling and recovery isn't an optional feature.

On the other hand, it doesn't work at all when you want to generate anything that doesn't look like code. Because the implementation is built to be as safe as possible, it intentionally specifies nearly everything it can. From the point of view of creating readable, language-oriented output, it's a failure.

The best way I've found to handle this scenario is to build your own DSL writers that understand the language and conventions, and how to express things in the most meaningful way.

10.4.2 Specific DSL writers

A DSL writer is exactly what it sounds like. It's a class that, given some sort of input, will produce textual output that's valid input for a DSL. How's that for an extremely dry definition?

A DSL writer is a glorified name for a class that writes to a TextWriter. The only thing of importance about this class is that it understands how to output the DSL well enough to generate readable output, instead of the usual cautionary output that the CodeDOM API generates, with everything explicitly specified and tediously repeated.

I intentionally put the DSL writer definition in those terms to make it clear that there is absolutely nothing special about DSL writers. And yes, that does leave you on your own to escape strings, handle keywords, and so on. Again, this is mostly intentional; we need to move away from the code-centric way of thinking about the DSL, to get human-readable[1] output. In practice, this isn't much of an issue, because there tends to be a fairly limited set of inputs for a DSL writer, but it's important to note that we do have to deal with issues like keyword escaping on our own.

Let's look at how we can implement a DSL writer for the Authorization DSL, which will allow us to save modifications that are made in the UI in figure 10.10.

NOTE The scenarios in which you use DSL writers tend to be narrowly focused. That's the whole point. You have enough information to make a lot of important assumptions, instead of having to support all the possible options.

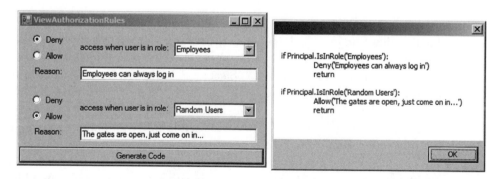

Figure 10.10   The output of a simple DSL writer

---

[1] I have very strict standards about what is human-readable. Most XML formats aren't human-readable, for example.

The implementation of this DSL writer is as simple as you might imagine. You can see it in listing 10.18.

Listing 10.18   A simple DSL writer can have a lot of value

```
public class AuthorizationDslWriter
{
    public string Write(IEnumerable<Control> controls)
    {
        var sw = new StringWriter();
        foreach (var control in controls)
        {
            var role = control as AllowByRole;
            if (role != null)
                WriteRoleRule(role, sw);
        }
        return sw.GetStringBuilder().ToString();
    }

    private void WriteRoleRule(AllowByRole role, StringWriter sw)
    {
        sw.WriteLine("if Principal.IsInRole('{0}'):", role.Role);
        if(role.Allow)
            sw.WriteLine("\tAllow('{0}')", role.Reason.Escape());
        else
            sw.WriteLine("\tDeny('{0}')", role.Reason.Escape());

        sw.WriteLine("\treturn");
        sw.WriteLine();
    }
}

public static class Extensions
{
    public static string Escape(this string self)
    {
        return self.Replace("'", "\\'");
    }
}
```

As you can see in listing 10.18, the implementation of DSL writers can be simple. The value that they bring is in being able to understand the DSL that they're writing.

In this case, we're feeding the DSL writer directly from the UI, although in most scenarios we'd have an intermediate object model in place. In fact, the most common scenario is to use the DSL instances themselves as the source for the DSL writer. This allows us to take a DSL instance, modify it, and save it back to text.

Another scenario where DSL writers are useful is when you want to use code generation to create a whole bunch of DSL scripts. In my opinion, it doesn't make a lot of sense to code-gen the DSL scripts. They're being created to be human-readable and -editable, and if you need to code-gen them with some other tool, something there needs a tune-up. Nevertheless, this is an important technique when you want to deal with migration from one form of DSL to another (such as when performing automatic version updates on existing DSL scripts), or when you're creating the system for the first time and duplicating rules that exist in non-DSL format.

This is a good tool to have in your toolbox, but its usage should be considered carefully. It's all too easy to reach for the code-generation hammer without considering whether there is another way to express what you want, perhaps with a different DSL that has more expressiveness than the existing one.

And with that, we're nearly done creating a professional DSL. We have one last important topic to talk about: error handling.

10.5 *Handling errors and warnings*

There is nothing that screams "Unprofessional!" like sloppy error handling. That nasty message box with "Unexpected Error" that pops up is about the most annoying thing that can happen, short of a blue screen just before you hit the Save button.

When dealing with a DSL, you need to be prepared to deal with scripts that are invalid. They may contain garbage, invalid code, code that's valid but will fail at runtime, code for a completely different DSL dialect, or even valid, but nonsensical, code. Those can all be divided into two broad categories: compiler errors and warnings, and runtime errors and warnings.

> **NOTE** What are these *warnings*? You're familiar with compiler warnings, which let you know that you're doing something that you probably shouldn't. Well, you can generate the same types of warnings at runtime, to actively detect and alert against behavior that's likely to cause issues or errors at a later date.

Compiler errors mean that you can't execute the script, and you have to be able to handle that gracefully. Usually this means showing the user the error message and allowing them to navigate to the precise location of the fault. Rhino DSL will automatically throw a detailed exception (aided by the Boo compiler) for any compiler errors, so it's fairly easy to deal with these.

Remember to take care of the lexical info when you extend the language. It allows the compiler to report exactly where an error occurred, and that can be important in troubleshooting. The lexical information is also important when runtime exceptions are raised, because the runtime will use this information to trace back the exception location to the DSL code.

With both compiler and runtime errors, you want to expose them to the user and offer the ability to go directly to the offending line in the DSL script. Think about the Errors & Warning pane in Visual Studio, where a double-click will take you to a compiler error. You want this kind of experience because it makes troubleshooting so much easier.

Compiler warnings occur when the compiler notices something that isn't quite right, but that isn't wrong enough to be a bug. The use of obsolete members is a good example of code that would generate a warning.

In addition to compiler warnings, your own code can issue warnings (by adding them to the `CompilerContext`'s `Warnings` collection). You can, and should, do that any time you discover some behavior that's likely to be wrong, but about which you aren't certain.

Because warnings are, well, warnings, Rhino DSL won't force you to deal with them the way it does with errors. You can access the warnings collection for the current compilation by overriding `DslEngine.HandleWarnings()`. I strongly recommend you do that and find a way to show them to the user in a meaningful way.

The rest of it is standard error handling, and that's not what this book is about.

10.6   *Summary*

In this chapter, I focused on the DSL mechanics rather than the UI particulars. This makes explaining the concepts easier, and it allows you to easily transfer your knowledge from one particular technology to another.

In many cases, the solutions I have presented are the trivial ones, just barely functional. That's intentional. Covering code completion in depth, for instance, would be a topic for a book of its own (and I recommend reading the free #develop ebook to get an idea of what building a full-fledged IDE means).

That doesn't mean you shouldn't use the techniques shown here. Indeed, I'm using them in several projects. They aren't appropriate for complex scenarios, but they're suitable for most reasonable situations, and they can take you a long way before you have to consider alternative approaches.

We covered two different approaches for creating UIs in this chapter. First, we looked at how to create a good text-editing experience for the DSL, providing such features as syntax highlighting and code completion. Then we looked at creating visualizations and a graphical editing experience for the DSL. We saw two different approaches to that: one using the DSL runtime itself, and the second using the AST of the code as it was provided by the Boo parser.

Finally, we touched on how to move from the graphical representation back to a textual representation, using an intentionally simple approach whose main advantage is the embedded knowledge of DSL operation modes.

Error handling is an important part of the UI in any application, and it must be considered when building a UI for a DSL. Compiler and runtime errors and warnings should have a well-thought-out place because they will happen, and the user will expect a good experience when they do.

Now it's time to move on to another topic that's critical for producing professional DSLs, although one that most developers would prefer to avoid: documenting the DSL.

DSLs and documentation

Documentation is a task that most developers strongly dislike. It's treated as a tedious, annoying chore, and it often falls to the developer who protests the least. Furthermore, developers trying to document their own work often don't do a good job. There are too many things they take for granted in their own code, and they tend to write to developers, in a way that makes little sense to non-developers.

At least, that's what I say when I'm asked to write documentation. It doesn't usually get me out of the task, but the problems are real.

Solid documentation is an important part of quality software. If the developers of the system are needed to handle routine matters, something is wrong. DSLs are no different in this regard. In fact, documentation is extremely important for DSLs, because you don't have a friendly UI that you can explore using trial and error.

You also need to keep in mind that DSLs are still rare in the industry (although they're a rapidly growing trend). Handing another developer a real-world DSL implementation will require some effort if the DSL implementation isn't documented.

221

11.1   Types of documentation

The anticipated users of your DSL will determine the level of the documentation and the assumptions you can make in that documentation. If the users are expected to be developers (or hobbyist developers), you can assume they'll know some things that non-developers would not.

The documentation for a DSL can be divided into two main parts:

- *User documentation*—The Getting Started Guide and User Guide, and perhaps some executable documentation
- *Developer documentation*—The Developer Guide and executable documentation, discussing the actual language implementation

NOTE   There are whole books written about documentation approaches, and I'm not going to attempt to cover the whole subject. Instead, I'll touch on several approaches that I have found useful when creating documentation for DSLs. This is the tip of the iceberg in terms of proper documentation, so take that into account.

In this chapter, we'll assume that the DSL will be used by business users with minimal programming experience. This is one of the toughest audiences to write documentation for. Teaching someone who doesn't know even the basics of programming to understand and use a DSL is a challenge. I haven't seen any DSL that has managed to avoid this issue (nor have any of the graphical tools I've seen).

Let's consider the Quote-Generation DSL. At first glance, it seems that no programming knowledge is required to write a script—it's a simple listing of requirements. The problem is that when you're writing such a script, you need to understand the execution environment and how the scripts will interact with each other.

There isn't a *lot* of programming knowledge required. You need to understand how the `if` statement works and that your script might not be the only one to run (so it might not produce the final results), but that's about all.

Let's consider what information we'd need to give someone who doesn't have a lot of programming knowledge in order for them to use our DSL:

- The syntax of the DSL
- The conventions used (if the folder structure has meaning, this should be spelled out)
- A list of commands that can be issued
- An overview of the execution semantics of the DSL—when and in what order the scripts are executed
- Tooling support—what kind of tools are provided for use with the DSL (IDE, trace viewer, GUI, and so on)
- Samples that shows how to do common things (for the express purpose of allowing copy, paste, and modify cycles)
- An explanation of how to deploy scripts

- An explanation of how to execute DSL scripts
- An explanation of how to get the results of a DSL execution
- An explanation of how to handle common errors and issues

This list isn't final, but it's still pretty big—each DSL is likely to have a slightly different list of things that need documenting. The list also uses some technical terms that users probably wouldn't understand. This is the kind of information you need to give users, but not how you should present it.

> ### Ensure a positive first impression
>
> I can't emphasize enough the importance of making a good first impression with your DSL. It can literally make or break your project. You need to make a real effort to ensure that the user's first impression of your system will be positive.
>
> This includes investing time in building a good-looking UI with snappy graphics. Such features might not have a lot of value from a technical perspective, and perhaps not even in day-to-day usage, but they're crucially important from a social engineering perspective. A project that looks good is pleasant to use, easier to demo, and generally easier to get funding for.
>
> From the documentation perspective, we want to give users some low-hanging fruit that they can grab easily—making the user feel that using the DSL is easy and that it can produce results quickly is important to gaining acceptance. The first stage should be an easy one, even if you have to specifically design to enable that.
>
> Nevertheless, you should be wary of creating a demoware project—one that's strictly focused on providing a good demo, but that doesn't add value in real-world conditions. Such projects may look good, and get funding and support, but they tend to become tortureware rapidly, making tasks harder to do instead of easier.

11.2 Writing the Getting Started Guide

The purpose of the Getting Started Guide is to get the user past the Hello World stage (or its equivalent) as quickly as possible. It's a highly focused document, meant to give someone who already understands the domain the basics of working with the DSL. It should be focused on giving clear instructions for achieving a specific set of tasks, for example, how to add a rule to calculate a new quote. In-depth discussion should be reserved for the User Guide.

The Getting Started Guide is the first thing that most users will see. Giving them a good first impression will create a lasting effect, and it can help tremendously in generating acceptance for the DSL.

The Getting Started Guide consists of an introduction to the DSL and its usage, and a set of examples that users can go through to familiarize themselves with the DSL at a high level.

11.2.1 *Begin with an introduction*

Ideally, the Getting Started Guide should begin with a short introduction explaining why you're utilizing a DSL. This introduction should not go beyond two or three paragraphs. Here's an example of how you could start the Quote-Generation DSL Getting Started Guide:

> The Quote-Generation Language aims to simplify the way that you set up and manage the quote-generation rules. It was built to express both the business and technical constraints involved in creating a quote for a customer.
>
> Using this approach, you will gain more control over how you generate the quote, and you'll see why certain items were added to the quote (by what rule, and based on what logic).
>
> The following screenshot shows a generated quote, with tracking from each item to the specific rule that added it ...

I like to use relatively informal language when writing the Getting Started Guide. I find that it forces me to speak in terms that are more readily understood. Note that there is no mention of a "DSL" or any other technical term in the introduction.

Interspacing your documentation with figures, screenshots, and other visual aids helps create a document that is more readable. It divides up the text, making it seems more approachable, and appropriate use of images can also significantly help readers. Appropriate images can clarify concepts better than any amount of text.

11.2.2 *Provide examples*

Following the introduction, it's a good idea to take users through the process of building a couple of example scripts from start to finish. You can talk about concepts for as long as you like, but until you take users through the motions of performing a task, it won't get through to many of them. Even those who are interested in the concepts and high-level overview will find it useful to see how things work.

I generally like to start the first example with something that can stand on its own. This doesn't include discussing the language in isolation. It's often better to show the language in use. If you can demonstrate how the DSL eliminates pain points in the current approach, do so. Relieving pain is great for acceptance.

The next step is to demonstrate how to create this script in the system, where to put it, how to get the application to accept it, and how to see that it's working. This part is important, and it should be as detailed as you can make it. Ideally, this is also an idiot-proofed scenario; try to anticipate all the mistakes a user might make.

There will always be something you'll miss, but do dedicate some time to addressing the obvious issues. For example, a simple common mistake is attempting to upload a Word document with the script in it. This is likely to fail, so outline that in the documentation and check for it in the code. I suggest accompanying each step in the walkthrough with a screenshot that shows what needs to be done. Text alone will not suffice.

TIP   Don't be shy about using screenshots to demonstrate functionality. A user is unlikely to be interested in the syntactic purity of the language, but they're most certainly interested in the tools and how they interact with it.

I tend to give three to five such examples, all at the same level of detail. They should be progressively more complex, although you should make sure that the first example is the most attractive one. You can skip the setup for each example if the setup is the same for all tasks; if it isn't the same, you should point out the differences explicitly.

Make sure you end each example with an explanation of how users can check that it worked. It's important to give users feedback that whatever they did produced the expected results.

You should also include examples that the user can copy, paste, tweak, and run. It's likely that you'll have several commonly repeated themes in the DSL, and providing an example of each of them that the user can immediately start experimenting with will be helpful.

That's it for the Getting Started Guide. Because the main purpose of this guide is to be short and to the point, it skips over a lot of details, most of which are important to users. That level of documentation belongs in the User Guide, our next topic of discussion.

11.3 *Writing the User Guide*

The Getting Started Guide is focused on taking users through their first steps, but the User Guide has a far bigger role. It's tasked with helping users understand how to use the DSL, the reasons behind the semantics of the syntax and behavior, and the full capabilities of the DSL. It also needs to cover the model and how to approach it, because you can't assume that anyone who learns to use the DSL is also a domain expert. (In fact, the DSL often is the way to become a domain expert.)

There are four main things that need to be documented in the User Guide:

- The domain and model
- The language syntax
- Other language aspects
- User-level debugging

Let's look at them each in turn.

11.3.1 *Explain the domain and model*

I usually start the User Guide with a discussion of the domain and the problems that the DSL is trying to solve. For the Quote-Generation DSL, I would write something like this:

> Generating quotes has always been a chore. The problem is that the dependency matrix between the various components of a system has exploded exponentially ever since [some business event]. As a result, the process of turning a client's requirements into

a quote (the list of items and components needed, the amount of onsite work, the support contracts and ongoing maintenance) became a laborious, error-prone, and manual process.

At the end of 2006, a quote for [client name] missed a dependency on [system name], causing over $250,000 in additional costs during system installation. As a result, the need for an automated and reliable quote-generation system became obvious.

This isn't part of any real-world documentation, but that's the style I would use. It gives users the relevant background on the business conditions that led to the development of the system. This is necessary for them to gain a good understanding of the system.

I then describe the model that's exposed to the user. This doesn't necessarily match perfectly with the way the DSL works, but it's the way I want the user to think it works. This is the mental model they'll develop in order to work with the system. I like to think about this part as telling a story that will affix the mental model of the system in the user's head.

NOTE   Although it's possible to diverge from the model in the implementation, I don't recommend it. It's best to give users an understanding of how the system really works, even if it's only at a very high level.

I also recommend explaining the model in the context of the business problem. Here's another snippet of the Quote-Generation DSL documentation:

A quote is generated using the concepts of components, dependencies, and constraints. With those concepts, you can build all the requirements for the Voice Mail system. When you generate the quote, you give the system all the relevant information (number of users, existing infrastructure, required features, and so on) and it will read all the dependencies and constraints of the components, resolving them to a valid quote.

For example, consider the Voice Mail component. It can support up to 5,000 mail boxes per machine (constraint) and it requires the IVR component (dependency). This is obviously a simplified example, but it will do. You can specify these requirements like this:

```
specification @VoiceMail:
    requires @IVR
    users_per_machine 5000
```

This specification is readable, and it specifies the constraints on the Voice Mail component and its dependencies. It can be written by the Voice Mail team without regard to constraints that other components have. It is the system's responsibility to generate the full quote for the customer based on the component specification that each team provides. Using this approach, you can unambiguously express all the requirements for the whole system.

It's important to understand that each component owner will have to write their own requirements specification, which is then rolled into the Quote-Generation System. The system is smart enough to be able to ...

The next step is to take a few examples from the Getting Started Guide and explain what is going on in detail. I suggest picking at least two examples, with enough differences to show different aspects of your language usage, or show things from different angles. Once you've worked through those, the user should have a good understanding of how things are supposed to work.

At that point, I usually move on to a reference style, instead of storytelling. And one of the first things that needs to be covered is the language syntax.

11.3.2 Document the language syntax

What makes for a good language reference? You'll need to cover the following topics at a minimum:

- Code file structure
- Keywords
- Notations
- Actions and commands
- Basic syntax rules
- Common operations

You will probably want to include additional documentation relevant to your specific scenario. For each of these points, you should also include examples, examples, examples. Let's look at them each in turn.

CODE FILE STRUCTURE

The code file structure is what a script file should look like. This section should outline whether users should include documentation comments, whether there are expected elements in the files, and so on. Let's look at how you might document the Routing DSL's file structure.

A typical file structure for the Routing DSL includes a documentation header, a filter, and one or more handle sections. A typical example is shown here:

```
"""
This is the documentation header;
Discussing what this file is doing
"""

# This is the filter; it decides whether
# we should handle this message
# or not
return if msg.type != "NewOrder"

# This is a handle section
HandleWith NewOrderHandler:
    # Inside the handle section we transform the
    # external message to its internal representation
    Return NewOrderMessage(msg.customer_id)

# There can be more than a single handle section
HandleWith LoggingHandler:
    # We can return the message in its raw form
    return msg
```

Should the User Guide contain the syntax for Boo?

That's a good question, and it usually depends on how technical your target audience is expected to be.

In almost all cases, I would include the syntax for common operations such as `if`, `unless`, and `for` statements. Those are too useful to keep from your users. Error handling (`try`, `except`, and `ensure`), resource management (`using`), and things of that nature should generally stay out of the DSL scripts, and I would avoid pointing them out.

Boo also has the notion of statement modifiers, and I recommend documenting and using them where it makes sense. For example, you can write a statement like this:

```
apply_discount 5.percent unless user.is_high_risk
```

Statement modifiers are applicable for `if` and `unless`. List comprehensions can use a similar syntax, but that's not usually something that you would want to use in a DSL.

After showing users an example file, you should go over each section and explain what they do while the user has the sample script in front of them.

The Routing DSL is a very technical DSL, so a lot of its syntax is derived from the Boo syntax, but that isn't always the case. The Quote-Generation DSL is a good example of a DSL that doesn't look much like a programming language. I would document the Quote-Generation DSL file structure as shown in listing 11.1.

Listing 11.1 The Quote-Generation DSL file structure

```
"""
This is the documentation header, where we document what
this file is doing.
"""
# A specification refers to a single module
specification @moduleName:
    # A specification denotes actions about
    # the system as a whole
    requires @anotherModuleName, "reason for requiring module"
    same_machine_as @anotherModuleName

# We can have multiple specifications
# in a single file
specification @anotherModuleName:
    users_per_machine 150
```

Like in the previous example, you need to explain the structure (how things are partitioned) but you don't need to discuss the actual details. The high-level details were already discussed in the Getting Started Guide, and the nitty-gritty stuff should be discussed when we talk about each keyword in isolation.

KEYWORDS

You need to document the keywords in the language. I don't mean only things like if, try, and using. I'm talking about the DSL keywords. In the Quote-Generation DSL, for example, that would include keywords such as specification, requires, same_machine_as, and so on. Those are the keywords of the language.

Here is how I would document specification for the Quote-Generation DSL:

```
specification @moduleName:
    << specification actions goes here >>
```

The specification keyword is used to set up a context for all the requirements of a particular module. The module is specified using the @name notation, described in the next section. Valid module names are names of components as specified in the ERP system.

The specification ends with a colon (:) and is followed by a list of requirements and constraints (see the Constraints section below). Those let the Quote-Generation system ...

I generally find that it's good to display the syntax of each keyword before discussing it. It gives the user something to glance at while reading the explanation.

NOTATIONS

A notation is a way of writing down something. Usually it allows a shorthand way to refer to something you use often, or to permit a better syntax. The @moduleName notation in the Quote-Generation DSL is a good example of that.

In the Quote Generation example, I would discuss notations as follows:

The @name notation is a shorthand for a component. This notation allows using component names (as defined in the ERP system under System > Administration > Setup > Components) directly in the text (replacing the hard-to-read Component IDs)

The @name notation is used whenever we want to refer to a component, in the specification, requires, and same_machine_as keywords.

Although we documented the @moduleName notation in the keywords example, it is important to also give them their own place, since users might want to refer to them specifically. This is especially true if you have a limited set of valid values in certain places, and they want to look at a particular value.

ACTIONS AND COMMANDS

Actions and commands are the operations that you allow the user to specify using the DSL. In the Quote-Generation DSL, requires and same_machine_as are operations (exposed as keywords), as are the Deny and Allow calls in the Authorization DSL.

For the Quote-Generation DSL, here is how I would document the requires keyword:

```
requires @moduleName
```

The requires keyword can appear inside a specification block. It has a single argument, a module name.

> This keyword creates a dependency between the component specification it appears on and the components specified as required. This dependency is taken into account
> ...

I usually like to make action documentation terse, because it is mostly used only for reference. Discussing the usage of each keyword in the context where it is used is usually left for the common operations section (discussed next).

BASIC SYNTAX RULES

Don't forget to document basic syntax rules, such as using indentation in the code (or using the end keyword, if you choose to use the whitespace-agnostic version of Boo). Or remembering to put the colon (:) character at the end of the line when you're creating a new block. And so on.

COMMON OPERATIONS

Take a look at common scenarios and show users what they look like. Show users how they can write their own scripts by giving them a wide range of examples to peruse.

Here's an example of documenting a common operation:

> This example will specify the required dependencies for a single component. In the Quote-Generation system, constraints are set at the component level. We can set the following constraints on a component specification:
>
> - `requires @moduleName`
> - `same_machine_as @moduleName`
> - `users_per_machine [numeric: number of users]`
>
> The following specification for the Voice Mail component sets dependencies on IVR and SMS components and specifies that 500 users are supported per machine.

```
specification @VoiceMail:
    requires @IVR
    requires @SMS
    users_per_machine 500
```

> As you can see, there is a direct translation between the way we think about the dependencies of the Voice Mail component and how we specify it. This is a fairly simple specification. A more interesting one would be handle conditions ...

So far we've only talked about the syntax, and the syntax is only a small part of a language. There are other things in a language implementation that need to be documented. We'll discuss those in the language reference.

11.3.3 *Create the language reference*

The difference between the language syntax and the language reference may sound artificial, but I consider it important. A language isn't just its syntax. The way a DSL is used is also part of the DSL, and you need to take that into account when documenting the DSL.

Usually, when the time comes to document a DSL, there is a lot of focus on the syntax, and some focus on how the engine works. There is little focus on how the environment and the usage of the DSL affect the DSL itself. Here are a few examples of topics that tend to be forgotten when documenting a DSL:

- *Naming conventions*—How to name script files and elements inside them
- *Script ordering*—How the engine determines the order of scripts to run and how to modify this order
- *Execution points*—What events will run the scripts

All of those are important in many DSLs, not only for the scripts' execution, but for how the scripts are written.

In chapter 9, we modified the Quote-Generation DSL to include a string that explains why a certain module is required by another, and the language reference should explain how we can get to that data from the final result of executing the script. After executing a set of scripts, we want to be able to examine the messages that the scripts generated. The documentation ought to contain detailed instructions about how to get them and include several references to the fact that you can get this information.

A final topic for documentation is the tools that are provided for the DSL, such as the IDE, the output viewer, and so on. I have seen users miss out on important tools because they weren't aware that they existed. It is preferable to avoid that.

And now, once you've documented how the DSL is supposed to work, you need to explain how to deal with the unexpected.

11.3.4 *Explain debugging to business users*

One of the key things you need to cover in the User Guide is how to deal with the unexpected. I generally think of this as debugging, but the actions users will perform are different from developer debugging (which is not a user-level concept).

When I talk about user-level debugging, I'm talking about looking at the result of a script's execution and understanding what has caused that particular result. If users can figure out what is happening on their own, it means one less debugging session that a developer has to go through. Increasing transparency in the application should be a key goal. These features should be documented prominently and referred to often.

Let's take the Quote-Generation DSL as an example again. The end result of the Quote-Generation DSL is a quote. It's a list of items and their prices (and also taxes, discounts, bundles, and offers, which we'll ignore here for the sake of simplicity). The Quote-Generation DSL figures out all the complex dependencies and configurations, and a common problem is figuring out why a particular item appears in the resulting quote.

We deal with that by adding the `reason` parameter to the `requires` action. The UI should also display all the reasons why an item was selected. This small feature alone provides a lot of value to the system. Expanding on that, you could allow the user to go from the quote item to all the scripts that mandated the item's selection. That would give the user a high level of control over what is going on in the application. (We'll look at this in more detail in chapter 12.)

That's the basics of the User Guide. The language syntax, the language reference, and the debugging and troubleshooting information are the key highlights. Now it's time to move on to documenting the language for other developers.

11.4   Creating the Developer Guide

Unlike the user documentation, you're on familiar ground when writing documentation for other developers. You can discuss things much more concisely, and you no longer have to deal with the pesky business details. You can discuss pure technological details to your heart's content. Okay, maybe not that last one.

But it's easier to write documentation for developers because there's a lot of ground you don't need to cover—they're already familiar with programming. That said, DSLs are still a niche topic, so they do require some explanation.

I strongly believe that the best documentation is the code itself, but not knowing *which* code to read can be a problem. That's why I recommend focusing your documentation on what the DSL does and where it happens, rather than on how it's implemented.

I usually partition the developer documentation using the following scheme:

- *Prerequisites*—Outline what you expect the developer will already understand when approaching the system.
- *Implementation*—Explore all the moving parts in the DSL implementation.
- *Syntax*—Document how the syntax for the DSL was implemented.

11.4.1   Outline the prerequisites

I like to start the Developer Guide by identifying the prerequisites for understanding what is going on. Usually, this comes down to having at least some understanding of the problem domain and the foundations of DSL building.

There are usually enough external resources on the problem domain that will give the developer a good idea about what you're trying to do. As for learning how to build DSLs ... that's what this book is all about.

Once you've covered the prerequisites, you can move on to the real meat: discussing the DSL implementation itself.

11.4.2   Explore the DSL's implementation

As I've explained elsewhere in this book, thinking about a DSL only in terms of syntax doesn't make sense. A DSL is composed of several parts, the syntax being the front end. The engine, the model, and the API are also intrinsic parts of the DSL and should be included in your documentation.

I don't intend to describe how to document the model or the API; those are fairly standard and there is nothing new that I can add here beyond outlining standard development documentation techniques. The syntax and the engine require special attention, because they are closely tied to the way the DSL works.

Using tests as documentation

I have several DSLs that have no documentation beyond their source and tests. They're usable, useful, and have been helpful. But I've run into situations where I, as the developer, could not answer a question about the language without referring to the code. I strongly recommend investing the time in creating good documentation for your DSLs.

Even behavior-driven design tests aren't quite enough. Those types of tests can help make it clear what the language is doing, but they aren't the type of documentation that you can hand to an end user to get them started using the language. Even if your users are developers, it's not a good enough approach.

It's your responsibility to make the system easy for users to use, and documentation is a key part of that. Handing users the tests is a good way to handle complex cases if your users are developers, but it's not a good way to reduce the learning curve.

Before diving into the details in the Developer Guide, it's important to provide a broad overview of how the different parts of the DSL work together. For example, if you're using the model directly in your DSL, you should make it clear that changing the model will also change the DSL.

On the other hand, as we've seen in chapter 9, this approach suffers from versioning problems, so we tend to use a facade layer between the model and the DSL to allow for easier versioning. In that case, we need to document that, outlining the versioning concerns and explaining how to add new functionality using the facade.

Giving developers a good grasp of how everything comes together is important in enabling them to work effectively with the DSL.

11.4.3 Document the syntax implementation

Documenting the syntax implementation is different from documenting the syntax (which we did in the User Guide). When we're talking about the *syntax*, we're mostly concerned with what to write and how to write it. When we talking about the *syntax implementation*, we're focusing on how to map the text to the language concepts.

When you have an internal DSL with a host language like Boo, you don't have a lot of work to do in this area, but you still have some. For example, your language will have keywords, behaviors, conventions, notations, and external integrations that you've built into it to talk about the problem domain in a meaningful way. You need to document how they work.

Developer documentation isn't just Word documents

Although the term *documentation* usually brings to mind wordy specifications and long sessions with a word processor, that isn't necessarily the best way to provide documentation when the target audience is developers.

Well-structured code with inline comments, accompanied by tests, is usually the best form of documentation that a developer could ask for.

We'll cover each of the syntax implementation parts, starting with the language keywords.

KEYWORDS

When documenting keywords, I tend to list each keyword, along with a short description of what it is responsible for and how it is implemented (method call, meta-method, macro, and so on).

That may not always be possible when you're extending the language externally (using the model or a facade, for example), so in those scenarios, I point out explicitly that extending the language is done externally to the actual language implementation and try to provide a tool that can automatically generate a reference for the documentation.

Building a list of keywords and their implementation semantics is a good first step toward documenting a language, but it isn't enough. You also need to document the implementation semantics—the way the DSL behaves.

BEHAVIORS

The term *behavior* refers to how the system performs operations, often complex ones. There are plenty of cases where what the DSL script appears to do and its behavior during execution are drastically different.

In the Quote-Generation DSL, for example, you execute the DSL to get a data structure and then process it further, without referring to the DSL itself anymore. In the Scheduling DSL, you're building both a description of how you want the system to behave as well as the condition and actions to be executed. Understanding the translation between the different parts of the DSL (the resulting model and the engine that processes it) and how a change in one can affect the other is a common cause for confusion in advanced scenarios.

Whenever the behavior of the system isn't obvious, it's a good idea to explain how and why it works. In chapter 12, we'll cover some advanced techniques that allow you to play with the language at a far deeper level. These techniques allow great freedom and the creation of very nice syntax and semantics for your DSLs, but they can be daunting if you come across them without some prior warning.

For example, take a look at listing 11.2, which shows a DSL that represents a rule engine for order processing.

Listing 11.2 A sample of an order-processing DSL

```
when customer.is_preferred and order.total_amount > 500:
    apply_discount 5.percent
```

In this example, we access both `customer` and `order` to make a decision. So far, it looks simple. But let's assume that `customer` can be `null` (if the `customer` doesn't have an account and makes a onetime purchase). How will we handle that?

One solution would be to rewrite listing 11.2 as shown in listing 11.3.

Listing 11.3 A sample of an order-processing DSL, with `null` handling

```
when customer is not null and customer.is_preferred \
     and order.total_amount > 500:
  apply_discount 5.percent
```

I'm pretty sure you'll find listing 11.3 less readable than 11.2, because in listing 11.3 the error-handling code obscures the way we handle the business scenario.

> **NOTE** A simple alternative approach to the problem of `null customers` would be to use the Null Object pattern (a null object is an object with defined neutral, *null*, behavior). Instead of a `null` reference, we could pass an anonymous customer. That's not always easy to do, however.

We could improve on this by checking whether the customer is null at the DSL level, instead of at the script level. We could state that if a rule references a variable that is null, we won't run it. This is an example of advanced behavior that's not self-evident in the code, but it's an important part of the DSL. This should be documented, both to point out this behavior and explain how it is implemented. (The full details on how to implement this are covered in chapter 12.)

Behaviors concern how the system does things, and it's closely related to how the system is organized. This is where the system's conventions come into play.

CONVENTIONS

A *convention* is a standard way of dealing with particular aspects of your application.

Conventions result in common, well-defined structures for our software, and that's a major plus, but it's just the tip of the iceberg. The fun part starts when the application is aware of those conventions and can make use of them. The use of naming and directory structures are typical conventions in our DSL implementations.

I mentioned earlier that these conventions should be documented in the User Guide; in the Developers Guide you need to document how they're implemented. For example, do you rely on external ordering? Is the ordering by filename?

I usually use the term *convention* for anything that's outside the code; I refer to conventions in the code as *notations*.

NOTATIONS

A *notation* is a way to express an idea in another manner, usually to gain either clarity or conciseness or both. In the Quote-Generation DSL, for example, you can use `@module-Name` as a notation to reference modules. Another notation might be the use of `underscores_between_words` instead of using `PascalCase`.

> **TIP** Notations and conventions seem innocent when you start to use them, but it's easy to forget about them. They're there to make things friction free, after all. But if you do forget about them, you may have to dig deep to figure out why something isn't working when you aren't following the proper convention or using a notation properly. It's important to make sure conventions and notations are documented explicitly.

As with conventions, notations should be documented in the User Guide, and the implementation semantics should be documented in the Developer Guide. In the two previous examples, those involve registering compiler steps to process the code during compilation, and usually you would use the `UseSymbolsStep` and `UnderscoreNaming-ConventionsToPascalCaseCompilerStep` compiler steps that are part of the Rhino DSL project. Spelling this out may seem redundant now, but it's likely to help in the future, particularly for more-complex DSLs that may contain many such notations.

One topic you still need to document is when you reach *outside* the DSL implementation to get your information.

EXTERNAL INTEGRATION

One of the more interesting DSL approaches I have seen is reaching outside the source files and the compiler into external systems to get additional information to solve a business problem.

For example, imagine that you're writing a Quote-Generation DSL and you have a typo in a module name. During compilation, the compiler interrogates the ERP system to check whether all the specified module names are valid. This allows it to give you a compiler error instead of a runtime error. Another example is generating code at the compiler level from external resources, such as a database, web service, and so on.

Those external resources are also part of the DSL, but they aren't things that you would usually notice (until they break, or are broken). Make sure that you document them adequately; I usually consider a list of all the external integration points and how they're configured to be adequate.

I mentioned earlier that I consider the code the best documentation. But that approach fails when you start to play underhanded tricks with the compiler.

11.4.4 *Documenting AST transformations*

An *AST transformation* is when you take a piece of AST (the compiler object model) and modify it during compilation, affecting the output of the compiler. A common AST transformation is the creation of the implicit base class.

Another example of AST transformation that you're probably familiar with is creating an XML document programmatically by manipulating the DOM—the DOM is the AST of the XML document. The code for doing that is usually long and complex, not because of what it's doing, but because it's full of details on how to manage the programmatic representation of an XML document. AST transformations written using the AST API directly require a lot of code. (Using quasi-quotation, which is covered in chapter 6, tends to simplify this by an order of magnitude or more, but it's only possible if your DSL is implemented in Boo.)

The main problem with code that performs AST manipulations is that it's hard to look at the code and see what the end result will be. For that reason, I recommend documenting most AST manipulation code with the code that it's generating. I usually do this as a comment directly in the code. An example of documenting AST manipulation can be seen in listing 11.4.

Listing 11.4 AST manipulation code with documentation

```
// compilerContext = BrailViewComponentContext(macroBodyClosure,
//          "componentName", OutputStream, dictionary)
block.Add(new BinaryExpression(BinaryOperatorType.Assign,
    new ReferenceExpression(componentContextName), initContext));

// AddViewComponentProperties( compilerContext.ComponentParams )
MethodInvocationExpression addProperties =
    new MethodInvocationExpression(
        AstUtil.CreateReferenceExpression(
            "AddViewComponentProperties"));
addProperties.Arguments.Add(
    AstUtil.CreateReferenceExpression(componentContextName +
                    ".ComponentParameters"));
```

The code in listing 11.4 comes from the Brail DSL, which is a text-templating language. As you can see, there is little to compare between the resulting code (which is shown in the comments) and the code that's used to generate the AST to produce the end result.

This is one of the few cases where I am in favor of verbose commenting, because there is such a gap between the concept and the code that creates it. Such commenting is particularly important for people who aren't used to reading this type of code.

So far, we've focused on documentation in the form of documents and comments, but that's not the only way to document code.

11.5 Creating executable documentation

Most documentation is inanimate words on paper (or on the screen). You can produce screencasts that provide much higher bandwidth communication, but they tend to be a poor way to discuss details. The details are usually left to documents, but they don't have to be.

Executable documentation is documentation that you execute in order to learn from. I consider tests a form of executable documentation, because I can look at the tests (and step through them) to see how various parts of the system are implemented. In fact, given a choice between a system with documentation but no unit tests, and one with unit tests but no documentation, I would take the system with the unit tests in a heartbeat.

Documentation goes out of date, and there is no real way to verify that it's accurate except by poring over the code. Tests tend to be up to date, and they can actively tell you if they aren't.

Tests as a form of documentation are usually only valuable to developers, but there's another option for creating executable documentation. You can create a set of examples that show how the system works. You can provide a tool that will allow users or developers to play with the examples and see the results of their actions. Microsoft did a good job of this with the 101 LINQ Examples. Not only did they provide a lot of examples, there's a GUI that allows you to modify them and play with different options. (The C# version of the examples can be found at http://msdn.microsoft.com/en-us/vcsharp/aa336746.aspx, and the VB.NET version is at http://msdn2.microsoft.com/en-us/bb688088.aspx.)

This type of documentation is valuable for both developers and users, and it's an approach you should consider when creating documentation for your DSL.

11.6   Summary

In this chapter, we've gone over the major points that should be documented in a DSL implementation, both from the end user's perspective and from the point of view of a developer coming on board the project.

Again, this is by no mean a comprehensive discussion of documentation. I've merely pointed out the highlights, indicating what should be documented and what type of documentation you should strive for.

Like most developers, I find writing documentation boring and maintaining documentation even worse, but it's important. You may never see the payoff of your documentation efforts yourself, because they usually come in the form of user acceptance of the DSL and an easier ramping-up process for new developers that are added to the team. But those are valuable results nevertheless.

We've now looked at documentation, user interfaces, versioning, and testing, all of which are high-level concepts in building DSLs. It's time to investigate common implementation issues and the patterns that are used to deal with them. That's the topic of chapter 12—DSL implementation challenges.

DSL implementation
challenges

The first part of this book dealt with building a DSL from scratch, and the second part with testing, documenting, versioning, and presenting the DSL. Between the two, there are still some gaps—details that are important for creating successful DSLs that we couldn't look at before you gained some experience building DSLs in Boo.

In this chapter, we're going to look at some of the more interesting challenges for DSLs, and in the next chapter we'll make use of many of the solutions outlined in this chapter to build a real-world DSL.

NOTE Many of the topics in this chapter involve AST manipulation, which we covered in chapter 6. As a quick reminder, the abstract syntax tree (AST) is how the compiler represents the code text internally. Boo allows you to access and modify the AST, and these modifications will affect the generated code, producing the result that you want.

12.1   Scaling DSL usage

A common goal for DSLs is to create a more transparent environment, one in which it's clear what the system is doing and why. It usually works beautifully in the demo, and as long as the system remains small. Where it often fails is when the system reaches a critical mass, when it has hundreds or thousands of scripts working together to produce the appropriate results. In one such system I worked on, we

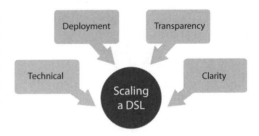

Figure 12.1   What it takes to scale a DSL

had well over 15,000 scripts; in another, we had close to 4,000. As you can imagine, we ran into several problems with these systems that we hadn't seen when they were small.

A lot of the solutions in this chapter resulted from working in that type of scenario. They're applicable and valuable in smaller-scale languages, but their value will truly become apparent after your system has become successful and sees a lot of use.

In general, the challenges (and their solutions) can be divided into several general areas, as shown in figure 12.1:

- *Technical*—Technical problems include startup time, response time, memory usage, and cold restart time (the time it takes to execute a script or a set of scripts the very first time). This generally covers the system not being ready for the scale of the problems it's given.
- *Deployment*—Unlike most code, DSL scripts are expected to be changed in production quite often. Doing so safely requires some prior planning.
- *Transparency*—In a big system, understanding why the system performed a particular operation can be decidedly nontrivial.
- *Clarity*—In a big system, it's often hard to make sure that you're expressing yourself clearly. This happens when the complexity of the problems increases, and you need to match that with complex solutions. Clarity is lost if you fail to take advantage of such a scenario to get to a higher level of expressiveness and understanding.

All the challenges we will deal with in this chapter can be assigned to one of these areas.

12.1.1 Technical—managing large numbers of scripts

Let's assume we have a system with several thousand scripts. What kind of issues are we going to run into?

- *Startup time*—Compilation time will be a significant factor, because the scripts will be compiled on the fly. Yes, we're caching the compiled assembly, but the startup time can be significant in such a system.
- *Memory*—There will almost certainly be a significant number of changes to the scripts that will have to be recompiled, loading more assemblies into memory.

Because we can't release assemblies on the CLR, we have to either accept this issue or deal with `AppDomains` to manage it.

Of the two, startup performance is the more worrying concern. An assembly isn't that big most of the time, and even a hundred changed scripts would add less than half a megabyte to the application. It's not ideal, but it's something we can live with. The startup time can be measured in *minutes* if you have enough scripts.

NOTE In this scenario, a large number of scripts is several hundred that need to be accessed immediately after system startup. If you have fewer scripts than that, or if not all the scripts need to be accessed shortly after system startup, you generally won't have to worry about startup performance issues.

There are two factors that relate to the speed of compiling a set of scripts: the number of the files and the number of times the compiler is called.

In general, it's best to invoke the compiler as few times as possible, with as many scripts as possible. This tends to produce fewer bigger assemblies, which is preferred over smaller, but more numerous, assemblies. There is also a cost for invoking the compiler itself, but this is usually only significant if you invoke it for each individual script, rather than compiling in batches.

It's a fine balancing act. On the one hand, it's slower to compile more files, but it's even slower to compile each script independently. The solution chosen for Rhino DSL (and described in chapter 7) is to compile all the scripts in the target script directory (though this can be overridden if you choose). This approach compiles scripts in batches but doesn't attempt to compile all the scripts in one go. In that way, it balances the need to keep the system responsive and overall system performance.

But even that's not a good enough solution in some cases. There are situations where you must compile a large number of scripts quickly. You have several options in that scenario. You can live with the performance hit, perform precompilation, or perform background compilation.

12.1.2 *Performing precompilation*

Although I tend to refer to DSL code as "scripts" to express how flexible they usually are, there is no real reason to treat them as such. In a mostly static system, you could easily compile all the scripts as part of the build process, and be done with them.

Listing 12.1 shows how you could compile a set of scripts ahead of time. We will discuss its usage immediately.

Listing 12.1 Precompiling a directory of scripts

```
public class DslPreCompiler
{
    public static void PreCompile(DslEngine engine,
        string directory, string destinationFile)
    {
```

```
        var allFiles = FileHelper.GetAllFilesRecursive(directory, "*.boo");
        // Compile all the files
        var compilerContext = engine.Compile(allFiles);
        // Copy generated assembly to destination
        File.Copy(compilerContext.GeneratedAssemblyFileName,
                destinationFile, true);
    }
}
```

As you can see, the `DslPreCompiler` takes a DSL engine and a directory of scripts, and it produces the compiled output.

But that only deals with the first part of the problem, compiling all the scripts in one go. How do you tell Rhino DSL that it should look for those scripts in the assembly? You can override the cache behavior to look at the compiled assembly file, as shown in listing 12.2.

Listing 12.2   Overriding the cache behavior

```
public class PrecompiledCache : IDslEngineCache
{
    private readonly Assembly assembly;

    public PrecompiledCache(Assembly assembly)
    {
        this.assembly = assembly;
    }

    public Type Get(string path)
    {
        var type = assembly.GetType(
                Path.GetFileNameWithoutExtension(path));
        if(type!=null)
            return type;
        throw new InvalidOperationException("Could not find " + path
                    + " in the precompiled assembly");
    }

    // Other methods omitted for brevity's sake; they all
    // throw NotSupportedException
}
```

In this example, the precompiled cache always goes to the assembly to find its types, and the `PrecompiledCache` intentionally throws an error if the type isn't found. That's done to keep the implementation simple. A more complex implementation would also handle the case where the scripts are modified from the precompiled version.

Now all you have to do is execute the precompilation:

```
DslPreCompiler.PreCompile(
    new QuoteGenerationDslEngine(), scriptDirectory, "test.dll");
```

Then you need to let the DSL engine know about the cache, as in listing 12.3.

Listing 12.3 Letting the DSL engine know about the precompiled cache

```
var factory = new DslFactory();
factory.Register<QuoteGeneratorRule>(new QuoteGenerationDslEngine
{
    Cache = new PrecompiledCache(Assembly.LoadFrom("test.dll"))
});
var rule = factory.Create<QuoteGeneratorRule>(
    Path.Combine(scriptDirectory, "sample.boo")
    , new RequirementsInformation(50));
```

As you can see, this is pretty easy and noninvasive. All requests for a DSL instance will be satisfied from the precompiled assembly.

12.1.3 Compiling in the background

Rhino DSL caches the results of compiling a script, so all you need to do to perform background compilation is create a thread that will ask for instances of all the scripts. This will cause all the scripts to be compiled before the first request, saving you the compilation time.

Rhino DSL is thread-safe, so you can spin off a thread that would request an instance of all the scripts. A simple example is shown in listing 12.4.

Listing 12.4 Compiling all the scripts in a background thread

```
var factory = new DslFactory();
factory.Register<QuoteGeneratorRule>(new QuoteGenerationDslEngine());
ThreadPool.QueueUserWorkItem(delegate
{
    var allFiles = FileHelper.GetAllFilesRecursive(
                            scriptdirectory, "*.boo");
    foreach (var file in allFiles)
    {
        factory.Create<QuoteGeneratorRule>(file,
                            new RequirementsInformation(50));
    }
});
```

Because the scripts are cached once they're compiled, all you have to do is request them once and, presto, they're cached.

NOTE By default, Rhino DSL caching is persistent, so it survives application restarts. Take that into account when you consider system performance.

12.1.4 Managing assembly leaks

I already mentioned that an assembly isn't a resource that can be freed easily. If you want to unload assemblies, you must load the entire AppDomain. Assembly leaks will only be an issue if you expect a large number of changes in production between application restarts. Again, a *large number*, in this context, is thousands of changes occurring regularly.

This is a common issue for development, but system uptime in development is rarely long enough for this to be a problem. In production, this situation occurs much less commonly than it's talked about, so I'll merely identify the solutions for this problem rather than demonstrate them in detail.

The first option, as I've mentioned, is not dealing with the issue. This is a valid response if you don't expect to have many changes in production. It's what I usually recommend doing.

The second option is to move the DSL to a separate `AppDomain` and perform all communication with the DSL instance over an `AppDomain` boundary. This has its own performance issues, and it requires that all the objects you send to the DSL instance either be serializable or inherit from `MarshalByRefObject`. It's not a solution that I like much.

The third option is to move much of the application itself to an `AppDomain` and rely on a small core to manage those `AppDomains`. This way, at given times, the application core could spin off a new `AppDomain` and unload the old one, freeing the memory. This approach is similar to the way IIS and Windows Process Activation work, and I suggest taking a look at them as well, because it's entirely possible to make use of the existing infrastructure for this purpose.

As you can see, the technical challenges are easily overcome using well-known technical solutions, such as background compilation, caching, and precompilation.

A more complex problem isn't strictly technical in nature: deployment. We've looked at the implications of editing scripts in production from the technical side, but not from the control and management sides.

12.2   *Deployment—strategies for editing DSL scripts in production*

Once the application is in production, how are users supposed to edit the DSL scripts? It's likely that some important behaviors are defined in the DSL and that users will want to make modifications to them. This is a question that comes up often. Yes, the DSL is easy to change, but how should you deal with changes that affect production?

Let's first assume we're talking about a web application or a backend system, not a Windows application. There are several aspects to this problem. First, there is the practical matter of creating some sort of UI to allow users to make the changes. This is generally not something trivial to produce as part of the admin section of an application.

There are also many other challenges in this scenario that need to be dealt with, such as handling frequent changes, cascading updates, debugging, invasive execution, error handling, and so on. Just making sure that all the scripts are synchronized across all the nodes in a web farm can be a nontrivial task. You also have to deal with issues such as providing auditing information, identifying who did what, why, and when, and you need to be able to safely roll back a change.

In development mode, there is no issue, because you can afford to be unsafe there. The worst thing that can happen is that you'll need to restart the application or revert to a clean checkout. For production, this isn't an option. This is *not* a simple matter.

My approach, usually, is to avoid this requirement as much as possible. I don't allow such changes to be made in production. It's still *possible*, but it's a manual process that's there for emergency use only. Like the ability to log in to the production database and run queries, it should be avoided if possible.

But disallowing changes isn't always possible. If the client needs the ability to edit DSL scripts in production, you need to provide a way for them to do so. What I have found to be useful is to provide a way to not work directly on production. Instead, we work on scripts stored in a source control server that is considered part of the application itself. You can see how it works in figure 12.2.

If you want to access the scripts, you check them out of source control. Then you can edit them with any tool you want (often the same tools that you use during development), and finish by committing them back to the repository. The application monitors the repository and will update itself when a commit is done to the production branch.

This approach has several big advantages. First, you don't have the problem of partial updates, you get a pretty good audit trail, and you have built-in reversibility. In addition to that, you avoid the whole problem of having to build a UI for editing the production scripts; you use the same tools that you used during development.

As a side benefit, this approach also takes care of pushing script changes to a farm, so you don't have to provide a separate solution for that. And yes, this method of editing scripts in production incorporates continuous integration as part of the application.

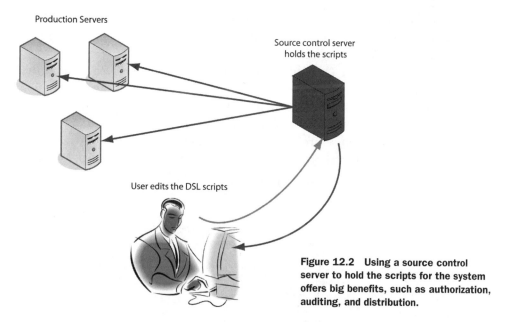

Figure 12.2 Using a source control server to hold the scripts for the system offers big benefits, such as authorization, auditing, and distribution.

12.3   *Ensuring system transparency*

Ensuring that the system is transparent (that it's possible to understand what goes on in the bowels of the system) can be hard work, particularly if you don't have a good grasp of the system's internals. In this section, we'll discuss the tooling that you have available to make the system transparent.

We'll also look at a new DSL that will allow us to discuss those patterns in greater depth. Chapter 13 discusses the implementation of the DSL in detail; this is a short overview.

12.3.1   *Introducing transparency to the Order-Processing DSL*

The Order-Processing DSL is used to define business rules regarding (surprise!) order processing. The syntax of the Order-Processing DSL is as follows:

```
when someBusinessCondition:
    takeAction1
    takeAction2
```

Listing 12.5 shows an example of an Order-Processing script.

Listing 12.5   An example of the Order-Processing DSL

```
when customer.IsPreferred:
    apply_discount 5.percent()
```

With that knowledge, let's take on our first challenge. Users want to know which rules took active part in the processing of a specific order. If there is a problem, that would make it much easier to track down. Users would know what rules had executed, in what order, and what the result of that execution was. With that feature in mind, let's go about implementing it.

When I built the Order-Processing DSL, I choose to use when, rather than if, for the common conditional. That's because when makes for a clearer distinction between business conditions and code conditions. If is a keyword, and when isn't, but it's possible to make a keyword out of when using a meta-method or a macro.

In most scenarios, I prefer to use a meta-method (though there is no real objective reason). Listing 12.6 shows one possible implementation of the when() meta-method.

Listing 12.6   The when() meta-method

```
[Meta]
public static MethodInvocationExpression when(
            Expression condition, BlockExpression action)
{
    var conditionBlock = new Block(condition.LexicalInfo);
    conditionBlock.Add(new ReturnStatement(condition));
    return new MethodInvocationExpression(
        // the init method
        new ReferenceExpression("Initialize"),
        // a delegate with the condition
        new BlockExpression(conditionBlock),
```

```
        // a delegate with the action
        action
    );
}
```

The when() meta-method decomposes the when keyword into its component parts and sends each part to the Initialize() method.

The when() meta-method shown in listing 12.5 will transform the code in listing 12.3 into the code shown in listing 12.7 (translated to C# to make it easier to understand).

Listing 12.7   The when() meta-method output (translated to C#)

```
Initialize( delegate { return customer.IsPreferred; }, delegate
{
    apply_discount(5.percent());
});
```

We have decomposed the code using the when keyword into two parts, the conditions and the action. Now we can implement the OrderRule implicit base class, as shown in listing 12.8.

NOTE   The when keyword implementation is split between the when() meta-method, which captures the appropriate information at compile time, and the Execute() method, which executes the code. The Initialize() method is called from the code generated by the when() meta-method, which is placed in the Prepare() method. We'll walk through this in chapter 13, so don't worry if you don't fully understand it yet.

Listing 12.8   The OrderRule implementation of conditional semantics

```
public void Initialize (Func<bool> condition, Action action)
{
    Condition = condition;
    Action = action;
}

public void Execute()
{
    // Execute the condition
    var result = Condition();
    // Log the result of this condition

    RuleContext.AddConditionResult(this, result);
    if (result) // Execute the action if condition evaluates to true.
        Action();
}
```

Using this approach, we can create what is effectively an auditable if statement. The only thing we have left to do is to display the results of the execution to the user. The when() meta-method generates the code to call the Initialize() method with the condition and actions wrapped in delegates. We later execute those delegates when calling the Execute method and then record the result of the condition.

That's not quite the end of adding transparency to a DSL. It would be nice if we could go directly from a script instance to its source. That would allow us to show the user the source of each rule, so they can understand what it does.

12.3.2 Capturing the script filename

We want to capture a script's filename so we can display it. The question is, how? We have the filename of the script during compilation, so what we need to do is record this in the script in a manner that will allow us to access it at runtime.

One way of doing this is to pass the filename to the `Initialize()` method. The new implementation is shown in listing 12.9.

Listing 12.9　Recording the filename

```
[Meta]
public static MethodInvocationExpression when(
            Expression condition, BlockExpression action)
{
    var conditionBlock = new Block(condition.LexicalInfo);
    conditionBlock.Add(new ReturnStatement(condition));
    return new MethodInvocationExpression(
        // The init method
        new ReferenceExpression("Initialize"),
        // A delegate with the condition
        new BlockExpression(conditionBlock),
        // A delegate with the action
        action,
        new StringLiteralExpression(condition.LexicalInfo.FileName)
    );
}

public void Initialize(Func<bool> condition, Action action,
                       string filename)
{
    Filename = filename;
    Condition = condition;
    Action = action;
}
```

That was pretty easy, wasn't it? We could also go with more complex semantics, using a compiler step to add a property to all the scripts. But the solution in listing 12.9 is short and simple and it works, so there's no reason to go there yet.

Because we now have access to the filename of the script at runtime, we can show the user which script it is, and let them immediately see what caused a particular decision. But that might be too cumbersome for some scenarios. We don't necessarily want the entire script—we only want the condition. How do we get that?

12.3.3 Accessing the code at runtime

Let's take a deeper look at the problem. Assume the condition in use is the code in listing 12.10.

Listing 12.10   Sample code in the Order-Processing DSL

```
when Order.Amount > 10:
    print "big sale!"
```

We'd like to give users the following information: "Because 'Order.Amount > 10' eval-uated to true, executing the rule action." The problem is how to get the string that represents the rule.

It turns out it's simple to do. We ask the compiler nicely, as shown in listing 12.11.

Listing 12.11   Providing the `Initialize()` method with the condition string
---

```
[Meta]
public static MethodInvocationExpression when(
    Expression condition, BlockExpression action)
{
    var conditionBlock = new Block(condition.LexicalInfo);
    conditionBlock.Add(new ReturnStatement(condition));
    return new MethodInvocationExpression(
        // The init method
        new ReferenceExpression("Initialize"),
        // A delegate with the condition
        new BlockExpression(conditionBlock),
        // a delegate with the action
        action,
        new StringLiteralExpression(condition.LexicalInfo.FileName),
        // Will translate the code into a string, and turn that into
        // a string Literal, so we can pass that as a parameter
        // to the When method
        new StringLiteralExpression(condition.ToCodeString())
    );
}

public void Initialize(Func<bool> condition, Action action,
                        string filename, string conditionString)
{
    Filename = filename;
    Condition = condition;
    Action = action;
    ConditionString = conditionString;
}
```

The important part here happens in the `when()` meta-method. We translate the call to the `when` keyword into a call to the `Initialize()` method. We're passing the argu-ments that we got, and also a string literal with the code that was extracted from the relevant expression.

Our ability to play around with the AST has allowed us to handle this scenario gracefully. What this means is that now we can access the condition as a string at run-time by accessing the property. We can display that information to the user, log it, or store it as part of the audit process.

Strings are good if you need the information for display purposes, but if you want to process a piece of code at runtime, and you want to get access to the code object model, strings aren't useful. For that, there's another solution.

12.3.4   *Processing the AST at runtime*

We don't have to do anything complex in order to implement the ability to inspect the compiler AST at runtime. As we saw in chapter 6, when we talked about quasi-quotation, Boo already has the facilities to take a compiler's AST and translate that into the code that would re-create the originating AST.

This makes our task a lot easier, because we can utilize this functionality instead of trying to roll our own (been there, done that, wasn't fun). Listing 12.12 shows what we need to do.

Revisiting serialized AST nodes

The code in listing 12.12 contains something we haven't looked at so far: a call to `CompilationHelper.RevisitSerializedExpression`. What is this, and why is it needed?

Each step in the compiler pipeline adds additional information to the AST, which is required by the following steps. Meta-methods are executed fairly late in the compiler pipeline, after some of the steps required to compile serialized AST have been run.

We solve the problem of wanting to serialize AST too late in the pipeline by re-executing the steps to serialize the AST on the serialized node, which means that we can continue with the compilation process successfully.

Listing 12.12   Serializing the condition expression and passing it to `Initialize()`

```
[Meta]
public static MethodInvocationExpression when(
    Expression condition, BlockExpression action)
{
    //Translate the expression to code that will recreate this expression
    //at runtime
    Expression serializedCondition =
                new CodeSerializer().Serialize(condition);
    // Revisit condition to ensure proper compilation.
    CompilationHelper.RevisitSerializedExpression(serializedCondition);

    var conditionBlock = new Block(condition.LexicalInfo);
    conditionBlock.Add(new ReturnStatement(condition));
    return new MethodInvocationExpression(
        new ReferenceExpression("Initialize"),
        new BlockExpression(conditionBlock),
        action,
        new StringLiteralExpression(condition.LexicalInfo.FileName),
        new StringLiteralExpression(condition.ToCodeString()),
        serializedCondition
        );
}

public void Initialize(Func<bool> condition, Action action,
                    string filename, string conditionString,
                    Expression conditionExpression)
{
```

⊟ ◈ rule		{Script}
⊞ ◈ [Script]		{Script}
⊞ Action		{Method = {Void Prepare$closure$2()}}
⊞ Condition		{Method = {Boolean Prepare$closure$1()}}
⊟ ConditionExpression		{Order.Amount > 10}
⊟ ◈ [Boo.Lang.Compiler.Ast.BinaryExpression]		{Order.Amount > 10}
⊞ ◈ base		{Order.Amount > 10}
⊞ Left		{Order.Amount}
NodeType		BinaryExpression
Operator		GreaterThan
⊞ Right		{10}
⊞ ◈ Non-Public members		

Figure 12.3 Executing the code in listing 12.12 on the script in listing 12.10 allows access to the ConditionExpression property as an AST node at runtime.

```
    Filename = filename;
    Condition = condition;
    Action = action;
    ConditionString = conditionString;
    ConditionExpression = conditionExpression;
}
```

Using this code, we can take the script in listing 12.10 and get the results shown in figure 12.3.

It displays both the compiled expression and the AST that describes it. This is critically important, because you can now take this piece of AST and do transformations or views on it.

There are a lot of things that you can do with the AST once you have it. In fact, this is how LINQ works (see sidebar on the similarities between LINQ and the AST). A simple enough example is that you could take the condition AST and translate it to some graphical representation. But we covered the UI exhaustively in chapter 10; let's explore a more interesting use for processing the AST at runtime.

12.4   *Changing runtime behavior based on AST information*

One of the more annoying problems when building an internal DSL is that you have to deal with code-related issues, such as the NullReferenceException.

For example, let's say that we have the following order rule:

```
when Order.Amount > 10 and Customer.IsPreferred:
    ApplyDiscount 5.percent
```

We have a problem with this rule because we also support an anonymous-checkout mode in which a customer can create an order without registering on the site. In that

---

Similarities between LINQ and the AST

You might have noticed that there is a remarkable similarity between LINQ's expression trees (Expression<T>) and the AST. Indeed, an expression tree is an AST that's limited to expressions only. You can use the AST to do everything that you do with expression trees, and usually do it the same way.

If you have any prior knowledge of expression trees, it'll be applicable to AST manipulation, and if you understand the Boo AST, that knowledge is transferable to working with expression trees.

mode, the `Customer` property is `null`, and trying to access the `IsPreferred` property will throw a `NullReferenceException`.

We could rewrite the rule to avoid the exception, like this:

```
when Order.Amount > 10 and Customer is not null and Customer.IsPreferred:
    ApplyDiscount 5.percent
```

But I think this is extremely ugly. The business meaning of the code gets lost in the technical details. We could also decide to return a default instance of the customer when using anonymous checkout (using the Null Object pattern), but let's look at another way to handle this.

We can define the rule as invalid when `Customer` isn't there. This way, a rule shouldn't run if it references `Customer` when the `Customer` is null. The dirty way to hack this is shown in listing 12.13.

Listing 12.13   Hacking around the `NullReferenceException`

```
var referencesCustomer = File.ReadAllText(ruleName).Contains("Customer");
if(referencesCustomer && Customer == null)
    return;
```

If you grimaced when looking at this code, that's a good sign. Let's solve this properly, without hacks.

First, we already have help from the compiler because we have access to the condition expression (as shown in listing 12.12). We can utilize this to make decisions at runtime. In this case, we'll use this to detect when we're referencing a `null` property and mark the rule as invalid. You can see this in listing 12.14.

Listing 12.14   Deciding whether to execute the rule based on the `Customer` property

```
public void Execute()
{
    var visitor = new ReferenceAggregatorVisitor();
    visitor.Visit(ConditionExpression);
    if (visitor.References.Contains("Customer") && Customer == null)
        return;// Rule invalid

    bool result = Condition(); // Execute the condition
    RuleContext.AddConditionResult(this, result);
    if (result) // Execute the action if condition evaluates to true.
        Action();
}
```

The `ReferenceAggregatorVisitor` that's used in listing 12.14 is shown in listing 12.15.

Listing 12.15   `ReferenceAggregatorVisitor` finds references in a piece of code

```
public class ReferenceAggregatorVisitor : DepthFirstVisitor
{
    public IList<string> References = new List<string>();

    public override void OnReferenceExpression(ReferenceExpression node)
    {
```

```
        References.Add(node.Name);
        base.OnReferenceExpression(node);
    }
}
```

This is a simple example of how you can add smarts to the way your code behaves, and this technique is the foundation for a whole host of options. I use a similar approach for adaptive rules and for more complex auditable actions.

12.5 *Data mining your scripts*

Working with the AST doesn't just mean dealing with compiler transformations. There is a lot of information in the AST that you can use in ways you may find surprising.

For example, suppose you have a set of DSL scripts, and you want to see what users are using the DSL for. You can try to read it all, but it's much more interesting (and feasible) to use the compiler to do so, because this opens more options.

Take a look at the DumpExpressionsToDatabaseVisitor in listing 12.16. It extracts all the information from a script, breaks it down to the expression and statement level, and puts it in a database.

Listing 12.16   Extracting expressions from a script for use in data mining

```
public class DumpExpressionsToDatabaseVisitor
    : DepthFirstVisitor
{
    readonly string connectionString;

    public DataMiningVisitor(string connectionString)
    {
        this.connectionString = connectionString;
    }

    public override bool Visit(Node node)
    {
        using (var con = new SqlConnection(connectionString))
        using (var command = con.CreateCommand())
        {
            con.Open();
            command.CommandText = @"
            INSERT INTO Expressions (Expression, File)
            VALUES(@Expr,@File)";
            command.Parameters.AddWithValue("@Expr", node.ToString());
            command.Parameters.AddWithValue("@File",
                    node.LexicalInfo.File);
            command.ExecuteNonQuery();
        }
        Console.WriteLine(node);
        return base.Visit(node);
    }
}
```

You can make use of the DumpExpressionsToDatabaseVisitor by executing it over all your scripts, as shown in listing 12.17.

> **Listing 12.17 Extracting expression information from all scripts in a directory**

```
foreach (var file in Directory.GetFiles(dsl, "*.boo"))
{
    var compileUnit = BooParser.ParseFile(file);
    new DumpExpressionsToDatabaseVisitor (connectionString)
        .Visit(compileUnit);
}
```

Note that this is *disposable code,* written for a single purpose and with the intention of being thrown out after it's used. But why am I suggesting this?

Well, what would happen if you ran this code on your entire DSL code base and started applying metrics to it? You could query your code structure using SQL, like this:

```
select count(*), Expression from Expressions
group by Expression
order by count(*) desc
```

This will find all the repeated idioms in your DSL, which will give you a good idea about where you could help your users by giving them better ways of expressing themselves.

For example, let's say you found that this expression was repeated many times:

```
user.IsPreferred and order.Total > 500 and \
    (order.PaymentMethod is Cash or not user.IsHighRisk)
```

This is a good indication that a business concept is waiting to be discovered here. You could turn that into a part of your language, with something like this:

```
IsGoodDealForVendor
```

Here we aren't interested in the usual code-quality metrics; we're interested in business-quality metrics. Getting this information is easy, and it'll ensure that you can respond and modify the language based on user actions and input.

12.6 *Creating DSLs that span multiple files*

It's common to think about each DSL script independently, but this is a mistake. We need to consider the environment in which the DSL lives. In the same way that we rarely consider code files independently, we shouldn't consider scripts independently.

For example, in the Message-Routing DSL we might have a rule like this:

```
priority 10
when msg is NewOrder and msg.Amount > 10000:
    dispatch_to "orders@strategic"
```

While building our DSL our focus might be mainly on the actual language and syntax we want. But we may need to perform additional actions, rather than just dispatch the message, such as logging all strategic messages. As you can see, we can easily add this to the DSL:

```
priority 10
when msg is NewOrder and msg.Amount > 10000:
    log "strategic messages" , msg
    dispatch_to "orders@strategic"
```

routing_scripts
  behaviors
    after
      dispatch_to_error_queue_if_not_dispatched
      log_strategic_messages
  routes
    orders
      dispatch_big_new_orders_to_strategic_customers_handling   **Figure 12.4   A suggested folder**
      dispatch_standard_new_orders_to_normal_customers_handling   **structure for the Message-Routing DSL**

But this is a violation of the single responsibility principle, and we care about such things with a DSL just as much as we do with code. So we could leave the original snippet alone and add another script:

```
when destination.Contains("strategic"):
    log "strategic messages", msg
```

Now the behavior of the system is split across several files, and it's the responsibility of the DSL engine to deal with this appropriately. One way to arrange this would be to use the folder structure shown in figure 12.4.

The DSL engine can tell from the information in the message that it needs to execute only the routing rules in /routes/orders, and it can execute the after actions without getting the routing scripts tied to different concerns.

If you want to be a stickler, we're dealing with two dialects that are bound to the same DSL engine. In this case, they're similar to one another, but that doesn't have to be the case.

Multifile DSLs don't have to combine the execution of several scripts for the different dialects; they could also be used to execute different scripts in the same dialect. Consider the possible folder structure shown in figure 12.5.

In this case, the DSL is based on the idea of executing things in reverse depth order. When a message arrives, we try to match it to the deepest scope possible (in this case, handling strategic customers), and we go up until we reach the root.

Nevertheless, this is still just another way of bringing several scripts of the same DSL together, albeit in a fairly interesting way. In section 12.8, we'll deal with a single DSL that's built of several files, each of them belonging to a different DSL implementation. We still have a bit to cover before going there, though.

For now, remember that when you're designing and building a DSL, thinking about a single file is the easiest way to go, but you ought to consider the entire environment when you make decisions. A language that doesn't support separation of concerns (the process of separating a computer program into distinct features that

routing_scripts
  routes
    orders
      dispatch_big_new_orders_to_strategic_customers_handling
    convention_based_dispatching   **Figure 12.5   A convention-based folder**
    log_strategic_messages   **structure for the Message-Routing DSL**

overlap in functionality as little as possible, discussed in detail at http://en.wikipe-dia.org/wiki/Separation_of_concerns) is bound to get extremely brittle quickly.

12.7 Creating DSLs that span multiple languages

Another common misconception about DSLs is that you can only have a single language in a DSL. We've already looked at including several dialects of a language in a DSL for versioning purposes, but that's not what I'm talking about here. What I have in mind is a single DSL composed of several different languages, each with its own purpose. Each language implementation contributes toward the larger collective DSL.

Conceptually, those different languages compose a single DSL with a single language that has different syntax for different parts of the system. From the implementation perspective, we are talking about different DSLs with a coordinator that understands how they all work and how to combine them.

As a simple example, let's consider the Message-Routing DSL again. Currently it is used for two separate purposes: message routing, and translating the message from an external representation to its internal one. This works for now, but it's likely to cause problems when the system grows. How will we handle a single message arriving at multiple endpoints and needing to be dispatched to several endpoints, but having to go through the same transformation?

A good solution would be to split the functionality of translating messages from that of the message routing. We'd have a DSL for translating messages, and another for routing messages, and both would work in concert to achieve their goals.

I know that this is a bit abstract, but the next section will go into all the implementation details you could want.

12.8 Creating user-extensible languages

Developers aren't the only ones who can extend languages. You can build a language that allows users to extend it without requiring any complex knowledge on their part.

Once you release a language into the hands of your users, it will take a while before you can release a new version. That means that if users don't have a way to solve a problem right now, they will brute force a solution. By giving users the ability to extend the language themselves (and remember, we're talking about business users here, not developers), you can reduce the complexity that will show up in your DSL scripts (reducing the maintenance overhead).

12.8.1 The basics of user-extensible languages

Suppose we wanted to build a DSL to handle order management. Here's a typical scenario:

```
when is_preferred_user and order_amount > 500:
    apply_discount 5.percent
```

This rule sounds reasonable, right? Except that it isn't a good example of a business rule. A business rule usually has a lot more complexity to it.

Listing 12.18 shows a more realistic example.

Listing 12.18   A typical order-management business rule

```
when user.payment_method is credit_card and \
    ((order_amount > 500 and order_amount < 1200)\
     or number_of_payments < 4) and \
     user.is_member_of("weekend buy club") \
     and Now.DayOfWeek in (DayOfWeek.Sunday, DayOfWeek.Saturday)
     and applied_discounts < 10:
     apply_discount 5.percent
```

At a glance, it's hard to understand exactly what this rule does. This is a good example of a stagnant DSL. It's no longer being actively developed (easily seen by the use of framework terms such as DayOfWeek, which in most cases you'll want to abstract away), and the complexity is growing unchecked.

Usually, this happens when the DSL design has not taken into account new functionality, or when it relies on the DSL developers to extend the language when needed. Because it requires developer involvement, it's often easier for users to solve problems by creating complex conditionals rather than expressing the business logic in a readable way.

A good way to avoid additional complexity and reduced abstraction is to incorporate known best practices from the development side in your DSLs, such as allowing encapsulation and extensibility.

As a simple example, we could allow the user to define conditions, as shown in listing 12.19. Those conditions allow users to define their own abstraction, which then becomes part of the language.

Listing 12.19   Defining business conditions in a user-editable script

```
define weekend_club_member:
    user.is_member_of("weekend club member")

define sale_on_weekend:
    Now.DayOfWeek in (DayOfWeek.Sunday, DayOfWeek.Saturday)

define good_payment_option: # Yes, I know, it is a bad name, sorry
    ((order_amount > 500 and order_amount < 1200) \
        or number_of_payments < 4)
```

Now the condition becomes much simpler, as shown in listing 12.20.

Listing 12.20   With user-defined abstractions, the rule becomes much simpler

```
when user.payment_method is credit_card and good_payment_option \
        and sale_on_weekend and weekend_club_member and \
        applied_discounts < 10:
    apply_discount 5.percent
```

This is important, because it avoids language rot and allows the end user to add abstraction levels. But how can we implement this?

> **Build the facilities for abstractions**
>
> If you want to create a language that's both usable and maintainable, you have to give users the facilities to create and use abstractions. This is a common theme in this chapter.
>
> Just because the code that users write is a DSL script doesn't mean that good design guidelines should be ignored. The separation of concerns principle and the DRY (Don't Repeat Yourself) principle are important even here.
>
> We can ignore them to some degree when we're building our languages, because with languages that aren't aimed at developers, too much abstraction can cause the language to be inaccessible, but we can't truly disregard them.

We'll do it by integrating another DSL into our DSL. You've already seen that DSL (the Business-Condition DSL) in listing 12.19—it's focused on capturing business conditions, and it works alongside the Order-Processing DSL to give users a good way of capturing common conditions and abstracting them.

And now, let's get into the implementation details.

12.8.2 *Creating the Business-Condition DSL*

The first thing you need to know about the Business-Condition DSL is that it's hardly a DSL. In fact, we'll cheat our way out of implementing it.

The problem is simple. If we wanted to make this a full-blown DSL, we'd have to deal with quite a bit of complexity in making sure that we map the concepts from the Business-Condition DSL to the Order-Processing DSL. Instead, we're going to simply *capture* the business condition and transplant it whole into the Order-Processing DSL.

Listing 12.21 shows how we can extract the business condition from a set of definition files that follow the format shown in listing 12.18.

Listing 12.21   The Business-Condition DSL extracts definitions from the file

```
public class Define
{
    private Expression expression;

    public Expression Expression
    {
        get { return expression == null ? null : expression.CloneNode(); }
        set { expression = value == null ? null : value.CloneNode(); }
    }

    public string Name {get;set; }
}

public class BusinessConditionDslEngine
{
    private readonly string path;
```

```
public BusinessConditionDslEngine(string path)
{
    this.path = path;
}

public IEnumerable<Define> GetAllDefines()
{
    foreach (var definition in
        FileHelper.GetAllFilesRecursive(path, "*.define"))
    {
        var compileUnit = BooParser.ParseFile(definition);

        foreach (MacroStatement defineStatement in
            compileUnit.Modules[0].Globals.Statements)
        {
            string name = ((ReferenceExpression)
                          defineStatement.Arguments[0]).Name;
            var statement = ((ExpressionStatement)
                            defineStatement.Block.Statements[0]);
            Expression expression = statement.Expression;

            yield return new Define
            {
                Name = name,
                Expression = expression
            };
        }
    }
}
```

What is going on here? The Define class is trivial, but it has a subtle gotcha that you should be aware of. You *must not* share an AST node (expression or statement) if you intend to reuse it afterward. AST nodes are mutable, and the compilation process *will* change them. When you need to share an AST node, always share a copy of the node.

The code in the GetAllDefines() method in listing 12.21 is a lot more interesting, though. Here we use the Boo parser to get the AST from the file, and then we walk through the AST and extract the information that we want.

The AST is structured as a compilation unit, containing a list of modules, each mapping to a single input file. A module is composed of namespace imports, type definitions, and globals; all the free-floating statements end up in the globals section in the AST. Because we only passed a single file, we have only a single module.

Listing 12.21 assumes that the file is composed of only macro statements (there is no error handling in the code, because we also assume correct input). For each of those statements, we get the define name (which is the first argument) and the single expression inside the macro block. We stuff them into the define class, and we're done.

> ## Why is `define` a macro?
>
> We haven't created a `DefineMacro` class inheriting from an `AbstractAstMacro`, so why does the compiler think that this is a macro?
>
> The short answer is that the compiler doesn't; the compiler isn't even involved. It's the Boo parser we're using here, and the parser doesn't care about such things. The parser contains a rule for recognizing things that look like macro statements.
>
> When the parser finds something that looks like a macro statement, it creates an instance of the `MacroStatement` AST node. Later in the compiler pipeline, there is a step (`MacroExpander`) that will look at the macro statement and decide whether there is a matching macro implementation.
>
> Because we never involve the compiler pipeline in listing 12.21, we can directly access the AST and rely on the parser to do this work for us.

Once we have those definitions, plugging them into the Order-Processing DSL is easy. Listing 12.22 shows the important details.

Listing 12.22   Finding references to definitions and replacing them with values

```
public class ReplaceDefinitionsWithExpression :
    AbstractTransformerCompilerStep
{
    private readonly Define[] defines;

    public ReplaceDefinitionsWithExpression(Define[] defines)
    {
        this.defines = defines;
    }

    public override void Run()
    {
        Visit(CompileUnit);
    }

    public override void OnReferenceExpression(ReferenceExpression node)
    {
        Define define = defines.FirstOrDefault(x => x.Name == node.Name);
        if (define != null)
        {
            ReplaceCurrentNode(define.Expression);
        }
    }
}
```

This is a pretty straightforward implementation. This compiler step will search for all reference expressions (the names of things, such as variables, methods, types, and so on). If it finds a reference expression whose name matches the name of a definition, it will replace the reference expression with the definition expression.

For example, given the following definition,

```
define strategic_order:
    Order.Amount > 1000
```

and the following order rule,

```
when strategic_order:
    print "big sale!"
```

the strategic_order reference expression will be replaced with Order.Amount > 1000.

Now, all we have left to do is to plug ReplaceDefinitionsWithExpression into the DSL engine. Listing 12.23 shows how this is done.

Listing 12.23 `OrderRuleDslEngine` modified to understand definitions

```
public class OrderRuleDslEngine : DslEngine
{
    private readonly Define[] defines;

    public OrderRuleDslEngine(Define[] defines)
    {
        this.defines = defines;
    }

    protected override void CustomizeCompiler(BooCompiler compiler,
        CompilerPipeline pipeline, string[] urls)
    {
        compiler.Parameters.References.Add(typeof(BooCompiler).Assembly);
        pipeline.Insert(1,
                    new ImplicitBaseClassCompilerStep(
                        typeof(OrderRule),
                        "Prepare"));
        pipeline.Insert(2, new ReplaceDefinitionsWithExpression(defines));
    }
}
```

The OrderRuleDSLEngine class accepts the definitions in the constructor and registers the ReplaceDefinitionsWithExpression compiler step as the second step in the pipeline. That's all we need to do. Because the step is one of the first to run, as far as the compiler is concerned, we're compiling this:

```
when Order.Amount > 1000:
    print "big sale!"
```

Listing 12.24 brings it all together.

Listing 12.24 Adding `defines` to a Quote-Generation script

```
DslFactory factory = new DslFactory();
var defines = new BusinessConditionDslEngine("Defines").GetAllDefines();
factory.Register<OrderRule>(new OrderRuleDslEngine(defines));
var rule = factory.Create<OrderRule>("Script.boo");
```

Now, users can introduce new keywords and concepts into the language themselves, without requiring developers to modify it for them.

> **The difference between Business-Condition DSL defines and C or C++ defines**
>
> If you have ever worked with C or C++, you're probably familiar with the `#define` statement, which allows you to do pretty much what I have outlined in section 12.8.2.
>
> The main difference between the two approaches is that in the C/C++ approach, defines use text substitution, which exposes a whole host of problems. You only have to remember the guidance about proper use of parentheses in defines to realize that.
>
> The approach outlined here uses AST substitution, which means that it's far more robust, easy to extend, and safer to use.

In one project where I introduced this approach, I also allowed users to extract a business condition from a rule and automatically refactor. Not only did it create the appropriate definition file, but it also scanned all the other existing rules and modified them if they had the same extracted rule. (If you want to try this yourself, consider using `Node.Matches()` to compare the different nodes.)

12.9   *Summary*

In previous chapters, we focused on the baseline knowledge, on building simple DSLs in Boo, and on understanding the AST and how DSLs fit in with the development lifecycle. In this chapter, we finally started to bring it all together.

We looked at scaling a DSL up (in terms of numbers of scripts and usage), managing deployment, and ensuring that we have sufficient control over how we deploy new DSL scripts to production.

We also focused on AST manipulation, and how we can use that to get all sorts of interesting results from our DSL. I am particularly fond of the ability to capture and manipulate the AST at runtime, because that gives us almost limitless power.

Finally, we touched on refactoring and giving users the ability to build their own abstractions. I find this to be an essential step for giving users a rich language that can evolve over time with minimal developer effort. It also helps keep language rot from setting in. (If users have to call a developer to get a change, that change will often either not be made or be made late, necessitating awkward workarounds.) We'll talk more about abstractions and how to ensure that we build the right ones in chapter 13.

This chapter has been a whirlwind of various implementation details and ways to utilize them. At the moment, it may seem hard to tie all of them together, and, indeed, they're used in different stages of the project and for different reasons. I hope that the next chapter, in which we build a full-blown DSL implementation from scratch, will clear things up. Let's begin ...

13

A real-world
DSL implementation

In this chapter

- Building real-world DSLs
- Exploring the language usage
- Going beyond the code

We've covered a lot of ground in our journey to learn about and build DSLs. We've explored the reasons for building them, the intricacies of their implementation, and how to extend a language to meet specific needs. We considered what's involved in creating a good language: testing, versioning, documentation, user interface, and supporting tools. We also spent the previous chapter reviewing a host of implementation challenges related to particular needs, along with approaches for solving them.

The only thing we haven't done yet is use all that knowledge in a cohesive manner. The languages we've built so far were meant to showcase specific features, so they were fairly focused and simplistic.

This chapter will demonstrate how to create and use a DSL, how to evolve it along with a project, and how to understand the domain and the requirements. The first half of the chapter is dedicated to concepts, and to designing and building a DSL. The second half is dedicated to the implementation details of that DSL. We'll start as we would in the real world, by looking into the scenario where a DSL might be useful.

13.1 Exploring the scenario

In this chapter, suppose we're building an order-processing backend for an online shop. These types of systems tend to grow in both size and complexity quickly, because they're the heart and soul of the store—the place where the business can truly differentiate itself from countless other competitors. Having a better backend system allows you to change the business direction more rapidly, and this is a significant competitive advantage.

We'll put special emphasis on the extensibility of the system, and we'd like to define the policy of the system externally, because this is the aspect that so often changes. To that end, we have settled on the following design decisions:

- Much of the policy of the system will be defined using a DSL or a set of DSLs.
- The system behavior will be implemented normally, using our standard programming language.
- At various points in the lifetime of the system, we'll shell out decisions to the DSL (or DSLs), and then act upon them.

We'll use a DSL because we need the flexibility. We want a clear separation between implementation and policy, and we want to be able to define the policy in terms the customer can grasp, follow, and extend. Remember, no business system ever succeeded because it was good at parsing XML. The value of a system comes from being able to change in response to market conditions.

Given all of that, what usage do we expect for our DSL? I generally start with the explicit assumption that whatever I come up with will need recalibration later on. Trying to figure out everything up front is expensive, and will blind us to better options along the way. Even if we get it perfect, the business will have changed by the time we finish writing the system, and we'd need to change it anyway. Because of that, I prefer

---

Separating policy and execution behavior

An approach that I take in most of my projects is to create a strict separation between the policy of the system and the execution behavior.

What do I mean by that? Being able to process a discount on an order is part of the *execution behavior* of the system. Deciding who should get a discount is a *policy decision*.

The execution behavior of a system tends to be fairly fixed, but the policy changes frequently. If you maintain a proper separation between the two, you'll find that you can make changes to the policy in isolation. Putting much of the policy in a DSL creates an explicit boundary between the two.

to start working in a changing environment from the get go. It usually means that I get good at handling changes.

With that said, we will initially plan for the DSL to be used in two ways:

- *Order authorization*—We may want to perform different actions based on credit rating, payment plans, and purchase history. This is a place where I want to be able to express myself in a way that is both unambiguous and crystal clear, so it is a good candidate for a DSL.
- *Shopping cart modifications*—This is where we manage offers, packaging, and similar order choices. For example, perhaps buying two books by the same author will give you a discount for a third one by the same author. Or buying three DVDs may grant you free shipping. The result of the DSL will affect the user interface of the system.

Implementing this will be a challenge, even though I've limited the scope of the project to fit it in a single chapter. Let's get to work.

13.2 Designing the order-processing system

We need to build the system in such a way that we can easily communicate intent and move between the DSL view of the world and the system implementation view of the world. I'm not going to expand on the subject of building systems that express intent. That's a subject for a book all its own, and Eric Evans did a great job of that when he wrote *Domain-Driven Design*.

I *will* touch on the parts of the system that relate directly to system implementation and interaction with the DSL. We'll start by looking at what we know we're going to need, and then start drafting an *application design* for it. Note that this isn't a *DSL design*; we're going to think about how the application will behave. This is important, because we don't want to tie the logic and behavior of the application to our DSL. Instead, we want the DSL to use the application behavior.

Let's look at the shopping cart as a specific example. We already know that we have rules that allow us to modify the shopping cart, and we can envision those rules performing the following actions:

- Add and remove shopping cart items
- Add and remove item discounts
- Add and remove shopping cart discounts
- Add messages to items
- Add messages to shopping carts

Using those simple rules, it's possible to produce complex behavior.

But how are we going to implement this? Figure 13.1 shows a rough outline of the initial design. This is still a simplified example, and in the real world you'd likely need to do more, but it's a good example of an important concept.

It's likely that you've created a shopping cart in the past, but this design is slightly different. In figure 13.1, you can see that we have the fairly standard ShoppingCart,

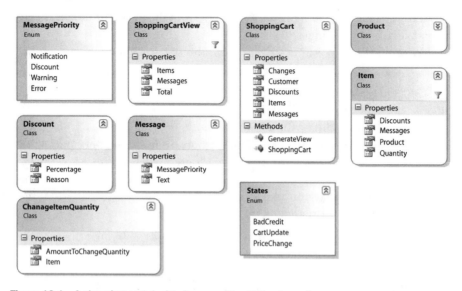

Figure 13.1   A shopping cart design for use with a DSL rule engine

Product, and Item classes, where the Item class's Quantity property specifies the quantity of a particular product in the shopping cart.

But why do we need Discount and ChangeItemQuantity classes? And why does a shopping cart need the concept of messages?

This shopping cart is built in this manner to make sure that we can easily integrate a versatile backend without creating cascading changes throughout the system. It's also a good way to structure things in general, because it gives us an object model in which we're mostly adding to the shopping cart, and only rarely modifying the user choices directly. This is important, because by using the addition-only approach we have a domain model that's auditable. This means that we can ask any shopping cart to explain what caused it to reach that particular total.

Another important design consideration is differentiating between items users place in the cart from item quantity changes the backend may have changed based on some policy decision.

As usual, an example tends to make everything clearer. Suppose we have the following requirement: if you buy all seven Harry Potter books, you'll pay for the Harry Potter bundle (a reduced price). This means the user either can select the bundle explicitly or can order each of the books without being aware of the existence of that special deal.

In the domain model in figure 13.1, we'll model the second case as a shopping cart with one item for each of the Harry Potter books. The backend will then make the following changes:

- Create one ChangeItemQuantity for each of the Harry Potter books, with AmountToChangeQuantity set to -1 (removing all the books that the user has selected from the cart, but not changing the ShoppingCart.Items collection)

- Create one `ChangeItemQuantity` for the Harry Potter bundle, with `Amount-ToChangeQuantity` set to 1 (adding it to the cart)
- Add a message saying that you're now buying the Harry Potter bundle for a reduced price

Note that to get that requirement working, we didn't have to modify the items that the user has selected—that list is still unmodified in the `ShoppingCart.Items` collection. For presentation purposes, we also have a simplified view on top of the shopping cart, called `ShoppingCartView`.

The `ShoppingCartView` is similar to a traditional shopping cart, but it only has the concepts of items and messages. Items are what the user will end up buying (one bundle of Harry Potter books, in this example), and messages are information for the user. A discount, for example, is translated in the view into a modified price for an item and a message notifying the user of the discount. You'll see the advantages of this approach when we start to implement the DSL engine.

Having designed our application and having a firm idea about how we'll build the system behavior, we can move on to see what kind of language and semantics we can put on top of that.

13.3 *Thinking in tongues*

The next step to take is to build a DSL that would integrate with the design of our Shopping-Cart DSL. That DSL will be a rule engine, which is almost the default starting place for DSLs because they're the easiest to build. I have a default syntax and approach for such rule engines, as shown in listing 13.1.

Listing 13.1 Default syntax for a rule engine

```
when [some business condition]:
    [some action]
    [another action]
```

In listing 13.2, you can see the syntax used for a real scenario: giving a preferred member a discount for large orders.

Listing 13.2 An example of using the rule engine syntax for a real-world rule

```
when cart.Total > 1000 and customer.TotalPurchaseAmount > 5000:
    msg = "Preferred members get 5% discount for orders over 1,000$"
    add_cart_discount 5, msg
```

By now you should be familiar with the mechanics of building such a DSL. If you need a refresher, take a look at the languages we built in chapter 4 and the syntax options in chapter 12.

Beyond the basics, tracing and auditing support is important, and you'll probably want to keep that in mind as you write your DSLs. This means that all actions that originate from a DSL script should be traced back to that DSL script, and hopefully also back to the business decision that prompted them.

Ordinarily, I would start implementing the DSL at this point, and we'll do that in the second half of this chapter. But for now, let's focus on the design considerations and on how different needs can (and should) influence a DSL's implementation and syntax to fit the DSL's requirements and purposes. In keeping with this, let's look at how we'll apply the syntax we used for the Shopping-Cart DSL to order authorization, and then we can identify the problems that will lead us to a better design.

From the syntax point of view, the Order-Processing DSL initial syntax is similar to the Shopping-Cart DSL, as listing 13.3 shows.

Listing 13.3   Initial syntax for the Order-Processing DSL

```
when state is auth_denied and customer.TotalPurchaseAmount > 5000:
    delay_order_until_payment_is_authorized "preferred customer benefit"

when state is auth_denied and customer.TotalPurchaseAmount <= 5000:
    cancel_order "no pay, no product"
```

The problem with this syntax is that there is something missing here. It's not nearly as expressive as it could be, and we're drowning in the details. Listing 13.4 shows an alternative, in which we make the concept of the order state an explicit notion in the language.

Listing 13.4   Order-Processing DSL with explicit order state

```
upon auth_denied:

    when customer.TotalPurchaseAmount > 5000:
    delay_order_until_payment_is_authorized "preferred customer benefit"

    when customer.TotalPurchaseAmount <= 5000:
        cancel_order "no money, no order"
```

The DSL now makes the concept of order state explicit. Before it was part of the condition to check, and now it's an explicit concept in the language, which allows us to discuss what is going on more clearly.

We can make use of this syntax to handle the behavior of the system in other states, such as the rule in listing 13.5.

Listing 13.5   Using the syntax to handle a customer having a low credit rating

```
upon low_credit_rating:

    when customer.TotalPurchaseAmount > 5000:
        authorize_funds cart.Total * 0.5,  \
            "Preferred customers authorize half the amount"

    when customer.TotalPurchaseAmount <= 5000:
        authorize_funds cart.Total,  \
            "Full authorization for low credit rating scenarios"
```

One thing that's implicit in listings 13.2 through 13.5 is the notion of preferred customers being those whose total purchase amount exceeds 5,000. In general, it's best to avoid implicit concepts, and to make them explicit instead. The problem is that although this example is very narrow, showing only a few concepts and examples, there will be many more in real-world situations. We can't turn them all into explicit language concepts, if only because that would make the language so much bigger and heavier than it needs to be.

This is where the notion of allowing users to add their own concepts to the language comes into play. We've looked at the implementation details for this feature in chapter 12. By implementing this feature, we can make our language much more expressive and allow users to extend it without requiring developer involvement.

WARNING When you give users the ability to extend the language, you should beware of unauthorized extensions. The DSL is a communication tool, not a programmatic tool. As such, new concepts should only be introduced into the language once they've been discussed and agreed upon by the users and business experts.

But even after this feature is implemented, there is still an implicit concept in place that we need to take care of. In fact, there are several. What we have at this point is a language that works, but it's not polished yet. It's important to find those missing concepts and add them to the language—that will change your language implementation from an acceptable to a truly excellent language. With DSLs, we want to turn implicit concepts into explicit ones.

13.4 *Moving from an acceptable to an excellent language*

The difference between acceptable and excellent languages is hard to define. Often, it's a small difference from the language implementer's point of view, but one that allow us to express our intent in a much clearer fashion. It's also a difference that you

---

Avoid implicit concepts

The whole purpose of a DSL is to make things clearer, and implicit concepts are anything but that. In many cases, you'll find your domain model and domain thinking getting bent out of shape until you realize that there's an implicit concept involved. At that point, you'll realize that you need to introduce a new explicit concept.

A quick way to find out if you have an implicit concept is to check whether there are any questions about the model that can only be answered by looking at all the DSL scripts. With the preferred customer example, that question is, "What are the benefits of a preferred customer?" As it stands (in listings 13.4 and 13.5), we would have to look at all the scripts where we make a decision about whether a customer is preferred or not in order to answer that question.

Because making policy decisions based on customer type is a common occurrence, we have an implicit concept here that we need to make explicit. The notion of a customer type needs to be explicit in both the Shopping-Cart DSL and the Order-Processing DSL.

can't plan for; you just need to be aware of friction points in the language and try to eliminate them.

Let's look at some implicit concepts. In listings 13.4 and 13.5 there is an implicit concept waiting to be discovered—the notion of the *preferred customer.*

Can we fix it by changing the way we define *preferred customer?* Using the same method we discussed in section 12.8.2 (Creating the Business-Condition DSL), we can define what a preferred customer is explicitly. Listing 13.6 shows a refactored version of 13.4.

Listing 13.6   Refactoring listing 13.4 to introduce explicit preferred customer notion

```
upon auth_denied:
    when preferred_customer:
        delay_order_until_payment_is_authorized "preferred customer benefit"

    when default_customer:
        cancel_order "no money, no order"
```

Well, not quite. We have the notions of preferred customers and default customers, but we haven't defined what they *mean*—what does it mean to be a preferred customer? I'm not referring to the selection criteria for being a preferred customer (that you have to buy over some amount). What I am looking for is what being a preferred customer *entails (what the benefits are of being a preferred customer).*

You could try to identify the benefits of a preferred customer now, but doing so would require going through many scripts and trying to figure out which of them reference a preferred customer. The special treatment of certain customers is based on their characteristics, and that's something that can and should be made explicit. The business gives benefits to certain customers as a grouping of actions in certain scenarios. Gold customers get a 5 percent discount and free shipping, silver customers get free shipping and a coupon code, and so on. Businesses do not usually think first about the action and then about the cause.

The of keyword

I introduced a new concept in listing 13.7, from a syntactic point of view: the use of the of keyword in the language. We'll talk about this particular feature of the language in greater detail in section 13.5. I considered using for instead, which might have been more natural, but that's not valid Boo code and would require modifying the parser. of is just as good, and we can make direct use of it without any modifications.

Listing 13.7 shows how we can take the notion of making decisions based on the customer type and make it an explicit concept in the language.

Listing 13.7   A new syntax for the language, making the role of the customer explicit

```
treatment of preferred_customer

upon bad_credit:
    msg = "For preferred customers we only authorize half the amount"
    authorize_funds cart.Total * 0.5,  msg
```

```
upon cart_update:
    when cart.Total > 1000:
        msg = "Preferred members get 5% discount over 1,000$"

        add_cart_discount 5, msg
```

Now that we've made the state of the customer explicit, we can take it one step further and ask the system to give us a description of how different types of customers are treated. In several cases, the result can be quite surprising for the business.

The code in listing 13.7 also implies the existence of a treatment specification for a default customer, and the DSL engine needs to take care of selecting the appropriate specification based on the customer selection criteria.

Don't get caught on the exact syntax

The syntax in listing 13.7 is one way of representing the concepts we've talked about, but it's an approach that's suitable when the number of rules and states is low. If we're going to have several hundred of each, we'll likely need help in managing that. One way of doing this is through a UI, based on the syntax shown in listing 13.7.

For example, we could show the user what will happen to a preferred customer with a low credit rating, or what the treatment is for all customer types with a low credit rating. We looked at how to do such things in chapter 10, and we'll see another example of that in section 13.7.2.

Another way of handling this is to use the directory structure we discussed in chapter 5 to help organize the different aspects of the DSL's behavior in each state and for each customer type.

But that's enough theory for now. Let's move on to the second part of this chapter, and implement this DSL.

13.5　*Implementing the language*

To discuss the language implementation properly, we'll first look at the syntax, then discuss how it's implemented, and finally consider the implications of the implementation decisions.

The DSL syntax that we'll focus on is shown in listing 13.8. Figure 13.2 shows an overview of the DSL implementation.

Listing 13.8　An example of the Shopping Cart DSL

```
treatment of preferred_customer

upon bad_credit:
    authorize_funds cart.Total * 0.5,  "..."

upon cart_update:
    when cart.Total > 1000:
        add_cart_discount 5, "..."
```

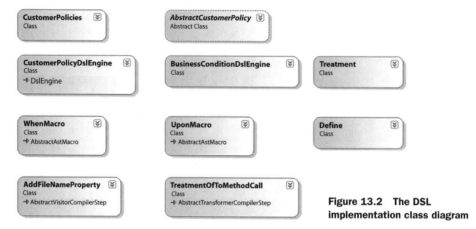

Figure 13.2   The DSL implementation class diagram

We'll tackle each of the components in figure 13.2 in turn:

- CustomerPolicies—This class is the engine, which is in charge of taking a set of DSL scripts and turning them into something that the application can make use of. This is the entry point to the DSL, and it should completely hide all details of the DSL from the application.

- AbstractCustomerPolicy—This is the implicit base class and is similar to the ones we've used elsewhere. This class describes the treatment in a given state for a particular type of customer.

- Treatment—This class contains the action that's taken for a particular customer type in a particular state.

- CustomerPolicyDslEngine—This class hooks together everything required to get the DSL compiled and running. We'll take a deeper look at it in the rest of this section.

- BusinessConditionDslEngine *and* Define—These classes were discussed in chapter 12; they allow users to define their own abstractions. In this implementation, I've adapted and extended how it works slightly. We'll look at this in detail when we look at how the first line in listing 13.8 works.

- WhenMacro *and* UponMacro—These classes are the macro implementations of the when and upon keywords.

- AddFileNameProperty—This class is a compiler step that adds a FileName property to the compiled code, which allows us to track which script generated the compiled code.

- TreatmentOfToMethodCall—This class implements the treatment of statement. We'll look at it in depth in the next section.

We will spend the rest of the chapter going over how all of those classes fit together to build a usable DSL.

13.5.1 *Exploring the treatment of statement's implementation*

As promised, we're going to dig into the implementation of the treatment of statement.

The first line in listing 13.8 uses a syntax we haven't talked about so far. The of keyword is used to specify generic arguments in Boo, and we're taking advantage of that syntax to parse this line, but this line isn't handled by the compiler. We're handling it ourselves, using the TreatmentOfToMethodCall compiler step.

The reason we're going that route is because the language has no other facilities that allow us to get what we want (or rather, no facilities that won't cause us too much trouble during implementation). Luckily, compiler steps are simple to write.

Listing 13.9 contains the full code of the TreatmentOfToMethodCall.

Listing 13.9 Converting treatment of into a TreatmentOf method call

```
public class TreatmentOfToMethodCall:
                 AbstractTransformerCompilerStep
{
    private readonly Define[] defines;

    public BehaviorOfToBehaviorMethodCall(Define[] defines)
    {
        this.defines = defines;
    }

    public override void Run()
    {
        Visit(CompileUnit);
    }

    public override void OnGenericReferenceExpression(
                     GenericReferenceExpression node)
    {
        // Verify that we are indeed trying to work with
        // 'treatment of' generic reference expression
        var methodName = node.Target as ReferenceExpression;
        if (node.GenericArguments.Count != 1 ||
            methodName == null ||
            methodName.Name != "treatment")
            return;

        // Get the generic argument, which is the business definition name
        var genericArg = ((SimpleTypeReference)node.GenericArguments[0]);
        // Find a business-level definition matching the arg name
        var define = defines.Where(x => x.Name == genericArg.Name)
            .First();
        // Create a method call for this
        var replacement = new MethodInvocationExpression(
            new ReferenceExpression("TreatmentOf"),
            define.ExpressionAsFunction,
            new StringLiteralExpression(define.Expression.ToCodeString())
            );

        ReplaceCurrentNode(replacement);
    }
}
```

The gist of this compiler step is that it takes a line such as this,

```
treatment  of preferred_customer
```

and turns it into one like this:

```
TreatmentOf(customer.TotalPurchaseAmount > 5000,
    "customer.TotalPurchaseAmount > 5000")
```

As you can see, the `preferred_customer` symbol was resolved into something meaningful. We make use of our ability to create a business-level definition to resolve the `preferred_customer` to the preferred customer selection criteria. We specify the mapping between the `preferred_customer` and its selection criteria in a definition file, which looks like listing 13.10.

Listing 13.10   Defining business-level concepts

```
define preferred_customer:
    customer.TotalPurchaseAmount > 5000

define default_customer:
    customer.TotalPurchaseAmount <= 5000
```

We parse the definitions in listing 13.10 and pass them to the `TreatmentOfToMethod-Call` compiler step, which then searches for generic type references named `behavior`. When it finds them, it turns them into `TreatmentOf` method calls, using the definitions in listing 13.10 to turn the generic argument name into the appropriate customer-selection specification. By doing this, we get a fairly natural syntax for specifying which customer type we're processing.

Unlike the `treatment` keyword, when and upon, the next most important keywords in our language, don't rely on a compiler hack but use the compiler extensibility mechanism that we explored in chapter 6. Let's look into them in detail.

13.5.2 *Implementing the upon and when keywords*

The upon keyword is implemented using a macro that is responsible for translating the upon keyword to the `UponState` method. The `UponMacro` macro is shown in listing 13.11.

Listing 13.11   The `UponMacro` implementation

```
public class UponMacro : AbstractAstMacro
{
    public override Statement Expand(MacroStatement macro)
    {
        // Get the first argument for the macro
        var name = (ReferenceExpression)macro.Arguments[0];
        // Resolve that name to a reference to the particular state
        // in the States enumeration
        var stateExpr = new MemberReferenceExpression(
            new ReferenceExpression("States"),
            UnderscoreCaseToPascalCase(name));
```

```
            // Create new anonymous delegate with single parameter 'cart'
            var action = new BlockExpression(macro.Body);
            action.Parameters.Add(new ParameterDeclaration("cart",
                new SimpleTypeReference(typeof(ShoppingCartView).FullName)));

            // Call the UponState method with the state enumeration,
            // the delegate to execute, and a string representation of
            // the action to be executed.
            return new ExpressionStatement(
                new MethodInvocationExpression(
                    new ReferenceExpression("UponState"),
                    stateExpr,
                    action,
                    new StringLiteralExpression(macro.Body.ToCodeString())
                    )
                );
        }
    }
}
```

The implementation is fairly straightforward. We grab the name of the first argument, change the naming convention from using underscores to Pascal casing, and generate a reference to the States enumeration. Then we take the body of the macro statement and generate a delegate from the macro body. We add a cart parameter to the generated delegate. Finally, we return a call to the UponState method, with the States enumeration value, a delegate that specifies what actions should be taken, and a string representation of those actions.

The end result is that this code,

```
upon bad_credit:
    authorize_funds cart.Total * 0.5,  "..."
```

is translated to this code:

```
UponState(States.BadCredit,
    delegate(ShoppingCart cart)
    {
        AuthorizeFunds(cart.Total * 0.5, "...");
    },
    "authorize_funds( (cart.Total * 0.5 ), '...')"
    );
```

In contrast, the when keyword is merely aliased to the if statement, as shown in listing 13.12. Ideally, this should be implemented as an auditable if, but I'll leave the implementation of that to you.

> **Listing 13.12 The when keyword is merely an alias for the if statement**

```
public class WhenMacro : AbstractAstMacro
{
    public override Statement Expand(MacroStatement macro)
    {
        return new IfStatement(macro.Arguments[0],
                               macro.Block, null);
    }
}
```

The auditable `if` is an important concept in creating debuggable DSLs. In essence, it's an `if` that tracks what the `if` condition evaluated to and records that in a place that's available for the user to inspect. (Other variations include creating a true audit log for regulatory purposes.) This gives the user a lot of information when they want to know why the system behaved in this way or that.

Speaking of audit information, it's not only decisions that need to be tracked. Source files and DSL scripts are also important, and we should make them as explicit as possible. Let's look at how.

13.5.3 *Tracking which file is the source of a policy*

Tracking which file was the source of a policy is a great help during auditing and debugging, so I usually make this an integrated part of my DSLs. The implementation is simple, as shown in listing 13.13.

Listing 13.13   Adding a property identifying the script that generated the class

```
public class AddFileNameProperty : AbstractVisitorCompilerStep
{
    public override void Run()
    {
        Visit(CompileUnit);
    }

    public override void OnClassDefinition(ClassDefinition node)
    {
        var fileNameProperty = new Property("FileName")
        {
            Getter = new Method("GetFileName")
        };
        var fileName = new StringLiteralExpression(
                        node.LexicalInfo.FullPath);
        fileNameProperty.Getter.Body.Add(new ReturnStatement(fileName));
        node.Members.Add(fileNameProperty);
    }
}
```

The code in listing 13.13 looks for a class definition, and when it finds one, it adds a syntactic property, `FileName`, to the class. This property will return the filename that represents the source of that class definition. Adding this property allows us to inspect, at runtime, the source of a particular class without trying to parse PDB files full of debugging symbols.

And now we just need to bring our DSL implementation back together.

13.5.4 *Bringing it all together*

The final implementation aspect we need to explore is how to take all of those components and turn them into a real language. The answer, as you've probably guessed, is that we use the `CustomerPolicyDslEngine` and `AbstractCustomerPolicy` classes, the second of which is shown in figure 13.3.

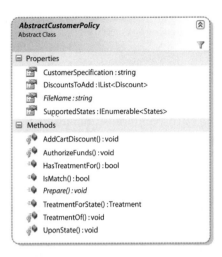

Figure 13.3 The AbstractCustomerPolicy class diagram

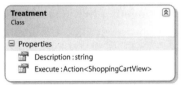

Figure 13.4 The Treatment class diagram

Note that the protected methods (`AddCartDiscount`, `AuthorizeFunds`, `TreatmentOf`, and `UponState`) are all part of either the DSL syntax (the first two) or the DSL implementation (the last two).

The public methods are how we'll work with the policy. As you can see in figure 13.3, this is mostly a simple matter. The only interesting tidbit here is the `TreatmentForState()` method's result, the `Treatment` class, which is shown in figure 13.4.

The `Treatment` class holds the `Description` (a string representation of the treatment code), and the delegate held in the `Execute` property will be executed to perform the action this treatment is supposed to have.

It starts to get interesting in the `CustomerPolicyDslEngine`, which is presented in listing 13.14. It brings everything we've seen so far together.

Listing 13.14 The `CustomerPolicyDslEngine` brings everything together

```
public class CustomerPolicyDslEngine : DslEngine
{
    private readonly Define[] defines;

    public CustomerPolicyDslEngine(Define[] defines)
    {
        this.defines = defines;
    }

    protected override void CustomizeCompiler(
        BooCompiler compiler, CompilerPipeline pipeline, string[] urls)
    {
        pipeline.Insert(1,
            new ImplicitBaseClassCompilerStep(
                typeof (AbstractCustomerPolicy),
                "Prepare",
                "Chapter13.DSL",
                "Chapter13.Model"));
```

```
    pipeline.Insert(2, new TreatmentOfToMethodCall(defines));
    pipeline.Insert(3, new AddFileNameProperty());
    pipeline.InsertBefore(
      typeof (ProcessMethodBodiesWithDuckTyping),
        new UnderscoreNamingConventionsToPascalCaseCompilerStep());
  }
}
```

There isn't much here that's special. It's all fairly common stuff, although we haven't seen it used together in the past. We mostly add a set of steps at the beginning of the compilation process to add the implicit base class, to handle the `treatment` of keyword, and to add the `FileName` property.

There are two subtleties you should be aware of in the `ImplicitBaseClassCompilerStep` class. First, we're adding Chapter13.DSL and Chapter13.Model as namespaces to be imported by default. We do this often enough, but here it's important because it's the import of Chapter13.DSL that makes the `when` and `upon` macros visible to the DSL and transforms them into keywords.

Second, we add the `AddFileNameProperty` after the `ImplicitBaseClassCompilerStep`. This is mandatory, because it is the `ImplicitBaseClassCompilerStep` that will create the `ClassDefintion` that `AddFileNameProperty` adds the `FileName` property to.

So far, though, we've only explored the infrastructure-level implementation. We still need to see how this DSL is being used.

13.6   *Using the language*

Usually, when you build a DSL, you won't want the rest of the system to directly use low-level constructs like `DslFactory` to interact with it. You'll want to put a layer in between, to ensure that the DSL is accessed consistently, and that the application does things properly to make sure that everything works (like calling `Prepare()` before using the script instances).

In the Shopping Cart DSL, the class that's responsible for ensuring proper usage of the DSL is called `CustomerPolicies`. You can see how it's used in listing 13.15.

> **Listing 13.15   Using the `CustomerPolicies` class**

```
var preferredCustomer = new Customer
{
    TotalPurchaseAmount = 6000
};
var policies = new CustomerPolicies("Scripts");
var policy = policies.For(preferredCustomer);
Console.WriteLine("Selected policy for {0}: {1} ",
    policy.CustomerSpecification,
    policy);

var treatment = policy.TreatmentForState(States.BadCredit);
Console.WriteLine("Treatment for bad credit is: {0}", treatment.Description);
```

This is the output of listing 13.15:

```
Selected policy for customer.TotalPurchaseAmount > 5000: PreferredCustomer
Treatment for bad credit is:
    authorize_funds((cart.Total * 0.5), '...')
```

As you can see, this is pretty simple. If we wanted to execute that treatment, we'd need to get a `ShoppingCartView` instance (which we can get from a `ShoppingCart` instance) and execute the treatment on the cart view. The implementation is shown in listing 13.16.

Listing 13.16 `CustomerPolicies` is the entry point for our DSL

```
public class CustomerPolicies
{
    private readonly DslFactory dslFactory;
    private AbstractCustomerPolicy[] policies;

    public CustomerPolicies(string rootFolder)
    {
        dslFactory = new DslFactory();
        Define[] defines = new BusinessConditionDslEngine(rootFolder)
            .GetAllDefines();
        dslFactory.Register<AbstractCustomerPolicy>(
            new CustomerPolicyDslEngine(defines));
        policies = dslFactory.CreateAll<AbstractCustomerPolicy>(
                            rootFolder);
        foreach (var policy in policies)
        {
            policy.Prepare();
        }
    }

    public AbstractCustomerPolicy For(Customer customer)
    {
        return policies
                .Where(x => x.IsMatch(customer))
                .FirstOrDefault();
    }
}
```

There isn't much here. We start by scanning for definition files (*.define files), which we then send to the DSL engine. Then we create all the policies and prepare them. When we request a particular policy, we return the first policy whose selection criteria matches the given customer.

And that's about it. This is the entire implementation of the DSL. This isn't a real-world scenario in the sense that you couldn't take the DSL out and use it as is; you'd need to plug in implementations for things like authorizing funds, canceling orders, and so on. But it's a real-world example in the sense that the complexity of the DSL implementation (as opposed to the real system making use of the DSL) matches that of a real-world DSL.

But looking at the code isn't enough. There are some topics outside the realm of the DSL code that we should look at.

13.7 *Looking beyond the code*

One of the things I've tried to focus on in this book is that writing the code to make things work isn't enough. There is a whole host of additional responsibilities you need to take care of beyond giving users the ability to type in your DSL, such as creating tests, providing a UI, and permitting integration with tools such as the IDE or inspecting execution results.

In this section, we'll look at those responsibilities and see how we can apply them to the DSL we're creating. So far we've gone over those concepts only in isolated examples; here we'll look at them all in the context of the Shopping Cart DSL.

13.7.1 *Testing our DSL*

You can look at the sample code to see how I tested the Shopping Cart DSL, so I won't bore you with that. But I will repeat how important tests are for correctness, for versioning, and for creating a language that you can rely on over time. It's easy to break something in a language if you don't have tests to cover you when you modify the language, and it's not pleasant to figure it out only when users report problems.

Chapter 8 covers testing in detail, so I'll just make one last suggestion for testing your DSLs: make sure that you clearly distinguish between tests that test the language implementation and tests that test policy decisions made by the language.

What do I mean by this? Look at the code in listing 13.17, which is taken from the test suite of the Shopping Cart DSL.

Listing 13.17   A test from the test suite of the Shopping Cart DSL

```
[Test]
public void CheckIfCustomerHasTreatmentForState()
{
    var policies = new CustomerPolicies("Scripts");
    var preferredCustomer = new Customer
    {
        TotalPurchaseAmount = 5001m
    };
    var policy = policies.For(preferredCustomer);
    Assert.IsTrue(policy.HasTreatmentFor(States.BadCredit));
    Assert.IsFalse(policy.HasTreatmentFor(States.PriceChange));
}
```

In the context of the test, we've defined a treatment for bad credit, but we have no behavior for price changes because the test also assumes that you've defined a script like the one shown in listing 13.8.

This is a good test for the *language feature*, but tests for policy decisions made by the DSL should be separate from language tests. They're going to test a completely different set of scripts in a wildly different context.

It's easy, particularly when you begin to implement a DSL from ideas that you're going to immediately use in your application, to mix the two types of tests. The problem with doing so is that your language tests end up being tied to policy decisions that have nothing to do with the language implementation. If we add a treatment to change the price for preferred customers, the language implementation tests should not break. This sounds obvious, but I have seen this happen, so take care to avoid this mistake.

Now let's look at an even more challenging problem—creating a user interface for our DSL.

13.7.2 Integrating with the user interface

The user interface is often seen as an external piece of the DSL, something that's completely separate from the language. Although this is one way to handle things, it's not necessarily the only way.

When you design a DSL, you should also think about the user interface that you intend to give your users. That will often change the way you build the language, not only because you need to give the UI more information, but also

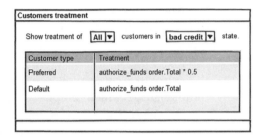

Figure 13.5 A mockup screen showing the DSL specification for treatment of the customers

because you can utilize the UI to make things easier for users.

In particular, a good UI will allow you to give users more information. For example, the Shopping Cart DSL can utilize the UI to show users what actions will be taken on bad credit for all types of customers, or what it means to be a preferred customer. This is an efficient way of writing documentation, and it's always guaranteed to be updated. Figure 13.5 shows a mockup of this UI.

Embracing external inputs as part of your domain

The UI isn't the only thing you can integrate your DSL with. In one project I worked on, the team made data a core concept in the DSL.

Many of the scripts in that project had to refer to specific items in the database and sometimes manipulate them. Instead of going with an API approach, we decided that because the items in the database had SKUs (stock-keeping units—IDs for the components in the system), and because users usually referred to them by their SKUs, we could make this an explicit concept in the model. Henceforth, the DSL knew that SKU1234 referred to an item SKU with the identifier 1234, and was able to pull it out of the database and give users access to its details by accessing its members. (Well, it was a bit more complex than that, because we had some performance concerns to deal with, but that was the gist of it.)

In another project, the DSL itself was composed of part Boo DSL and part XML files, which were used together to process the appropriate results. XML was mainly used to get a machine-readable format for lists and data, and the DSL was mainly used for logic and more complex operations.

These approaches do not always lead to good solutions, but they should be considered.

This interface shows the user data that the DSL scripts aren't able to show. It's displaying aggregated data across all treatments and in all states—something that you otherwise would have to remember or research every time you wanted to find out what is happening.

In short, don't limit yourself to the typical IDE options. A DSL can and should give you a lot more information, and using this information can give you a lot of insight into your business.

Now, although I've advised you not to limit yourself to the same old IDE clichés, there is one thing that you *should* limit: the scope of your DSL.

13.7.3 *Limited DSL scope*

When you're writing a DSL inside an existing language, you have the full power of the host language, which can provide great flexibility and also be a liability.

One of the most interesting capabilities of such a DSL is that it can go outside the box you've allocated to it. Occasionally, this approach can allow your DSL to jump the gap and become truly useful. This capability is what made Binsor (a Boo DSL for configuring the Windsor IoC container) a success.

But more often, this is a sign that your DSL isn't pulling its own weight and that you need to take action to rectify it. By definition, a DSL has a limited scope, and you should strive to make this scope as limited as possible. If you want a general-purpose programming language, I strongly suggest you don't write one yourself but use one of the hundreds that already exist.

I still remember quite distinctly the time when my configuration DSL morphed into an HTTP server to auto-update parts of the system on the fly. That kind of thing is a misuse, plain and simple, and should be avoided whenever possible. You should have a well-defined scope for what the DSL is supposed to do. There is a lot more value in having two DSLs, each of them focused on their own specific areas, than having a single DSL that attempts to serve both needs.

But even when you have several DSLs, you may still find yourself without the proper means of expressing what you want the way you want it using Boo. That's where Boo's openness comes to our aid again, allowing us to remake the basic language syntax to fit our needs.

13.8 *Going beyond the limits of the language*

Boo is a versatile language, and it can do quite a lot for you. We've spent this entire book playing within the confines of Boo, and it wasn't overly confining. Its flexible syntax can allow you to go a long way. That said, there will be situations in which what you want is beyond the scope of the language. In those cases, I have an alternative solution to creating an external DSL.

As I mentioned in chapter 1, Boo is an open language, but so far we've only talked about what you can do within the limits of Boo's default syntax. You can easily modify the parser that Boo uses to make it accept a different syntax, while keeping everything else the same so you still have the benefit of running on the CLR, using the open compiler to modify the code, and so on.

The Boo parser is defined using ANTLR, a parser generation tool (http://antlr.org). If you decide to modify the parser, I strongly recommend first reading Terence Parr's *The Definitive ANTLR Reference: Building Domain-Specific Languages*.

Before jumping headfirst into the Boo parser definition, there are a few other alternatives for generating parsers you may want to consider. The M language from Microsoft is, at the time of this writing, in early alpha stage, but it's supposed to deliver an easy syntax for defining languages. It also comes with a toolset that might well prove useful and interesting. I also find the GOLD parser (http://www.devincook.com/goldparser/) to be a very nice parser generator to work with. As it currently stands, both are useful for defining parsers for external DSLs, because they can turn a piece of text into an object graph.

An interesting experiment would be to use one of those parser generators to produce Boo AST, which you could then plug into the rest of the compiler pipeline. The Boo parser is just another step in the pipeline, which you can replace at will.

Another option, which I personally consider the most interesting one, would be to make use of Boo.OMeta. OMeta is a parser generator specification that is easy to work with and implement. The Boo compiler has been extended to support it, and in the future I expect to see not only compiler extensibility from Boo, but also parser extensibility using Boo.OMeta. You can see some of the experiments in that direction in the bamboozled archives: http://blogs.codehaus.org/people/bamboo/archives/001722_boo_ometa_and_extensible_parsing_i.html.

The future seems to be quite promising in this regard, and if you want to extend the Boo parser, I strongly suggest taking a look at Boo.OMeta before looking at other technologies.

13.9 *Summary*

The purpose of this chapter wasn't so much to impart new knowledge, but to set what we've already discussed in a real-world context, where you could see the forces and constraints that you'll need to deal with when building your own DSLs.

We started with a requirement to build an order-management system and then limited our scope to handling the shopping cart.

We proceeded to build a domain model that would allow us to plug in our behavior at runtime without undue difficulty. This was an important step, because actually managing the shopping cart is outside the responsibility of the DSL, yet it directly affects the DSL.

The model we built was designed to support external automated agents mucking about in the shopping cart. The explicit separation between actions that the user performs and actions that the DSL scripts initiate helps ensure system maintainability and debuggability in the long term.

After looking at the domain model, we started experimenting with various dialects of the DSL to see if we could devise one that would match our requirements. We went through three iterations before we settled on one that worked. In each case, the problem was an implicit concept that we sought to make explicit. Explicit concepts are important for clarity, because as long as they're implicit, their effect on the system is hard to understand and trace.

We then moved on to the implementation of the DSL, examining all the bits and pieces and assembling them together into a cohesive whole.

We also considered the separation between the DSL infrastructure and the interface that the rest of the application uses to communicate with the DSL. We kept them separated for a reason; that separation gave us the ability to contain the DSL implementation details in a small section of the application, instead of having it scattered all over the place.

Finally, we covered some advanced topics, like testing, UI integration, and integration with non-DSL sources in general.

In the space of a single chapter, I attempted to give you the sense of what it's like to create a real-world DSL project. A single chapter can't really cover all the details of a real-world project, but I hope that this has given you a good idea of what it's like.

The most important concept to take away from this chapter is that you should not try to fixate on a particular implementation, but be ready and willing to change the implementation of the DSL (indeed, of the application as a whole, sometimes) when new information makes it clear that the current path doesn't lead to a good place. I have been involved in several projects in which the first few months of DSL use exposed weaknesses in the model we were using. After we restructured the DSL, we had a far easier time dealing with the complexities that we had previously been struggling with. Flexibility is important, and not only when it comes to DSLs.

appendix A
Boo basic reference

This appendix deals with how to use Boo as a programming language, and aims mostly to get you familiarized with its syntax and behavior. It intentionally leaves out some details in order to speed the learning process and to provide a smooth path for learning to both write and read Boo programs. Appendix B supplies the details and is more rigorous in presenting the language.

For additional information about Boo, please visit Boo's site (http://boo. codehaus.org). For more information about the advanced features of Boo (those that make it so applicable as a DSL host language), please refer back to chapters 2 and 6.

NOTE This appendix was adapted from a Boo tutorial by Brent W. Hughes (http://home.comcast.net/~brent.hughes/BooWho.htm). I would like to thank Brent for writing this tutorial and allowing me to reuse it.

A.1 Prerequisites

It is assumed that you already know a little about programming—for example, what variables and functions are. It is also assumed that you have ready access to Boo's interpreter, complier, and interactive shell so you can experiment with the language as we go along. You can download these materials from Boo's website at http://boo.codehaus.org/.

A.2 The Boo interactive shell, interpreter, and compiler

For many of our examples, we will use booish, the Boo interactive shell. It acts much like a Boo-powered calculator, which is very convenient when you wish to quickly try out some ideas.

You start the Boo interactive shell by just entering booish at the command-line prompt. (If you're using Windows, you will first need to open a command-line window.) When booish is ready for you to type something in, it displays three greater-than signs as a prompt. After the prompt, you can calculate 2 + 2.

```
>>> 2 + 2
4
```

You could also type this:

```
>>> print 2 + 2
4
```

Why would you type print if you didn't need to? Well, you might not do this in the interactive shell, but when you're writing a program to be run by the interpreter (booi) or compiled by the compiler (booc), you will need to use print (or an equivalent function) to display the information on the screen. In our examples, we use print to help you keep this in mind.

For some of the longer examples in this documentation, we will use booi instead of booish. That is, we will use a text editor to create a source file that we will name with a .boo extension. For example, you might name the file test1.boo. You would then run the program from the command line using the Boo interpreter, like this:

```
booi test1.boo
```

You could also compile the program like this:

```
booc test1.boo
```

This would produce an executable file with the name test1.exe. You would then run it like this:

```
test1
```

Let's begin.

A.2.1 *Expressions*

Boo can display information. Here, we show a string of characters (or more simply, a string).

```
>>> print "Hello, world!"
Hello, world!
```

"Hello, world!" is printed (displayed) on your monitor's screen. Boo can also display numbers:

```
>>> print 23
23
>>> print 3.14
3.14
```

You can print more than one item at a time:

```
>>> print 42, 12.34, "Hi, there."
42 12.34 Hi, there.
```

Besides simple items, you can print the values of expressions:

```
>>> print 5 + 6 * 7
47
>>> print 7 * (5 + 6)
77
```

NOTE Operators, like addition and multiplication in the previous examples, each have an assigned precedence that determines the order in which the operators are applied. You can use parentheses to change that order.

Variables can be assigned values like this:

```
>>> a = 5
5
>>> b = 3 * a + 4
19
>>> c = 2.718
2.718
>>> print a, b, c
5 19 2.718
```

Since 5 is an integer, so is the variable a. And because 2.718 has a decimal point, the variable c is a floating-point number.

NOTE Variable names begin with either a letter or an underscore and may then contain letters, digits, and underscore characters.

Most programs take some input, process it in some way, and produce some output. So far, you've seen one way to output information using the print statement. You've also seen how to process data using expressions. Let's look at one way to input some information.

```
>>> Name = prompt("What is your name? ")
What is your name? Brent
'Brent'
>>> print Name
Brent
```

Here, we called the prompt function, which displayed the string "What is your name?" and then read what was typed at the keyboard ("Brent" in this example). It then returned that string, which was then assigned to the variable Name. Booish printed that out. On the next line we told booish to print Name, which it did.

A.2.2 *Boolean values and Boolean expressions*

The expression 3 + 5 is an integer expression because it evaluates to 8, which is an integer.

The expression 3 > 5 is a Boolean expression because it evaluates to False, which is a Boolean value. The other Boolean value is True. Boolean values can be combined with the and operator (which evaluates to True if both operands are True; otherwise, False) and with the or operator (which evaluates to True if either operand is True; otherwise, False). The not operator evaluates to True if its operand is False; otherwise, it evaluates to False.

Here are a few examples of Boolean expressions:

```
>>> print 23 + 46 > 50
True
>> print 4 > 5 and 6 > 3
```

```
False
>>> print 4 > 5 or 6 > 3
True
>>> print not 4 > 5
True
>>> gt1 = 10 > 8
true
>>> gt2 = 3 > 4
false
>>> gt3 = b and c
False
>>> print gt1, gt2, gt3
True False False
```

A.3   Comments

A *comment* in Boo is text that the Boo parser ignores; it is only there for the enlightenment of the programmer. A comment can begin with a # character or a double slash (//) and continues to the end of the line. Here are a few examples:

```
# get the age of the user
AgeStr = prompt("What is your age? ")
Age = int.Parse(AgeStr) // convert the string to an integer
InSeconds = Age * 365.25 * 24 * 60 * 60
print "You are ${InSeconds} seconds old."
```

A comment can also begin with a slash followed by an asterisk (/*) and end with the reverse (*/) making multiline comments possible, like this:

```
/*
This program was written by Brent W. Hughes
in July of 2005.
*/
```

Note that booish doesn't support multi-line comments unless you use the backward slash (\) line continuation character.

A.4   Control statements

Control statements allow you to change the flow of the program based on your logic. The most common control statement is the condition statement, of which Boo has two variants, the if statement and the unless statement. Loops are also control statements, and Boo has the while and for loops in its arsenal.

A.4.1   If statement

If evaluates the following Boolean expression, and, if True, executes the then part of the statement. (To understand the ellipses, see the sidebar.)

```
>>> a = 7
7
>>> if a > 3:
...     print a
... print "end of first part"
...
7
```

```
end of first part
>>> a = 2
2
>>> if a > 3:
...     print a
... print "end of second part"
...
end of second part
```

Here is a general way of describing the simple `if` statement:

```
if <BooleanExpression>:
        <Statement>
        <...>
```

That is, the `if` statement is followed by one or more contingent statements that we'll call a *statement block*. Here's an example from a Boo source file (rather than from booish):

```
if x > 1.5:
    y = 5.0
    z = 3.5
    print "Okay"
print "After the if statement."
```

In this example, if x is greater than 1.5, all three of the following statements (the statement block) will be executed; otherwise, none of them will be executed. In either case, the `following print` statement will be executed.

Here's another general form of the `if` statement:

```
if <BooleanExpression>:
        <StatementBlock>
else:
        <StatementBlock>
```

Indentations in booish

When booish sees a colon at the end of a line, it knows that the statement isn't complete. It will then prompt you with an ellipsis (. . .) instead of the regular prompt (>>>) until you enter an empty line. Booish will then execute the code. If this same code were entered into a file for later execution, it would look like this:

```
a = 7
if a > 3:
    print a
print "end of first part"
a = 2
if a > 3:
    print a
print "end of second part"
```

When run, the preceding code would output this:

```
7
end of first part
end of second part
```

And here is an example of using the `else` block in an `if` statement:

```
if Count > 100:
    Count = 0
    print "Goodbye"
else:
    a = a + 1
    print "Hi, again."
print "After the if statement."
```

This is one final form of the `if` statement:

```
if <BooleanExpression>:
        <StatementBlock>
elif <BooleanExpression>:
        <StatementBlock>
<more elif's>
else:
        <StatementBlock>
```

Here's an example of it in use:

```
Name = prompt("What is your name? ")
if Name == "Stanley":
    print "Hi, Stan."
elif Name == "William":
    print "Hi, Bill."
elif Name == "Robert":
    print "Hi, Bob."
else:
    print "How's it going, ${Name}"
```

A.4.2   *While statement*

The general form of a while statement is as follows:

```
while <BooleanExpression>:
        <StatementBlock>
```

First, the `BooleanExpression` is evaluated. If it is `True`, then the `StatementBlock` will be executed, and control then returns to the top of the `while` statement where the `BooleanExpression` will be evaluated again, and so on. If the `BooleanExpression` evaluates to `False`, the `StatementBlock` will be skipped, and control will continue after the `while` statement.

Let's look at some examples:

```
i = 1
j = 1
while i < 5:
    j = j * 2
    i = i + 1
    print i, j
print "The final value of j is ${j}."
```

The preceding code will print the following:

```
2 2
3 4
4 8
5 16
The final value of j is 16.
```

Here's another example:

```
Count = 10
while Count > 0:
    print Count
    Count = Count - 1
print "Done"
```

The preceding code is equivalent to this:

```
Count = 10
:loop
if not Count > 0:
    goto next
print Count
Count = Count - 1
goto loop
:next
print "Done"
```

You can exit a while loop early with the break statement:

```
i = 0
while i < 100:
    i = i + 1
    if i > 10:
        break
    print i
# next statement will print "The final value of i: 11"
print "The final value of i: ${i}."
```

You can start the next iteration of the while loop early with a continue statement:

```
i = 0
while i < 100:
    i = i + 1
    if i % 10 == 0:        # if the remainder of i divided by 10 is 0
        continue
    print i                # prints 1 to 99 except for multiples of 10
```

A.4.3   *For statement*

A for statement has the following general form:

```
for <Variable> in <RangeOrSequence>:
        <StatementBlock>
```

Here's an example:

```
>>> for i in [2,4,6,8]:
...     print i + 1
...
3
5
7
9
>>> for Name in ["Stephanie", "Jody", "Jill"]:
...     print Name
...
Stephanie
Jody
Jill
```

The `for` statement may be combined with the `range` method (which will be described in section A.5.2):

```
>>> for i in range(5):     # see below for range
...     print i * i
...
0
1
4
9
16
```

You can exit a `for` loop early with the `break` statement:

```
>>> for i in range(100):    # see below for range
...     if i >= 5:
...         break
...     print i * i
...
0
1
4
9
16
```

You can start the next iteration of a `for` loop with the `continue` statement:

```
>>> for i in range(5):     # see below for range
...     if i % 3 == 0:     # if the remainder of i divided by 3 is 0
```

```
...          continue
...      print i * i
...
0
1
4
16
```

A.5   Types

Boo is a CLR language, and as such it uses the usual .NET types. Nevertheless, there are several types that have built-in support directly in the language, such as lists, hashes, and arrays.

A.5.1   Lists

A list in Boo is a sequence of items, each of which is an int, a double, a string, another list, and so on. A literal list can be typed by separating the items by commas and surrounding them with brackets. Here's an example using booish again:

```
>>> a = [4, 9.82, "Help"]
[4, 9.82, "Help"]
>>> b = [ ["cat", "mouse"], ["lion","gazelle"] ]
[ ["cat", "mouse"], ["lion","gazelle"] ]
# print the length (number of elements) in the lists
>>> print len(a), len(b)
3 2
```

An item in a list can be accessed using an integer index. The first item in a list is at index 0.

```
>>> MyList = [2, 4, 6, 8]
[2, 4, 6, 8]
>>> print MyList[0]
2
>>> print MyList[len(MyList)-1]
8
```

Negative indexes can be used to count from the end of a list, like this:

```
>>> print MyList[-1]
8
>>> print MyList[-2]
6
```

New items can be added to the end of a list using the list's Add method.

```
>>> MyList.Add(10)
[2, 4, 6, 8, 10]
```

You cannot access the list beyond its length:

```
>>> print MyList[5]     # Error: index is out of range
```

A.5.2   *Range*

Boo doesn't really have anything like C's `for` statement, so we need another way to handle iterating over numeric ranges. For that, we use the following syntax:

```
for i in range(5):
    print i
```

Here, `range(5)` returned the integer values 0 through 4, which were, one at a time, assigned to the variable `i`. In general, `range(Max)` will return the values 0 through Max − 1.

Another form of the range method is `range(Min,Max)`. This returns the integers Min through Max − 1:

```
>>> for i in range(5,10):
...     print i
...
5
6
7
8
9
```

Another form is `range(Min,Max,Step)`:

```
>>> for i in range(5,10,2):
...     print i
...
5
7
9
```

And let's see if you can figure this one out:

```
>>> for i in range(10,5,-2):
...     print i
...
10
8
6
```

A.5.3   *Arrays*

An array, like a list, is a sequence of items of any type. The difference is that an array isn't as flexible as a list, but it's generally faster to manipulate.

An array literal can be typed with its items separated by commas and enclosed in parentheses:

```
MyArray = (3, 5, 7, 9)
MyStrArray = ("one", "two", "three")
```

An item of an array is accessed with an integer index. The first item has index 0:

```
# displays a 3
print MyArray[0]
# displays "three"
```

```
print MyStrArray[2]                         MyArray[0] = MyArray[1] + MyArray[2]
# displays 12
print MyArray[0]
# displays the length of MyArray, namely, 4
print len(MyArray)
```

Here's one way of swapping two items in an array:

```
Temp = MyArray[2]
MyArray[2] = MyArray[3]
MyArray[3] = Temp
```

Here's a way of swapping the items without needing a temporary variable:

```
MyArray[2], MyArray[3]  =  MyArray[3], MyArray[2]
```

Here's another way of creating an array; notice the parentheses around the int to the left of the equals sign (=). This stands for int array. To the right of the equals sign, we indicate that we want a new array with room for 5 integers. The integers will be initialized to 0.

```
theArray as (int) = array(int,5)
```

A.5.4 *Hashes*

A hash is a way of associating pairs of items. The first item in each pair is called the *key*, and the second item is called the *value*.

A literal hash can be typed by separating the key and value of each pair with a colon, separating the pairs from other pairs with a comma, and surrounding the whole series of pairs with braces:

```
MyHash = { "Susan":3, "Melanie":9, "Cathy":27 }
```

Given the key, you can access the value like this:

```
# get the value 9 and assign it to Age
Age = MyHash["Melanie"]
# Set the value associated with Melanie to 10
MyHash["Melanie"] = Age + 1
```

Both the key and the value can be any type.

Here are some other things you can do with a hash:

```
Passwords = { }                     # create an empty hash

Passwords["John"] = "Spot"          # add the pair John:Spot
Passwords["Mary"] = "Fluffy"        # add the pair Mary:Fluffy
Passwords["Chris"] = "Sniffles"     # add the pair Chris:Sniffles

Print "The number of pairs is #{Passwords.Count}"

for Item in Passwords:              # print out all of the pairs
    Print Item.key, ":", Item.Value

for Key in Passwords.Keys:          # also print out all of the pairs
    print Key, "=>", Passwords[Key]
```

A.5.5   *Strings*

A string variable can hold a sequence of characters:

```
>>> Color = "green"
'green'
>>> Food = "tomato"
'tomato'
```

Strings can be concatenated (joined together) using the plus (+) operator:

```
>>> Meal = "fried " + Color + " " + Food
'fried green tomato'
```

Boo also supports a feature called *string interpolation*:

```
>>> Meal = "fried ${Color} ${Food}"
'fried green tomato'
```

Strings can be repeated using the asterisk (*) operator:

```
<<< print 'Help' * 3
'HelpHelpHelp'
```

Individual characters of a string can be accessed using integer indexes. However, they cannot be changed; strings are immutable.

```
>>> print Meal[1]
r
>>> Meal[1] = Meal[2]
ERROR: Property 'System.String.Chars' is read only.
```

A.5.6   *Slicing*

Slicing is a way of specifying a part of a sequence:

```
>>> Vowels = "aeiou"
'aeiou'
>>> print Vowels[2:4]
'io'
>>> print Vowels[0:3]
'aei'
>>> print Vowels[1:-2]
'ei'
```

The first number within the brackets specifies the first item in the slice. The second number within the brackets specifies one beyond the last item in the slice.

The following table might make the previous example more clear:

-5	-3	-3	-2	-1
a	e	i	o	u
0	1	2	3	4

If you leave out the first number within the brackets, 0 is assumed. If you leave out the second number within the brackets, the length of the rest of the sequence is assumed.

```
>>> print Vowels[:3]
'aei'
>>> print Vowels[3:]
'ou'
>>> print Vowels[:]
'aeiou'
```

Besides strings, slicing also works with arrays and lists:

```
>>> MyArray = (0,1,2,3,4)
(0, 1, 2, 3, 4)
>>> print MyArray[1:4]
(1,2,3)
>>> MyList = ["zero","one","two","three"]
['zero', 'one', 'two', 'three']
>>> print MyList[2:3]
['two']
```

A.5.7 *Declaring types explicitly*

In Boo, all data must have an associated type determined at compile time (except for duck types, which were covered in chapter 2). Much of the time, Boo can determine the type of a variable just by the way it is used. You don't have to explicitly specify the type in those cases. However, if the type is ambiguous, you must specify it in your code.

Here's an example of declaring types:

```
Count as int
Cost as double

Count = 5
Cost = 1.98
```

In the preceding example, we first specified the types of the two variables and then assigned values to them. In the next example, we do both at once:

```
Count as int = 5
Cost as double = 1.98
```

And, of course, in the following case, we don't have to explicitly specify the types because Boo can figure it out:

```
Count = 5
Cost = 1.98
```

In method definitions, you will usually have to specify the types of the parameters as well as the return type.

A.6   *Creating real programs*

When building real programs with Boo, we need more structure than just statements and variables. Boo, being an object-oriented language, offers us methods, classes, namespaces, and assemblies as the main ways to structure our programs.

A.6.1   *Methods*

A method is like a mini-program. It can have input, processing, and output. It has a name by which you can refer to it. It is defined beginning with the keyword def, like this:

```
def GetTotal(Product as string, \
             Price as double, \
             Quantity as int) as double:
    Total = Price * Quantity
    print "Total cost of ${Product} is ${Total}"
    return Total

thePrice = 1.98
TotalCost = GetTotal("Widget", thePrice, 5 * 2)
```

NOTE   Here we're showing code within a source file rather than code typed into booish.

The preceding code defines a method named GetTotal. It takes three pieces of information as input: the variables Product, Price, and Quantity. These variables are referred to as the *parameters* or *arguments* of the GetTotal method. Product is declared as a string, Price is declared as a double (a floating-point number), and Quantity is declared as an int (an integer). In general, a parameter can be any type. The last as double on the def line before the colon specifies that the method returns a floating-point number as its output value.

Note that the names of the actual arguments that are passed to the method when calling it may be different than the names of the formal parameters used in the declaration of the method. Also, you can pass expressions as arguments to a method. These expressions are evaluated before assigning them to the formal parameters.

Some methods might not have any parameters or might not return a value, and types do not need to be declared in that case:

```
def SayHi():
    print "Hi, Mom!"

SayHi()
```

A.6.2   *Classes and objects*

Think of a *class* as a box that contains variables and methods. You can create objects (other boxes) based on that class. Each object (box) gets its own independent copy of the variables, whereas all of the objects share the methods. Creating an object from a class is called instantiation, and the object that's created is often called an *instance* of its class. We will use both terms interchangeably.

Let's explore that with the usual bank account example:

```
class BankAccount:
    public Balance as double
    def constructor():
        Balance = 0.0
```

```
    def Deposit(Amount as double):
        Balance = Balance + Amount
    def Withdraw(Amount as double):
        # note: no error checking for simplicity
        Balance = Balance - Amount
```

The `BankAccount` class contains one variable and three methods. We can instantiate as many objects as we like from this one class. Here we create two new instances of the class:

```
Account1 = BankAccount()
Account2 = BankAccount()
```

`Account1` and `Account2` each have their own independent copy of the variable `Balance` (which is declared public for pedagogical purposes). Both objects share the three methods.

An element of one of the objects can be accessed by using the object name, followed by a period, followed by the element name:

```
Account1.Deposit(400.0)
Account1.Withdraw(50.0)
print Account1.Balance                 # prints 350
print Account2.Balance                 # prints 0
```

The *constructor* method is special. It is automatically called when a new object is created. This is where the initialization of the object occurs.

Sometimes you'll have a variable that you want to be shared among all the instances of a class. We call this a *class variable or a static variable*. To create a static variable, precede the declaration of the variable with the keyword `static`:

```
class BankAccount:
    static InterestRate as double = 4.5
    public Balance as double
    def constructor():
        Balance = 0.0
    def Deposit(Amount as double):
        Balance = Balance + Amount
    def Withdraw(Amount as double):
        # note: no error checking for simplicity
        Balance = Balance - Amount
```

A.6.3 Imports

Suppose you want to use System.Console.WriteLine as found in the .NET Framework. At the top of your program, you would use the `import` statement:

```
import System

Console.WriteLine("Hello, Mom!")
```

You could also do this:

```
import System.Console

WriteLine("Hello, Mom!")
```

A.7   *Generators*

Generators are similar to LINQ expressions in C# 3.0. They provide a special syntax for processing a set of items. Consider the following code:

```
SquareList = [ ]                        # initialize to empty list
for i in range(5):
    SquareList.Add(i * i)       # append to end of SquareList
print SquareList
```

This prints [0, 1, 4, 9, 16].

  Now consider this:

```
SquareList = [i * i for i in range(5)]
print SquareList
```

This is called a *list generator* or *list comprehension*, and it also prints [0, 1, 4, 9, 16].

  Now consider this example:

```
EvenSquareList = [ ]
for i in range(5):
    if i % 2 == 0:                     # % is the mod or remainder operator
        EvenSquareList.Add(i * i)
print EvenSquareList
```

It prints a list containing the squares of all even integers from 0 to 4, namely [0, 4, 16].

  Now look at the comparable list generator:

```
EvenSquareList = [i * i for i in range(5) if i % 2 == 0]
print EvenSquareList
```

It also prints [0, 4, 16].

  Let's generalize what we've just done.

```
aList  = [ <Expression>  for i in <Range>  if <BooleanExpression> ]
```

is equivalent to

```
aList = [ ]
for i in <Range>:
    if <BooleanExpression>:
        aList.Add(<Expression>)
```

Now let's talk about generator expressions. The following code assigns a list expression to a variable:

```
>>> Cubes = Num * Num * Num for Num in range(4)
generator(System.Int32)
```

Cubes is now a generator of integers. You can use it like this:

```
>>> for n in Cubes:
...     print n
...
0
1
8
27
```

Generator expressions can be used as arguments to functions:

```
def ShowSquare(Num as integer):
    print Num * Num

ShowSquare(i for i in range(5))
```

Generator expressions can also be returned from functions:

```
def CubeGen():
    return c*c*c for c in range(5)

cg = CubeGen()
for n in cg:
    print n          # prints 0, 1, 8, 27, 64 on separate lines
```

Let's now look at a generator method. Any method that uses the yield statement rather than the return statement is a generator method.

The Fibonacci series is 0, 1, 1, 2, 3, 5, 8, 13, 21, and so on, where, except for the first two, each number is the sum of the previous two numbers. We can write a method that returns the Fibonacci numbers like this:

```
def Fibonacci():
    a,b = 0,1
    while true:
        yield a          # returns a
        a,b = b,a+b

g = 0
for f in Fibonacci():
    print f
    g = g + 1
    if g > 10:
        break;           # Without the break, this would be an infinite loop.
                         # Actually, an exception would be thrown when
                         # a+b got too big.
```

This appendix is intended as a language reference. It lists the Boo syntax, compares it to the C# equivalent, and provides a few words of explanation. In many cases, the Boo and C# syntax are similar, in both shape and intent.

NOTE For a more explanatory guide to Boo, see appendix A.

B.1 Interesting keywords

Assuming that you are already familiar with another programming language, the Boo syntax should be familiar to you. Table B.1 compares Boo syntax to the equivalent C# syntax.

Table B.1   Boo syntax compared to C# syntax for keywords

Boo syntax	C# equivalent

`class Car:`
`    pass`
	`public class Car`
	`{`
	`}`

Because Boo has significant whitespace, specifying an empty declaration can be a bit of a problem. The `pass` keyword solves this issue nicely.

`employee is null`	`employee == null`

The `is` keyword is used to make reference equality checks.

`"foo" is "bar"`	`ReferenceEquals("foo","bar")`
`employee isa Manager`	`employee is Manager`

The `isa` keyword is used to ask about the type of the object.

`employee is not null`	`employee != null`

The ability to use `is not` makes statements like this example extremely readable.

Table B.1 Boo syntax compared to C# syntax for keywords *(continued)*

Boo syntax	C# equivalent
`not employee.IsTemporary`	`!employee.IsTemporary`
You can use `not` in a standalone manner.	
`employee is not null and` `employee isa Manager`	`employee != null &&` `employee is Manager`
Boo uses the `and` keyword, where C-based languages use `&&`. This helps make Boo easier to read.	
`employee isa Manager or not` `employee.IsTemporary`	`(employee is Manager) ||` `(!employee.IsTemporary)`
You use `or` in Boo instead of `||` in C#.	
`cast(int, variable)`	`(int)variable`
You usually won't need casting in Boo, because the compiler does it for you, but when you do, you can use the built-in `cast()` method.	
`name = variable as string`	`string name = variable as string;`
You can do conditional casting using the same `as` syntax.	
`typeOfString = typeof(string)`	`Type typeOfString = typeof(string);`
The built-in `typeof()` method is identical in Boo and C#.	
`typeOfString = string`	`Type typeOfString = typeof(string);`
The use of `typeof()` can be skipped if the meaning is unambiguous. This is useful in many APIs that accept type parameters.	

TIP   Boo supports both significant-whitespace and whitespace-agnostic modes, which can be controlled by a compiler switch. That choice gives you a lot of flexibility in deciding which mode your language should use. This is discussed in more detail in chapter 2.

That's the bare bones of the syntax, and it should indicate why Boo makes a good language for DSLs. It's already quite expressive on its own, before you start to add on top of it.

B.2   *Conditionals*

Boo supports the `if` and `unless` conditionals. Boo doesn't support `switch/case`, but that is arguably a good thing. Case statements are frowned upon as code smells in certain circles.

Also note that Boo doesn't have `when` as a keyword. This is important for building DSLs, because you can use `when` in your DSLs more easily.

Table B.2 compares the Boo conditionals' syntax to the equivalent C# syntax.

Table B.2   Boo syntax compared to C# syntax for conditionals

Boo syntax	C# equivalent
```if lives == 0:``` ``` print "game over"```	```if (lives == 0)``` ``` Console.WriteLine("game over");```
A simple `if` statement.	

```if lives == 0:```
```   print "game over"```
```   game.Finish()```
	```if(lives == 0)```
	```{```
	``` Console.WriteLine("game over");```
	``` game.Finish();```
	```}```

Boo syntax compared to C# syntax for conditionals	
```if not lives:``` ``` print "game over"```	```if (lives == 0)``` ``` Console.WriteLine("game over");```
Boo considers 0 and `null` to be equivalent to `false` when used in a conditional.	
```unless lives:``` ``` print "game over"```	```if (lives == 0)``` ``` Console.WriteLine("game over");```
The `unless` keyword simply translates to `if not` and has all the usual semantics.	

```print "game over" unless lives```
 	
```print "game over" if lives == 0```
	```if (lives == 0)```
	``` Console.WriteLine("game over");```

Boo supports statement modifiers. This allows you to form a fairly natural statement: do this if *X*, do this unless *Y*.	

```if lives == 0:```
``` print "game over"```
```else:```
``` print "carry on"```
	```if (lives == 0)```
	``` Console.WriteLine("game over");```
	```else```
	``` Console.Writeline("carry on");```

An `if` statement with an `else` clause.	

```if lives == 0:```
``` print "game over"```
```elif lives == 1:```
``` print "Last life"```
```else:```
``` print "carry on"```
	```if (lives == 0)```
	``` Console.WriteLine("game over");```
	```else if (lives == 1)```
	``` Console.Writeline("last life")```
	```else```
	``` Console.Writeline("carry on");```

Boo has a special syntax for multilevel `if` statements. This compensates for not having the `switch/case` statement.	

As you can see, Boo has quite a few options for expressing conditionals. When it comes to writing a DSL, these will be very useful.

Some people say that this is confusing to them:

```
raise ArgumentNullException("username") if not username
```

For me, this is a very natural read, especially since you can also write this:

```
raise ArgumentNullException("username") if username is null
```

Now this is very nearly grammatically correct English statement.

B.3   *Loops and iterations*

Loops work just as you would expect them to. Boo's `for` loop is equivalent to C#'s `foreach` loop. Boo does have the `range()` function that allows a very similar construct, though. Table B.3 compares the loop syntax in Boo and C#.

Table B.3   Boo syntax compared to C# syntax for loops

Boo syntax	C# equivalent
`while lives != 0:` `    PlayRound()`	`while(lives!=0)` `    PlayRound();`
You could just say `while lives:`, but clarity should be preferred.	
`for i in range(0,10):` `    print i`	`for(int i=0;i<10;i++)` `    Console.WriteLine(i);`
Boo doesn't have a `for` loop that matches the one in C-based languages. The Boo `for` loop is the equivalent of the C# `foreach` loop, but Boo has the `range()` function, which allows very nearly the same syntax.	
`for user in users:` `    print user.Name`	`foreach(User user in users)` `    Console.WriteLine(user.Name);`

`for user in users:`
 	
`    if user.Name is null:`
`    continue`
`    print user.Name`
	`foreach(User user in users)`
	`{`
	`    if(user.Name == null)`
	`        continue;`
	`    Console.WriteLine(user.Name);`
	`}`

`continue` works as expected, and it will work on `while` loops as well.	

`index = 0`
`for user in users:`
`    break if index > 10`
`    print user.Name`
`    index += 1`
	`int index = 0;`
	`foreach(User user in users)`
	`{`
	`    if(index > 10)`
	`        break;`
	`    Console.WriteLine(user.Name);`
	`    index += 1;`
	`}`

`break` will terminate the current loop, and works exactly like it does in C#.	
`while ie.Busy:` `    Thread.Sleep(50ms)`	`while( ie.Busy)` `    Thread.Sleep(50);`
Statement modifiers work with loops as well.	

I haven't touched on generators here, although they are arguably related, because this is a syntax form that is rarely used in DSLs. Generators are too programmer-focused to be useful in that arena.

B.4   Type declarations

Now that we've gone through all the syntax that we can define inside a method's block, let's climb a bit higher and take a look at the real building blocks: the types that make our programs.

Table B.4 explores the differences between the Boo and C# syntaxes for defining types.

Table B.4   Boo syntax compared to C# syntax for type declaration

Boo syntax	C# equivalent
| ```
class Car:
    wheels as int
    def StartEngine():
        pass
``` | ```
public class Car
{
  protected int wheels;
  public void StartEngine()
  {
  }
}
``` |
| Type declarations are public by default.
 Field declarations are protected by default.
 Method and property declarations are public by default. | |
| ```
internal class Car:
    pass
``` | ```
internal class Car {}
``` |
| You can explicitly state the visibility of a class, specifying `internal`, `protected`, and so on. | |
| ```
struct Point:
    X as int
    Y as int
``` | ```
public struct Point
{
    public int X;
    public int Y;
}
``` |
| You can define structures, as well. | |
| ```
class Truck(Car):
    pass
``` | ```
public class Truck : Car
{

}
``` |
| Inheritance is simple. | |
| ```
class Car(IDisposable):
    def Dispose():
        pass
``` | ```
public class Car : IDisposable
{
    public void Dispose()
    {
    }
}
``` |
| You inherit from an interface in order to implement it. | |

Table B.4 Boo syntax compared to C# syntax for type declaration *(continued)*

Boo syntax	C# equivalent
| ```
enum TddStages:
    Red
    Green
    Refactor
``` | ```
public enum TddStages
{
    Red,
    Green,
    Refactor
}
``` |

An example of defining an enumeration.

That's how you can deal with types, but there's still something missing here, for bridging the gap between the method's block and the type itself ...

B.5   *Methods, properties, and control structures*

We'll start with methods and move downward, trying to cover everything from errors to event handling.

Table B.5 compares the syntax options.

Table B.5 Boo syntax compared to C# syntax for methods

Boo syntax	C# equivalent
| ```
def Start():
    pass
``` | ```
public void Start()
{
}
``` |

In Boo, method declarations start with `def`.

Boo syntax	C# equivalent
| ```
def Start(async as bool):
    pass
``` | ```
public void Start(bool async)
{
}
``` |

Parameters are specified in the method parentheses, using the <param name> as <param type> syntax.

Boo syntax	C# equivalent
| ```
def Start(async as bool) as
WaitHandle:
    raise NotImplementedException()
``` | ```
public WaitHandle Start(bool async)
{
    throw new
NotImplementedException();
}
``` |

The method return type is specified after the closing parentheses using the as <return type> syntax.

Boo syntax	C# equivalent
| ```
def GetInteger():
    return 1
``` | ```
public int GetInteger()
{
    return 1;
}
``` |

You can let the compiler figure out the return type on its own.

Table B.5   Boo syntax compared to C# syntax for methods *(continued)*

Boo syntax	C# equivalent
| ```
def SetItem(key,val):
    pass
``` | ```
public void SetItem(object key, object
val)
{
}
``` |

If you skip specifying the type in the parameter list, Boo will assume that you want an object there.

| ```
def VarArgs(*args as (object)):
    pass
``` | ```
public void VarArgs(params object[]
args)
{
}
``` |

You can specify the last parameter as an array that can accept a variable number of arguments, so you can call this method like this:
```
VarArgs(1, "foo");
```

| ```
Name:
    get:
        return "Boo"
``` | ```
public string Name
{
    get { return "C#"; }
}
``` |

A simple read-only property.

| ```
Email:
    get:
        return email
    set:
        email = value
``` | ```
public string Email
{
    get { return email; }
    set { email = value; }
}
``` |

A read-write property.

| ```
Email:
    get: return email
    set: email = value
``` | ```
public string Email
{
    get { return email; }
    set { email = value; }
}
``` |

You can also use one-line blocks, in which case you don't need the line breaks.

| ```
[property(Email)]
email as string
``` | ```
public string Email { get; set; }
``` |

Automatic properties exist in Boo and in C# 3.0.

| ```
xml = XmlDocument()
``` | ```
XmlDocument xml = new XmlDocument()
``` |

Boo doesn't have the `new` operator. The type name followed by `()` is treated as a constructor invocation.

| ```
emp = Employee(Name: "foo", Id: 15)
``` | ```
var emp = new Employee{ Name = "foo",
Id = 15};
``` |

Boo can set named properties in the constructor. C# 3.0 introduced a similar feature.

Table B.5   Boo syntax compared to C# syntax for methods *(continued)*

Boo syntax	C# equivalent
| ```
class Car():
    def constructor():
        print "Car created!"
``` | ```
public class Car
{
    public Car()
    {
        Console.WriteLine("Car
created!");
    }
}
``` |

Boo uses an explicit `constructor` keyword rather than the class name.

| ```
class Car():
    def destructor():
        print "died"
``` | ```
public class Car
{
    public ~Car()
    {
        Console.WriteLine("died");
    }
}
``` |

Use the `destructor` keyword to define a destructor instead of using the class name prefixed with a tilde (~).

`raise NotImplementedException()`	`throw new NotImplementedException();`

Throwing an exception.

`raise "error happened"`	`throw new Exception("error happened");`

This is a nice feature for quick and dirty error handling. If you raise a string, it is automatically wrapped in `System.Exception`.

| ```
try:
    # do something
except:
    print "error happened"
``` | ```
try
{
    // do something
}
catch
{
    Console.WriteLine("error
happened");
}
``` |

Yes, this is as bad form in Boo as it is in C#.

Table B.5   Boo syntax compared to C# syntax for methods *(continued)*

Boo syntax	C# equivalent

``
try:
    # do something
except e as SoapException:
  print e.Detail
except e:
    print e
``
	``
	try
	{
	    // do something
	}
	catch(SoapException e)
	{
	    Console.WriteLine(e);
	}
	catch(Exception e)
	{
	    Console.WriteLine(e);
	}
	``

This is an example of much better error handling than in the previous example, but you will want more-legible error handling in real applications.

``
try:
  # do something
except e:
  print e
ensure:
  print "done"
``
	``
	try
	{
	    // do something
	}
	catch(Exception e)
	{
	    Console.WriteLine(e);
	}
	finally
	{
	    Console.WriteLine("done");
	}
	``

A try, catch, finally block in C# matches a try, except, ensure block in Boo.

``
try:
    # do something
except e:
    print e
    raise
``
	``
	try
	{
	    // do something
	}
	catch(Exception e)
	{
	    Console.WriteLine(e);
	    throw;
	}
	``

As with C#, calling raise in an except block will re-throw the exception while preserving the original stack trace.

``
save.Click += do(sender,e):
    print "Clicked"
``
	``
	save.Click += delegate(
	            object sender,
	            EventArgs e
	          )
	{
	    Console.WriteLine("Clicked");
	}
	``

This creates a closure (also called anonymous delegates, lambda, and blocks) that you can call at a later time. This is useful for events, and for a lot of other things.

Table B.5 Boo syntax compared to C# syntax for methods *(continued)*

Boo syntax	C# equivalent

`save.Click += { print "Clicked" }`	`save.Click += (sender, e) =>`
	
	`Console.WriteLine("Clicked");`

This is an inline block, contrasted with a lambda expression from C# 3.0.

Boo syntax	C# equivalent

`myList.Find( { i | i > 5 })`	`myList.Find(delegate(int i)`
	`{`
	`    return I > 5;`
	`});`

You can also specify the parameters of an inline block explicitly.

Boo syntax	C# equivalent

`namespace Foo.Bar.Baz`
 	
`class Foobar:`
`    pass`
	`namespace Foo.Bar.Baz`
	`{`
	`    public class Foobar`
	`    {`
	`    }`
	`}`

Namespaces in Boo are not blocks. You don't need to indent everything after them to include them in the namespace.

Boo syntax	C# equivalent
`self.name = "foo";`	`this.name = "foo";`

The `self` keyword in Boo has the same meaning as `this` in C#.

Boo syntax	C# equivalent
`super.name = "foo";`	`base.name = "foo";`

The `super` keyword in Boo has the same meaning as `base` in C#.

Boo syntax	C# equivalent

`# single line comment`
`// and this is one as well`
`/*`
` And here is a multi`
` line comment`
`*/`
	`// single line comment`
	`/*`
	`Multi line comment`
	`*/`

Boo has several ways to specify comments.

That about concludes the basic syntax. Now we can move on to the more interesting parts. For instance, major parts of Boo are implemented using Boo's own extension mechanism. Let's look at Boo's built-in macros.

B.6   *Useful macros*

One of the interesting features of Boo is macros. Those are so useful that some of the things that we think of as language features are actually implemented as extensions, instead. Table B.6 lists a few of the more common ones.

Table B.6   Useful built-in macros in Boo

Boo syntax	C# equivalent
`assert user is not null`	`Debug.Assert( user != null, "user is not null") ;`
The Boo version is definitely the clearer one.	
`print "foo"`	`Console.WriteLine("foo");`
Printing to the console.	

`using db = RhinoConnection():`
`    pass`
	`using(RhinoConnection db = new`
	`RhinoConnection())`
	`{`
	`}`

Boo supports a `using` statement with syntax similar to C#.	

`lock syncLock:`
`    #code under lock`
	`lock(syncLock)`
	`{`
	`    // code under lock`
	`}`

Boo supports locking objects with syntax similar to C#.	

This appendix has covered the basic building blocks of Boo, but I suggest taking a look at the Boo website (http://boo.codehaus.org/) for further information. A language is more than just its syntax, and if you want to program in Boo (and not just build DSLs using it), I strongly recommend reading the documentation on the site and joining the Boo community.

index

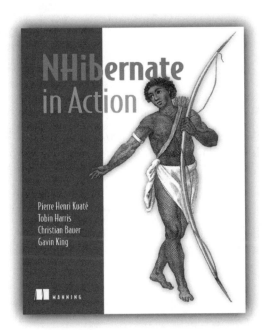

NHibernate in Action
by Pierre Henri Kuaté, Tobin Harris,
   Christian Bauer, and Gavin King

ISBN: 978-1-932394-92-4
400 pages
$49.99
February 2009

The Art of Unit Testing
with Examples in .NET
by Roy Osherove

ISBN: 978-1-933988-27-6
320 pages
$39.99
May 2009

For ordering information go to www.manning.com

MORE TITLES FROM MANNING

ASP.NET MVC in Action
by Jeffrey Palermo, Ben Scheirman,
  and Jimmy Bogard

  ISBN: 978-1-933988-62-7
  392 pages
  $44.99
  September 2009

*Brownfield Application Development
in .NET*

by Kyle Baley and Donald Belcham

  ISBN: 978-1-933988-71-9
  550 pages
  $49.99
  March 2010

For ordering information go to www.manning.com